DEVELOPMENT OF PERSON–CONTEXT RELATIONS

DEVELOPMENT OF PERSON–CONTEXT RELATIONS

Edited by

THOMAS A. KINDERMANN
Portland State University

JAAN VALSINER
University of North Carolina at Chapel Hill

 LAWRENCE ERLBAUM ASSOCIATES, PUBLISHERS
1995   Hillsdale, New Jersey   Hove, UK

Lawrence Erlbaum Associates, Inc., Publishers
365 Broadway
Hillsdale, New Jersey 07642

Library of Congress Cataloging-in-Publication Data

Development of person-context relations / edited by Thomas A.
Kindermann, Jaan Valsiner.
        p. cm.
    Includes bibliographical references and index.
    ISBN 0-8058-1568-6 (cloth)
        1. Context effects (Psychology)   2. Developmental Psychology.
I. Kindermann, Thomas A.   II. Valsiner, Jaan.
BF714.D48   1995
155.9--dc20   95-6935
                                                                 CIP

Books published by Lawrence Erlbaum Associates are printed on acid-free
paper, and their bindings are chosen for strength and durability.

Printed in the United States of America
10 9 8 7 6 5 4 3 2 1

Contents

Contributors

Michelle L. Batchelder Department of Human Ecology, University of Texas at Austin, Austin, TX 78712-1097

Annette Claar Institut für Psychologie, Technische Hochschule Darmstadt, Hochschulstr. 1, D-64289 Darmstadt, Germany

David P. Herbst late of Work Research Institute, P. B 8171 Dep. N-00341 Oslo, Norway

Thomas A. Kindermann Department of Psychology, Portland State University, P.O. Box 751, Portland, OR 97207-0751

Kurt Kreppner Max-Planck-Institut für Bildungsforschung und Humanentwicklung, Lentzeallee 94, D-14195 Berlin, Germany

Richard M. Lerner Institute for Children, Youth, and Families, 2 Paolucci Building, Michigan State University, East Lansing, MI 48824-1030

Christiane Spiel Institut für Psychologie, Universität Wien, Liebiggasse 5, A-1010 Wien, Austria

Warren Thorngate Department of Psychology, Carleton University, Ottawa, Ontario, Canada K1S 5B6

Gisella Trommsdorff Sozialwissenschaftliche Fakultät, Fachgruppe Psychologie, Universität Konstanz, Postfach 5560 D 14, D-78434 Konstanz, Germany

Jaan Valsiner Developmental Psychology Program, University of North Carolina at Chapel Hill, CB # 3270 Davie Hall, Chapel Hill, NC 27599-3270

Alexander von Eye Michigan State University, 321 Berkey Hall, East Lansing, MI 48824-1111

Holger Weßels National Institute of Child Health and Human Development—SSED, BSA Building, Room 331, 9190 Rockville Pike, Bethesda, MD 20814

Acknowledgments

We would like to thank Joyce Ahamad from the University of North Carolina at Chapel Hill for her help with manuscript preparation, and Nicole Sage, Penny Ross, Melissa Jillson, Cherissé N. Crooker, Tina Fitzgerald, Kristin Lyons, and Tanya McCollam from Portland State University for their help with editing of the manuscripts and the preparation of the author and subject indices. We are also very thankful to the staff at Lawrence Erlbaum Associates—to Judith Amsel for her conceptual help in preparing this volume, and to Sondra Guideman for her help and patience during the production process.

DEVELOPMENT OF PERSON–CONTEXT RELATIONS

Individual Development, Changing Contexts, and the Co-Construction of Person–Context Relations in Human Development

Thomas A. Kindermann
Portland State University

Jaan Valsiner
University of North Carolina at Chapel Hill

Traditionally, developmental psychology has its focus on individuals. Developmentalists aim to describe regularities in individuals' change and development across time, to explain the processes and mechanisms that are involved in producing change and regularity, and, eventually, to design strategies for optimization and modification of developmental pathways. Although the role of contexts has always been of central concern for these purposes, it is nevertheless surprising to note that, compared to the effort devoted to individuals, relatively little attention has been paid to the study of the nature and organization of their contexts.

This volume is an exploration of the idea that the way we describe and explain human development will be closely tied to our understanding of what contexts are, how individuals and contexts become influential for one another, what contexts do to and with individuals, and how contexts and their influences change themselves across time. A major theme is the issue of whether the traditional dichotomy between individuals and their contexts may be artificial, perhaps culturally biased, and, after psychologists have adhered to it for about a century, may have become an impediment to increasing our understanding of developmental processes.

Recent trends in developmental psychology propagate the study of *ecological systems* (Bronfenbrenner, 1989; Bronfenbrenner & Crouter, 1983; Ford & Lerner, 1992; Sameroff, 1983; Wachs, 1992; Wohlwill, 1983), the study of *relationships* between people and their environment (Hinde, 1992; see also Emde, 1994; Maccoby, 1992), or the study of *co-constructive processes* in

1

human development (Valsiner, 1987, 1989; Winegar & Valsiner, 1992). Common to these approaches is the insight that it is neither individuals nor contexts by themselves who determine the pathways of the human lifecourse, but the complex interconnections and relationships that exist between individuals and their contexts.

The scope of this book is consistent with these systemic frameworks. A basic premise is that instead of focusing on individuals (or their contexts), developmentalists may want to focus their attention on the *relations* that exist between people and their environments (see also Lerner, 1991). However, although individuals are units that appear to be well defined, there exists no natural unit of analysis for their environments. At best, we are able to identify specific people who serve as environmental agents of target individuals at specific points in time, or to differentiate between different levels of complexity in larger environmental systems. Hence, we think that adopting the umbrella-term of systems-oriented frameworks necessitates further clarifications, especially in terms of conceptual elaboration of the defining characteristics of developmental contexts, in terms of the psychological "active" characteristics of contexts, and in terms of the design of methodological strategies for their study.

We chose the term *person-context relations* for the title of this volume for several reasons. First, we want to highlight that, to take systemic notions seriously, as much attention would need to be paid to the characteristics that contexts may possess as is usually paid to characteristics of individuals under study. This is not the case in many of the existing systems-oriented frameworks. Thus, the term *relations* is used as a formal descriptor: Person-context relations include combinations of events, objects, and individuals that constitute an ecological system at a given time, and sets of relations that exist among these elements.

Second, the term *relations* is chosen for its overlap with the term *relationships*; we assume that most developmental contexts are phenomena that are constructed jointly by people and other people who act as their environments. Typically, these others are themselves not treated as individuals in psychological research and theorizing. In fact, it is a common feature of almost all existing conceptualizations of developmental contexts that they rarely include explicit notions that social environments, like individuals, have psychological characteristics of their own that are undergoing development themselves.

Third, the emphasis is on *change* in person-context relations (cf. Lerner, 1991; Gottlieb, 1992). Although it is a central tenet of most developmental theories to assume that individuals develop within changing environments, in terms of practical research, this insight seems to be of little consequence. Hetherington and Baltes (1988) stated, "much developmental research still presents a picture of the child developing within a rather static ecosystem. Certainly more attention is focused on individual change than on contextual change" (p. 12). Often intense effort is paid to control change in people's environment across time, in order to examine their "true" developmental change, instead of examining the connections between individuals' change and changes in their environments. We hope that the current volume can be a contribution toward the cause of incorporating notions of context change in our empirical endeavors.

Why should change in contexts be so important? This is most evident with regard to historical time frames; sociologists and life-span developmentalists have provided ample evidence for cohort differences in development (e.g., Baltes, Cornelius, & Nesselroade, 1979; Cain, 1987; Elder, 1985; Featherman, Spenner, & Tsunematsu 1988; Nesselroade & Baltes, 1984; Schaie, 1965; Stewart & Healy, 1989). However, is context change also as important for changes within individuals? We believe that this is so. First, societal change may have long-lasting influences and, by itself, must not always be slow in pace. Elder's work on the long-term developmental impact of young adults' experiences during the great depression, the work of Featherman and colleagues on the rates of change in children's socioeconomic status, or Claar's work on the impact of macrocultural change on children's economic understanding (this volume, chap. 7) provide examples.

In addition, frameworks that focus on change and adaptation of contexts as a primary force in development have also gained prominence with the increasing attention that has been paid in Europe and in the United States to the work of Vygotsky (see van der Veer & Valsiner, 1991, 1994; Wertsch, 1985). Key areas of interest are person-context transactions that target children's "zone of proximal development" (Valsiner, 1978; Vygotsky, 1984), in the form of "scaffolding" (Bruner, 1982; Hodapp, Goldfield, & Boyatzis, 1984), "apprenticeship" (Heckhausen, 1987; Kaye, 1982; Kindermann & Skinner, 1988; Rogoff, 1990), or "guided participation" (Rogoff, 1993).

Finally, many developmentalists concur with the view that scientific endeavors, psychological theorizing, and research are strongly influenced by ongoing historical and macrocultural trends (cf. Riegel, 1978). On that account, it is likely that the magnitude of current sociocultural changes in many different parts of the world (after a period of relative stability) may lead developmental psychologists to change the focus of their attention away from focusing on static context envelopes and toward considering the consequences of societal change, and even turmoil (e.g., Bronfenbrenner, 1993). Authors from European countries may be most sensitive to considerations of change in context conditions. In fact, we hope that it will turn out to be a strength of the current volume that the selection of contributors is quite international.

ORGANIZATION OF THE VOLUME

In outlining our framework on person-context relations we begin with a series of discussions about the implications of this framework for research, theorizing, and intervention efforts in developmental psychology. Lerner (chap. 1) argues for the need of an approach that is interwoven with a life-span perspective on human development (Baltes, 1989; Baltes, Reese, & Nesselroade, 1982; Lerner, 1991) and notions of developmental contextualism (Lerner & Kauffman, 1985). Starting from the basic question of what the target phenomenon should be for developmental psychologists, Lerner concludes that organismic/individualistic and mechanistic perspectives are insufficient and argues for a dialectic framework that is characterized by notions of interdependent levels and integrative organizations in reciprocal individual-context relations. According to his argumentation, if person-context relations became our target of investigation, we would need to focus on the diversity of pathways of human development, instead of normativity in individuals' trajectories; we would need to conduct studies more in the "real world"; policy and program design and their evaluation would become a means to examine contextual influences; and we would need to reach out to other disciplines like sociology, biology, and history for our efforts in studying, conceptualizing, and optimizing institutions and social systems. Accordingly, a full consideration of person-context relations requires teams of multidisciplinary researchers.

In Chapter 2 Thorngate examines conceptual and methodological implications of the study of person-context relations. In his view, description would need to become a primary goal. The question of how to describe development in person-context relations poses problems that entail the sum of complications normally encountered in studies of individuals' development, plus an at least similar amount of complications with regard to descriptions of their contexts. Beyond accounts of people, environments, and changes in people and environments, we would be in need of accounts for changes in their interrelations, and of accounts for how changes in people and environments are related to each other. Thorngate proposes a pluralistic approach to constructing accounts of person-context relations across time and offers perspectives on how to form these accounts. These perspectives include notions of purpose and familiarity of individuals with their contexts, notions about how individuals organize their time within contexts, and the notion of proliferation of individuals' activities across contexts. In essence, his chapter is a challenging plan for new conceptualizations and methodologies in the study of developing person-context relations.

In Chapters 3 and 4, Valsiner's and Herbst's contributions address the logical basis for focusing on person-context relations. What we today have come to regard as the "classical viewpoint," namely, to understand individuals and their context partners as separate entities, is contrasted with a perspective of co-genetic logic. The basic idea is that a relation can logically be conceived to be our target of study, instead of an individual. As Valsiner points out, this perspective is not new altogether but deeply rooted in the work of early psychologists and their search for a logic of change processes in development (e.g., Baldwin, 1906). (It is sad to note that Herbst died shortly after the current chapter was finished, so Valsiner, in an introduction to Chapter 4, gives an outline of the implications of a co-genetic logic for psychological studies.)

The second part of the volume addresses empirical consequences of a person-context relations approach to the study of human development. First, the chapters by Claar (chap. 5) and by Trommsdorff (chap. 6) illustrate how such an approach may be applied to the the study of cognitive and emotional development within macrocultural contextual frames.

Claar's chapter presents a unique perspective on context change: The converging frames of Germany's two formerly separate political and eco-nomical systems are examined in terms of their implications for children's understanding of economical concepts. Claar emphasizes individuals' efforts to actively make sense of their changing cultural frame. What is unique about the situation is that a historically homogenous culture had diverged into two different social systems for some time, and that these are now converging again. In addition, because in Western cultures one's economic standing and understanding is quite essential for one's place in society, the chapter targets a central phenomenon of person-context relations, which, probably because of its seemingly unpsychological nature, has traditionally received only little attention in psychological studies.

In contrast, Trommsdorff's chapter focuses on cross-cultural comparisons, and on processes of emotional attunement in children's person-context re-lationships. The main argument concerns index variables in cross-cultural studies. In Trommsdorff's opinion, an overarching cultural difference (in this case, a group-orientation in the Japanese culture, in contrast to an individu-alistic orientation in Western societies) should not be used as an index variable for examining interindividual differences in outcome variables (in this case, empathy, and its potential for activating prosocial behaviors). In-stead, the global system variables would need to be "translated" into the relevant psychological, interactional, and socializing conditions that exist for children who grow up in a given culture. Within the cultural frame, the detailed context conditions for children's behavior need to be examined at specific developmental stages.

By comparing Japanese and German children's empathic and procosocial behaviors in interactions with their mothers and peer playmates, Trommsdorff shows that despite similarities in children's behaviors across both cultures there are different activation systems in place that trigger the occurrence of these behaviors. In Trommsdorff's view, these differences can be explained by culturally different meanings of person-context relations and by differences in socialization processes.

The three last chapters of the volume focus more specifically on methods to examine *changes* in person-context relations. Chapters 7 through 9 use combinatorial perspectives; the chapters converge on the premise that the study of change in person-context relations involves the consideration of several changes at the same time: change within individuals, change within contexts, and changes in the match between "who" or "what" constitutes a context for a particular individual at a specific time. Several stategies are discussed for combining methods that examine change in individuals with methods that examine change within contexts.

First, the chapter by von Eye, Kreppner, Spiel, and Weßels (chap. 7) focuses on critical life events. Life events are perceived as turning points in people's life that bring about massive changes and alter people's developmental pathways. These events may be material or social changes in the environment, but they also include changes within individuals (e.g., biological changes) that affect their functioning even within stable environments. The central argument is that in all these cases the result is a change in person-environment relations that leads to alterations of people's future developmental pathways. In specific, the authors highlight the role of order and spacing in the occurrence of life events across time and suggest methods for analyses that are based on examination of event configurations.

Second, the chapter by Batchelder (chap. 8) provides a more qualitative analysis of adaptation and coping processes following a specific critical life event, namely, parental divorce. The focus is on the extent to which adaptation processes lead to reorganizations of children's relationships within their families, and the main theme is an argument for the study of selection processes in person-context relations. The chapter demonstrates that, after this life event, there is an enormous potential for children to form coalitions with different old or new family members. Specific attention is paid to the extent to which different kinds of person-context relations may provide different resources for adaptation processes.

Finally, Kindermann (chap. 9) presents suggestions for examining natural person-context relations in school environments. Again, a basic assumption is that children, to some extent, are able to select for themselves those others who become a member of their close peer context. Using the example of children's school motivation, it is argued that the psychological characteristics of self-selected context agents can be influential for individuals' further development. In specific, the chapter addresses three points: The psychological characteristics of natural peer contexts appear to be related to the characteristics of those individuals for whom they form a context; individuals' peer contexts seem to change in a predictable way across time in terms of their members and their psychological characteristics; and, in turn, socialization processes in self-selected peer contexts can influence a target individual's further development.

Taken together, the contents of this volume emphasize the potential virtues of a focus on person-context relations in the study of human development. Our epilogue summarizes the contributions and presents recommendations for further directions in the study of person-context relations. Focal points are notions of change and development within contexts as well as within individuals, attention to the processes by which people and their contexts become connected to one another, recognition of the psychological characteristics that contexts possess and attention to change in these characteristics, and recognition of change in the processes of reciprocal influences between individuals and their contexts across time.

With this volume, we hope to contribute a serious consideration of development and systematic change to emerging models of person-context relations, and to provide suggestions about how it may be possible to incorporate these notions in developmental research and theorizing. We are aware that only suggestions for starting points can be given here. However, we hope the book also provides encouragement for contextually oriented researchers to develop new conceptualizations of person-context relations, and new methodological approaches for their study.

REFERENCES

Baldwin, J. M. (1906). *Thought and things: A study of the development and meaning of thought, or genetic logic*. London: Swan Sonnenschein.

Baltes, P. B. (1989). Theoretical propositions of life-span developmental psychology: On the dynamics between growth and decline. *Developmental Psychology, 23*, 611–626.

Baltes, P. B., Cornelius, S. W., & Nesselroade, J. R. (1979). Cohort effects in developmental psychology. In J. R. Nesselroade & P. B. Baltes (Eds.), *Longitudinal research in the study of behavior and development* (pp. 61–87). New York: Academic Press.

Baltes, P. B., Reese, H. W., & Nesselroade, J. R. (1982). *Life-span developmental psychology: Introduction to research methods*. Hillsdale, NJ: Lawrence Erlbaum Associates.

Bronfenbrenner, U. (1989). Ecological systems theory. In R. Vasta (Ed.), *Annals of child development* (pp. 187–249). Greenwich, CT: JAI.

Bronfenbrenner, U. (1993). Living through societal chaos: Developmental risks and rescues. *Newsletter of the International Society for the Study of Behavioral Development, Serial no. 23*, 1–2.

Bronfenbrenner, U., & Crouter, A. C. (1983). The evolution of environmental models in developmental research. In P. H. Mussen (Series Ed.) & W. Kessen (Vol. Ed.), *Handbook of child psychology: Vol. 1. History, theory and methods* (pp. 357–414). New York: Wiley.

Bruner, J. (1982). The organization of action and the nature of the adult-infant transaction. In M. Cranach & R. Harre (Eds.), *The analysis of action* (pp. 280–296). New York: Cambridge University Press.

Cain, L. (1987). Theoretical observations on applied behavioral science. *Journal of Applied Behavioral Science, 23*, 277–294.

Elder, G. H. (Ed.). (1985). *Life course dynamics: Trajectories and transitions*. Ithaca, NY: Cornell University Press.

Emde, R. N. (1994). Individuality, context, and the search for meaning. *Child Development, 65*, 719–737.

Featherman, D. L., Spenner, K. I., & Tsunematsu, N. (1988). Class and the socialization of children: Constancy, change, or irrelevance. In E. M. Hetherington, R. M. Lerner, & M. Perlmutter (Eds.), *Child development in life-span perspective* (pp. 67–90). Hillsdale, NJ: Lawrence Erlbaum Associates.

Ford, D. H., & Lerner, R. M. (1992). *Developmental systems theory: An integrative approach.* Newbury Park, CA: Sage.

Gottlieb, G. (1992). *Individual development and evolution: The genesis of novel behavior.* New York: Oxford University Press.

Heckhausen, J. (1987). Balancing for weaknesses and challenging developmental potential: A longitudinal study of mother-infant dyads in apprenticeship interactions. *Developmental Psychology, 23,* 762–770.

Hetherington, E. M., & Baltes, P. B. (1988). Child psychology and life-span development. In E. M. Hetherington, R. M. Lerner, & M. Perlmutter (Eds.), *Child development in life-span perspective* (pp. 1–19). Hillsdale, NJ: Lawrence Erlbaum Associates.

Hinde, R. A. (1992). Developmental psychology in the context of other behavioral sciences. *Developmental Psychology, 28,* 1018–1029.

Hodapp, R. M., Goldfield, E. C., & Boyatzis, C. J. (1984). The use and effectiveness of maternal scaffolding in mother-infant games. *Child Development, 55,* 772–781.

Kaye, K. (1982). *The mental and social life of babies: How parents create persons.* Chicago: Harvester.

Kindermann, T. A., & Skinner, E. A. (1988). Developmental tasks as organizers of children's ecologies: Mothers' contingencies as children learn to walk, eat, and dress. In J. Valsiner (Ed.), *Child development within culturally structured environments* (Vol. 2, pp. 66–105). Norwood, NJ: Ablex.

Lerner, R. M. (1991). Changing organism-context relations as the basic process of development. *Developmental Psychology, 27,* 27–32.

Lerner, R. M., & Kauffman, M. B. (1985). The concept of development in contextualism. *Developmental Review, 5,* 309–333.

Maccoby, E. E. (1992). The role of parents in the socialization of children: An historical overview. *Developmental Psychology, 28,* 1006–1017.

Nesselroade, J. R., & Baltes, P. B. (1984). Sequential strategies and the role of cohort effects in behavioral development: Adolescent personality (1970–1972) as a sample case. In S. A. Mednick, M. Harway, & K. M. Finello (Eds.), *Handbook of longitudinal research* (Vol. 1, pp. 55–87). New York: Praeger.

Riegel, K. F. (1978). *Psychology mon amour: A countertext.* Boston: Houghton Mifflin.

Rogoff, B. (1990). *Apprenticeship in thinking: Cognitive development in sociocultural activity.* New York: Oxford University Press.

Rogoff, B. (1993). Children's guided participation and participatory action appropriation in sociocultural activity. In R. H. Wozniak & K. W. Fischer (Eds.), *Development in context: Acting and thinking in specific environments* (pp. 121–153). Hillsdale, NJ: Lawrence Erlbaum Associates.

Sameroff, A. J. (1983). Developmental systems: Contents and evolution. In P. H. Mussen (Series Ed.) & W. Kessen (Vol. Ed.), *Handbook of child psychology: Vol. 1. History, theory and methods* (pp. 237–294). New York: Wiley.

Schaie, K. W. (1965). A general model for the study of developmental problems. *Psychological Bulletin, 64,* 92–107.

Stewart, A. J., & Healy, J. M. (1989). Linking individual development and social changes. *American Psychologist, 44,* 30–42.

Valsiner, J. (1984). Construction of the zone of proximal development (ZPD) in adult-child joint actions: The socialization of meals. In B. Rogoff & J. V. Wertsch (Eds.), *Children's learning in the "zone of proximal development": New directions for child development* (pp. 65–76). San Francisco: Jossey-Bass.

Valsiner, J. (1987). *Culture and the development of children's action.* Chichester: Wiley.

Valsiner, J. (1989). *Human development and culture.* Lexington, MA: Heath.

van der Veer, R., & Valsiner, J. (1991). *Understanding Vygotsky: A quest for synthesis.* Oxford, UK: Blackwell.

van der Veer, R., & Valsiner, J. (Eds.). (1994). *The Vygotsky reader.* Oxford, UK: Blackwell.

Vygotsky, L. S. (1978). *Mind in society.* Cambridge, MA: Harvard University Press.

Wachs, T. D. (1992). *The nature of nurture.* Newbury Park, CA: Sage.

Wertsch, J. V. (1985). *Vygotsky and the social formation of mind.* Cambridge, MA: Harvard University Press.

Winegar, L. T., & Valsiner, J. (Eds.). (1992). *Children's development within social context (Vol. 2): Research and methodology.* Hillsdale, NJ: Lawrence Erlbaum Associates.

Wohlwill, J. F. (1983). Physical and social environment as factors in development. In D. Magnusson & V. L. Allen (Eds.), *Human development: An interactional perspective* (pp. 111–129). New York: Academic Press.

PART ONE

TOWARD A FRAMEWORK FOR THE STUDY OF DEVELOPING PERSON–CONTEXT RELATIONS: PRAGMATIC, THEORETICAL, AND METHODOLOGICAL ISSUES

Developing Individuals Within Changing Contexts: Implications of Developmental Contextualism for Human Development Research, Policy, and Programs

Richard M. Lerner
Michigan State University

Interest in the context of human development has a long history in philosophy and social science (for reviews see Dixon & Nesselroade, 1983; Kaplan, 1983). However, contextual philosophy (e.g., Pepper, 1942) began to attract increasing interest from psychologists during the late 1960s (e.g., see Bandura, 1978; Bronfenbrenner, 1979; Jenkins, 1974; Kuo, 1967; Rosnow & Georgoudi, 1986; Sarbin, 1977). There were at least two reasons for this burgeoning interest. They pertain to metatheoretical issues about models of human development and to empirical findings about relations between individual development and social or historical change.

In this chapter, I discuss a specific instance of this interest in contextualism—developmental contextualism—as a framework for studying development in general and children, youth, and families in particular. Two sources are noted for the increased interest in developmental contextualism—the growth in the importance accorded metatheories of human development and a burgeoning of the number of studies of organism-context relations. The concept of integrative levels in development is presented as a means to introduce the features of developmental contextualism and to discuss general characteristics of models of dynamic, person-context relations. Finally, I indicate the implications of developmental contextualism for understanding the basic process of development, that is, for understanding changing person-context relations; in turn, I explain how this view of the basic process of human development has implications for methods of research in human development and for the links between research, policies, and programs designed to enhance the course of life.

METATHEORIES OF HUMAN DEVELOPMENT

Attention to contextualism derived from altered conceptual emphases among scholars in the area of human development. In the early decades of the 20th century, and continuing through at least the beginning of the 1940s, much of developmental psychology was descriptive and normative in orientation (Bronfenbrenner, 1963; Looft, 1972). Change in this orientation was in part prodded by the infusion of European psychologists (such as Kohler, Lewin, and Wertheimer), who came to the United States in the years surrounding World War II (Dixon & Lerner, 1988). These scholars infused American psychology with ideas that provided contrasting accounts of the bases of norms of development. As a consequence, the middle decades of the century saw increasing discussions of the explanations of development.

For instance, in an early review of the history of developmental science, Bronfenbrenner (1963) noted that from the 1930s to the early 1960s there was a continuing shift away from studies involving the mere collection of data, and a shift toward research concerned with abstract processes and constructs. Some books and essays published during this period epitomized this trend by calling for the study of developmental processes and mechanisms (e.g., Harris, 1957; Spiker & McCandless, 1954). Accordingly, describing the status of the field in 1963, Bronfenbrenner (1963) wrote that "first and foremost, the gathering of data for data's sake seems to have lost favor. The major concern in today's developmental research is clearly with inferred processes and constructs" (p. 527). In a review almost a decade later, Looft (1972) noted continuation of the trends documented by Bronfenbrenner. Looft's review, like Bronfenbrenner's, was based on an analysis of major handbooks of developmental psychology published from the 1930s to 1972. Looft suggested that a shift toward more general, integrative concerns occurred by 1945 (after World War II), and that the trend continued through 1963 (Bronfenbrenner, 1963) to 1972.

Since the early 1970s, this trend toward attending to both the description and explanation of developmental processes has continued in a number of ways. Considerable interest has come to be focused on a variety of theories, on explanations, and on processes of development. Such emphases have led to the recognition that there are multiple adequate ways (theories) of accounting for the facts (descriptions) of development. This pluralistic perspective implies that theoretical concerns guide the collection and interpretation of data, and that theory and data should be evaluated in terms of each other. A second aspect of this trend toward explanation may be seen in an examination of the most recent compilations of research and theory. For example, in the fourth edition of the *Handbook of Child Psychology*, the first volume (Mussen & Kessen, 1983) is devoted to historical, theoretical, and methodological issues—topics not integrated within a single section of previous editions.

Indeed, the interest in conceptual and methodological issues has itself generated considerable scholarship. In particular, the theoretical and meta-theoretical bases upon which individual development is studied and inter-preted has become a focus of investigation (e.g., Overton, 1984; Reese & Overton, 1970). Following the work of such philosophers as Pepper (1942) and Kuhn (1970), Reese and Overton (1970) identified two major philo-sophical models that provided the basis for many extant assumptions about human development. These models provide a set of assumptions, or meta-theoretical ideas, about human nature and thereby influenced lower order theoretical and methodological statements.

The two models discussed by Reese and Overton (1970) were termed *organicism* and *mechanism*. The organismic position stresses the qualitative features of developmental change and the active contribution of the organ-ism's processes in these changes. The theories of Piaget (e.g., 1950) and to some extent of Freud (e.g., 1954) are examples of such organismically ori-ented approaches. In contrast, the mechanistic position stresses quantitative change and the active contribution of processes outside the primary control of the organism (e.g., in the external stimulus environment) as the major source of development. The behavioral analysis approach of Bijou (1976) and of Bijou and Baer (1961) is a major example of such mechanistically oriented approaches.

The discussions prompted by the work of Reese and Overton (1970) involved, as well, consideration of the "family of theories" associated with each model. For instance, as I previously noted, there are at least two types of organismically oriented theories, that of Freud and that of Piaget. Although there are differences among family members (Freud emphasized social and personality development and Piaget emphasized cognitive development), there is greater similarity among the theories within a family (e.g., the com-mon stress on the qualitative, stage-like nature of development) than there is between theories associated with different families (e.g., mechanistically oriented theories would deny the importance, indeed the reality, of quali-tatively different stages in development).

Due to the philosophically based differences between families of theories derived from the organismic and the mechanistic models, the period since the early 1970s has included several discussions about the different stances regarding an array of key conceptual issues of development, which are associated with the different metatheories of development. Examples are the nature and nurture bases of development (Lehrman, 1970; Lerner, 1978; Overton, 1973); the quality, openness, and continuity of change (Brim &

Kagan, 1980; Looft, 1973); appropriate methods for studying development (Baltes, Reese, & Nesselroade, 1977); and ultimately, the alternative truth criteria for establishing the "facts" of development (Dixon & Nesselroade, 1983; Reese & Overton, 1970).

This awareness of the philosophical bases of developmental theory, method, and data contributed to the consideration of additional models appropriate to the study of psychological development. In part, this consideration developed as a consequence of interest in integrating assumptions associated with theories derived from organismic and mechanistic models (Looft, 1973). For instance, Riegel (e.g., 1975, 1976) attempted to apply an historical model of development that seemed to include some features of organicism (e.g., the active organism) and some features of mechanism (e.g., the active environment). In turn, Riegel's interest in continual, reciprocal relations between an active organism and its active context (and not in either element per se), and the concern with these relations as they exist on all phenomenal levels of analysis, formed a basis for his proposing a dialectical model of human development (Riegel, 1975, 1976). Indeed, other developmentalists, focusing too on the implications for theory of viewing distinct levels of analysis as reciprocally interactive, proposed related models, ones termed *transactional* (Sameroff, 1975), *relational* (Looft, 1973), or *developmental contextual* (Lerner, 1978, 1984, 1986). This philosophically driven interest in bidirectional organism-context relations led several theorists to explore the application of a change-oriented contextual model to the collection and interpretation of developmental (and other psychological) data (see especially the volume on contextualism edited by Rosnow & Georgoudi, 1986). This last feature of the recent history of the field of human development is linked as well to the second basis for the growing interest in the context of human development.

THE EMPIRICAL STUDY
OF ORGANISM-CONTEXT RELATIONS

A second basis of the interest in contextualism that grew through the 1970s derived from the nature of empirical findings generated during this period. These findings were quite problematic to interpret when viewed from extant organismic- or mechanistic-derived theories. As a consequence, scholars sought to evaluate the use of a new philosophical, or metatheoretical, frame for their work because of the growing empirical literature that suggested that it was necessary to forego an exclusively psychological analysis of individual development; this literature pointed instead to explanations that emphasized the multilevel bases of human functioning and the connections among levels (e.g., Baltes, 1987; R. Lerner, 1984; Lerner & Busch-Rossnagel, 1981; Magnusson & Allen, 1983; Tobach & Greenberg, 1984).

For example, in 1980 Brim and Kagan edited a book (*Constancy and Change in Human Development*) that reviewed evidence from several disciplines about whether early experience provides a virtually immutable shaper of the entire life course—in other words, about whether events in early life necessarily constrain later development. Studies were reviewed that indicated that features of the person's historical setting often shape personality, social, and intellectual functioning to a much greater extent than maturational- or age-associated changes (Elder, 1974; Nesselroade & Baltes, 1974; Schaie, 1979). General historical events such as wars, economic privations, or political upheavals, as well as personal events such as marriage, divorce, illness, death, or career change, are seen often to provide potent shapers of the quantity of life changes and of the quality of the life course (e.g., Elder, 1974, 1980). These studies also indicate that there are multiple paths through life. As people age they become increasingly different from each other, and these different life paths are again linked to general historical or personal events (Baltes, Reese, & Lipsitt, 1980; Brim & Ryff, 1980).

To illustrate the kind of findings reviewed in the Brim and Kagan (1980) volume, I point to the research of Schaie (1979). He reported that the direction of age changes in intellectual aging is related to variables associated with birth cohort membership. Members of one birth cohort might show negatively accelerated changes in levels of cognitive abilities during their aged years; another cohort might show stability in these abilities during this period; and still another cohort might show continued growth in abilities during their aged years. The particular pattern depended on educational and pedagogical variables present in the context of a given cohort during the particular time in history when its members were educated.

Not only may contextual variables exist that differentiate people born at given times in history and thereby influence the particular direction of their ontogenetic changes, but there also may be contextual variables, present only at specific times of measurement, which may "cut across" cohorts and influence the direction of change of people from different cohorts. For instance, Nesselroade and Baltes (1974) studied about 1,800 West Virginia male and female adolescents in 1970, 1971, and 1972. These adolescents were from birth cohorts 1954 to 1957 and thus ranged in age at the time of first measurement from 13 to 16. Personality questionnaires and measures of intelligence were administered to these subjects. Contrary to what is stressed by those theorists who focus on personological components of adolescent development (e.g., Anna Freud, 1969), Nesselroade and Baltes found that change at this time of life was quite responsive to sociocultural–historical influences. In fact, age by itself was not found to be a very influential contributor to change. Rather, for these groups of adolescents, developmental change was influenced more by cultural changes over the 2-year historical period than by age-related sequences. For instance, adolescents as a whole, despite their age or birth cohort, decreased in "superego strength," "social-emotional anxiety," and achievement during the 1970 to 1972 period. Moreover, most adolescents, regardless of age or cohort, increased in independence during this period.

Accordingly, the Nesselroade and Baltes (1974) data show that it was the time at which all these differently aged adolescents were measured that was most influential in their changes. Perhaps due to the events in society of that time (e.g., events associated with the Vietnam War), all adolescents scored similarly in regard to these personality characteristics. Despite where they were (i.e., their age) upon "entering" the 1970 to 1972 historical era, members of different cohorts changed in similar directions, due presumably to events surrounding them at the times they were tested.

Perhaps the best example of how the changing social context provides a basis of individual development is derived from Elder's (1974) longitudinal study of the development of people who were children and adolescents during the Great Depression in the United States. Elder reported that among a group of 84 males and 83 females born in 1920 and 1921, characteristics of the historical era produced alterations in the influence of education on achievement, affected later adult psychological health for youths from working-class families suffering deprivation during this era, and enhanced the importance of children in later adult marriages for youths who suffered hardships during the depression.

Other components of a person's context that can influence individual development are the physical and social characteristics of the school environment. Indeed, Simmons, Rosenberg, and Rosenberg (1973) found that changes in the school context may influence personality. In a study of about 2,000 children and adolescents, they found that in comparison to 8- to 11-year-old children, early adolescents—and particularly those 12 and 13 years of age—showed more self-consciousness, greater instability of self-image, and slightly lower self-esteem. However, they discovered that contextual rather than age-associated effects seemed to account for these findings. Upon completion of the sixth grade, one portion of the early-adolescent group had moved to a new school—that is, a local junior high school—whereas the remaining portion of the early adolescents stayed in the same school (which offered seventh- and eighth-grade classes). The group of early adolescents who changed their school setting showed a much greater incidence of the personality changes than did the group that remained in the same school. Corresponding findings have been reported by Simmons and Blyth (1987). Thus, variables related to changes in the school context seem to influence the personality development of young people.

Empirical findings emerging throughout the 1970s indicated that organism-centered models of developmental change could not account for the multidirectionality of ontogenetic change. Instead, the context of human development needed to be incorporated into any adequate analysis of the diversity of developmental trajectories that was seen to characterize the life course. However, this context was not the simplistic, S–R environment of learning theorists (see White, 1970) or of those taking a behavior-analytic approach to development (e.g., Bijou, 1976; Bijou & Baer, 1961).

Indeed, the multiple levels of the context, which seem linked to the organism level over the course of the life span, cannot be reduced to the molecular elements of any extant mechanistic-behavioristic theory (Lerner & Kauffman, 1985). Instead, organism and context may be seen as two distinct, yet inextricably linked, components of the system of relationships comprising the ecology of human life (e.g., Bronfenbrenner, 1979; Ford, 1987).

This empirically driven view of organism-context relations meshed well with the view of organism and context being forwarded in the simultaneously developing literature on metatheoretical models, a literature that brought an interest in contextualism to the fore. Indeed, it is possible to see each of these two literatures—the philosophical and the empirical—as synergistically, if not dialectically—growing with the other. The view that has emerged as a consequence of this co-historical, philosophical-empirical evolution is one wherein theoretical reductionism is eschewed in favor of models that depict changing, synthetic relations among qualitatively distinct levels of analysis. It is important to understand the precise meaning of the term *levels* as it is used in this literature.

THE CONCEPT OF *LEVELS* IN THE DEVELOPMENTAL LITERATURE ON RECIPROCAL ORGANISM-CONTEXT RELATIONS

In the integrated philosophical-empirical literature I have been discussing, levels are conceived of as integrative organizations; that is, "the concept of integrative levels recognizes as equally essential for the purpose of scientific analysis both the isolation of parts of a whole and their integration into the structure of the whole. It neither reduces phenomena of a higher level to those of a lower one, as in mechanistic models, or describes the higher level in vague nonmaterial terms which are but substitutes for understanding, as in vitalism. Unlike other 'holistic' theories, it never leaves the firm ground of material reality. . . . The concept points to the need to study the organizational interrelationships of parts and whole" (Novikoff, 1945, p. 209). Moreover, Tobach and Greenberg (1984) stressed that:

> the interdependence among levels is of great significance. The dialectic nature of the relationship among levels is one in which lower levels are subsumed in higher levels so that any particular level is an integration of preceding

levels. . . . In the process of integration, or fusion, new levels with their own characteristics result. (p. 2)

If the course of human development is the product of the processes involved in the "fusions" (or "dynamic interactions"; Lerner, 1978, 1984) among integrative levels, then the processes of development are more plastic than often previously believed (cf. Brim & Kagan, 1980).

Given such a potential for plasticity, it is, then, a basic feature of the system of processes involved in human development that both constancy and change—both continuity and discontinuity—may exist across life. The presence of—or better, potentiality for—at least some plasticity means that the key way of casting the issue of continuity–discontinuity of development is not a matter of deciding what exists for a given process or function; instead, the issue should be cast in terms of determining the patterns of interactions among levels that may promote continuity and/or discontinuity for a particular process or function at a given point in ontogeny and/or history. The same process may exhibit either continuity or discontinuity with earlier life periods and/or may exhibit some features of both continuity and discontinuity, depending on the particular dynamic interaction that exists among levels at a given point in time. Thus, neither continuity nor discontinuity is absolute. Both are probabilistically present features of change, and the actualization of either is dependent on prevailing developmental conditions within the organism as well as its context.

For example, Simmons, Blyth, and their colleagues (e.g., see Simmons & Blyth, 1987) illustrated that either continuity or discontinuity in females' self-esteem across early adolescence is possible. Whether continuity or discontinuity in self-esteem occurs depends on the confluence of other organismic and contextual changes experienced by the females. For instance, discontinuity (in the direction of decrement) of self-esteem is most likely when the early adolescent female is experiencing simultaneously the organismic change associated with menarche and the contextual alterations associated with the transition from elementary school to junior high school.

The developmental literature suggesting these ideas about plasticity and the relativity of continuity and discontinuity has to a great extent been associated with the life-span view of human development (Baltes, 1987; Featherman, 1983; Lerner, 1984, 1986). Within this perspective, the context for development is not seen merely as a simple stimulus environment but, according to Bronfenbrenner (1979), rather as an "ecological environment . . . conceived topologically as a nested arrangement of concentric structures, each contained within the next" (p. 22) and including variables from biological, psychological, physical, and sociocultural levels, all changing interdependently across history (Riegel, 1975, 1976).

The life-span perspective is associated, then, with a concern with issues about the relations between evolution and ontogeny, about the role the developing person plays in his or her own development, about human plasticity, and therefore about life course continuity and discontinuity (Baltes, 1987; Lerner & Busch-Rossnagel, 1981; Scarr & McCartney, 1983; Tobach, 1981). These issues are linked by the idea that reciprocal relations (i.e., dynamic interactions; Lerner, 1978) between individuals and the multiple contexts within which they live characterize human development (Bronfenbrenner, 1979). In other words, all the issues raised by this perspective derive from a common appreciation of the basic role of the necessary link between an organism's development and its changing, multilevel context. The functional significance of this changing organism-context relation requires adoption of a developmental contextual (or probabilistic epigenetic; Gottlieb, 1970; Schneirla, 1957) view of an organism's development. In the next section I consider the key components of developmental contextualism.

FEATURES OF DEVELOPMENTAL CONTEXTUALISM

Since its inception as a specialization within the discipline, developmental psychology—or, as it was initially termed, *genetic psychology* (e.g., Hall, 1904)—has been dominated by a biological model of change. Indeed, the concept of development is biological in its scientific origin (Harris, 1957; von Bertalanffy, 1933). Although the particular version of biological change that has influenced developmental psychology has been and remains Darwinian in character (White, 1968), this common heritage has nevertheless led to the formulation of the quite diverse models of development; for instance, mechanistic-behavioral conceptions of developmental change (e.g., Bijou, 1976; Bijou & Baer, 1961) and organismic-dynamic (e.g., Freud, 1954) and organismic-structural (e.g., Piaget, 1950) theories may be interpreted as derived from this Darwinian heritage (Dixon & Lerner, 1988).

Despite this range of interpretations of the contribution of biology to psychological development, the organismic versions have been predominant in developmental psychology and in fact have been termed *strong* developmental models (e.g., Reese & Overton, 1970). Thus, to the field of psychology in general, and perhaps to the scholarly community as a whole, the organismic theories of Freud (1954), Erikson (1959), and Piaget (1950) typically are held to be the classic, prototypic, or exemplary ones within developmental psychology (e.g., see Emmerich, 1968; Lerner, 1986).

These instances of organismic theory, especially those of Freud and of Erikson, have been labeled predetermined epigenetic (Gottlieb, 1970). In this type of theory, biology is seen as the prime mover of development. Intrinsic (e.g., maturational) changes are believed to essentially unfold; although environmental or experiential variables may speed up or slow down these progressions, they can do nothing to alter the sequence or quality (e.g., the structure) of these hereditarily predetermined changes (e.g., see Gesell, 1946; Hamburger, 1957).

Another view of biological functioning exists: A probabilistic epigenetic one. Here biological and contextual factors are considered to be reciprocally interactive, and developmental changes are probabilistic in respect to normative outcomes due to variation in the timing of the biological, psychological, and social factors (or levels) that provide interactive bases of ontogenetic progressions (e.g., Schneirla, 1957; Tobach, 1981).

It is this probabilistic epigenetic view of biological functioning—or, better, of biology (or organism)-context relations—that I have noted provides the theoretical underpinning of the life-span view of human development (Lerner & Kauffman, 1985). Indeed, it is this particular organismic view, or better, this developmental contextual view (Lerner & Kauffman, 1985), that constitutes the new intellectual agenda of developmental psychology noted by Brim and Kagan (1980). For instance, within the field of adolescence the models of person-context relations advanced by Brooks-Gunn (1987), Lerner and Lerner (1989), and Petersen and Taylor (1980) are all consistent with the developmental contextual view of human development. In addition, Thompson and Lamb (1986) saw promise for the developmental contextual view associated with the life-span perspective to enrich the study of infancy. Similar prospects exist in regard to the multidisciplinary study of child development (Hetherington & Baltes, 1988). Thus, there are now, and there seem likely to continue to be, important links between developmental contextualism and other areas of psychological and developmental science.

Indeed, the developmental contextual conception of development can be traced to comparative biology (Novikoff, 1945) and comparative psychology (e.g., Gottlieb, 1970, 1976; Kuo, 1967; Maier & Schneirla, 1935; Schneirla, 1957). In this literature the concept of probabilistic epigenesis was not used to emphasize intrinsically predetermined or inevitable timetables and outcomes of development; instead, probabilistic epigenesis stressed that the influence of the changing context on development is to make the trajectory of development less certain with respect to the applicability of norms to the individual (Gottlieb, 1970; Tobach, 1981). Thus, such a conception emphasizes the probabilistic character of both the directions and outcomes of development and in so doing admits of more plasticity in development than do predeterministic conceptions. As I noted earlier, it is this plasticity that necessitates a revised formulation of the continuity–discontinuity issue. The plasticity that derives from the probabilistic (yet causal) interaction among levels makes both continuity and/or discontinuity a probabilistic feature of developmental change across life periods.

Probabilism in continuity and discontinuity is stressed, according to Gottlieb (1970), because of "the view that the behavioral development of individuals within a species does not follow an invariant or inevitable course, and, more specifically, that the sequence or outcome of individual behavioral development is probable (with respect to norms) rather than certain" (p. 123). But, do all possible instances of continuity and discontinuity have an equal probability of occurrence? I think not. Development occurs in a multilevel context. The nature of the changes in this context contributes to the probabilistic character of development; but one needs to appreciate too that the organism as much shapes the context as the context shapes the organism, and that—at the same time—both organism and context constrain, or limit, the other. In other words, the processes that give humans their individuality and their plasticity are the same ones that provide their commonality and constancies (Lerner, 1984, 1988).

Accordingly, although there is some probability that any process or feature of development could show continuity or discontinuity, constraints on change, arising from both organism and context, make some constancies and changes more probable than others. This differential probability complicates the study of continuity and discontinuity, because it requires not only an indication of "confidence intervals" around particular instances of continuity and discontinuity but, as well, a specification of the likely systemic ordering of such instances.

For example, it is less likely that a large and complex social institution such as a junior high school will alter its overall curriculum or educational policies to accommodate one child's individuality than it is that a single classroom will show such change. Nevertheless, there is some possibility that a particular instance of a child's individuality (e.g., consider a child with AIDS) will evoke a general change in the junior high school. Conversely, it is less likely that the experience of instruction within a single course will alter the lives of an entire cohort of adolescents than it is that the experience of an overall high school curriculum will have that influence. Yet, as the case of East Los Angeles Garfield High School mathematics teacher Jaime Escalante illustrates (in the 1988 film *Stand and Deliver*), a single class, or in this case teacher, can indeed alter the educational lives of an entire cohort of students. Thus, whereas one would have to order the effects of a single child on a classroom as more likely than the effects on an entire school, and whereas one would similarly have to order changes on a cohort of high school students as more likely to be evoked by an entire school curriculum than by a single course, there is nevertheless some probability in both cases that the less likely (lower order) change will occur.

A final point about the developmental contextual view needs to be highlighted. Although, in attempting to explain development, both this conception and mechanistic-behavioral views conceive of the context as enveloping an organism, it is clear that they do so in distinctly different ways. Developmental contextual theorists do not adopt a reductionistic approach to conceptualizing the impact of the context (Tobach, 1981). Instead, there is a focus on organism-context transactions (Sameroff, 1975), a commitment to using an interlevel, or relational, unit of analysis (Lerner, 1984), and, as emphasized before, a concept of the context as composed of multiple, qualitatively different levels (e.g., see Riegel, 1975, 1976).

Moreover, although both the mechanistic and the developmental-contextual perspectives hold that changes in the context become part of intraindividual changes in the organism's constitution, the concept of *organism* found in the two perspectives is also quite distinct. The organism in developmental contextualism is not merely the host of the elements of a simplistic environment. Instead, the organism is itself a qualitatively distinct level within the multiple, dynamically interacting levels forming the context of life.

As such, the organism has a distinct influence on the multilevel context that is influencing it. As a consequence the organism is, in short, an active contributor to its own development (Lerner & Busch-Rossnagel, 1981). The contemporary study of children, youth, and families provides an excellent illustration of these developmental contextual notions. In addition, this literature illustrates the change-oriented and relational nature of the basic developmental process conceived of within this view. Finally, this literature illustrates the importance of developmental contextualism's views of person-context relations for developmental research and for its link to interventions to enhance the course of life. Accordingly, I turn now to a discussion of the literature on children, youth, and families.

DIVERSITY AND CONTEXT IN RESEARCH, POLICY, AND PROGRAMS FOR CHILDREN AND ADOLESCENTS

Over the last two decades the study of children, youth, and their contexts, for example, their families, schools, and communities, has evolved in at least three significant directions. Each of these trends—involving changes in the conceptualization of the nature of the child, the emergence of a life-span perspective about human development, and a stress on the contexts of development—was product and producer of the developmental contextual perspective (Lerner, 1986, 1991; Lerner & Kauffman, 1985).

Indeed, within the context of a developmental contextual conceptualization of the dynamic interactions involved in the relations individuals have with the more molecular (e.g., biological) and the more molar (e.g., familial) levels of organization involved in human behavior and development, children have come to be understood as active producers of their own development (Lerner & Busch-Rossnagel, 1981; Lerner & Spanier, 1978; Lewis & Rosenblum, 1974). These contributions are believed to primarily occur through the reciprocal relations children have with their parents and with other significant people in their context, for example, other family members, caregivers and teachers, and peers.

Moreover, the content and functional significance of these "child effects" are seen to occur as a consequence of children's characteristics of organismic and/or behavioral individuality (cf. Schneirla, 1957). Individual differences in children evoke differential reactions in other people, reactions that provide feedback to children and influence the further, individual character of their development (Lerner, 1982). Accordingly, individuality is central in understanding the way in which the child is an active agent in his or her own development; that is, the unique fusion of biological, psychological, and sociocultural levels of organization makes the child individually distinct; this individuality provides the basis of further, distinct interactions with the context and promotes the continued development of an individual developmental trajectory.

The second trend that arose in the 1970s in relation to developmental contextualism promoted as well a concern with individual differences, and with diversity of human developmental pathways across life. The emergence of interest during the 1970s and 1980s in a life-span perspective about human development (e.g., Baltes, 1987; Baltes, Reese, & Lipsitt, 1980; Lerner, 1984; Lerner & Spanier, 1980) led to the understanding that parents as well as children develop as distinct individuals across life.

Parents develop both as adults in general and, more specifically, in regard to their familial and extrafamilial (for example, vocational or career) roles. Indeed, the influence of a child on his or her parents will depend in part on the prior experience the adult has had with the parental role *and* on the other roles in which the parent is engaged (e.g., worker and/or adult-child and—with increasing frequency in our society—caregiver for an aged parent). Thus, a person's unique history of experiences and roles, as well as his or her unique biological (e.g., genetic) characteristics (McClearn, 1981), combine to make him or her unique. Moreover, with time, given the accumulation of the influences of distinct roles and experiences, the person becomes increasingly more unique over the course of life (Lerner, 1988; Lerner & Tubman, 1989).

The life-span perspective underscores, then, the developmental contextual idea that changing relations between the person and his or her context provide the basis across life of the individual's unique repertoire of physical, psychological, and behavioral characteristics. This link between person and context was a product and a producer of the third trend emerging in the study of human development since the 1970s.

The study of children and their parents became increasingly "contextualized" (Lerner & Kauffman, 1985) or placed within the broader "ecology of human development" (Bronfenbrenner, 1979) during this period. This focus has involved a concern with the "real life" situations within which children and families exist, and with the study of the bidirectional relations between the family and the other social settings within which children and parents function, for instance, the workplace, the day care, and the formal and the nonformal educational and recreational settings present in a neighborhood or a community (e.g., see Kreppner & Lerner, 1989).

In essence, then, within the contemporary study of human development there has been an increasing focus on the connections across life between the active, developing individual and the changing, multiple contexts within which he or she is embedded. Indeed, within the field of human development this focus is legitimated through subscription to the developmental contextual notion that the basic process of development is one of changing person-context *relations* (Gottlieb, 1991; Lerner, 1991). This understanding of basic process results, then, in an emphasis in research on the appraisal of *the relations* between an individual's development and the changing familial, community, societal, and cultural contexts within which the person is embedded.

In sum, then, a developmental contextual perspective involves the study of active people providing a source across the life span of their individual developmental trajectories; this development occurs through the dynamic interactions people experience with the specific characteristics of the changing contexts within which they are embedded. Accordingly, developmental contextualism leads to a focus, across the course of life, on individual differences—of people and of settings—and on changes in person-context relations across time. These foci have important implications for research and for the policies and programs aimed at understanding and optimizing, respectively, the course of development in childhood and adolescence.

Implications for Research

The emphasis in developmental contextualism on the bidirectional connections between the individual and the actual ("ecologically valid") settings within which he or she lives has brought to the fore of concern in the social and behavioral sciences an emphasis on *diversity* (individual differences) and *context* (of people's specific array of sociocultural institutions). In turn, the developmental contextual stress on the relation between the individual and his or her context has resulted in the recognition that a synthesis of perspectives from multiple disciplines is needed to understand the multilevel (e.g., person, family, and community) integrations involved in human development. In addition, there has been a recognition that to understand the basic process of human development—the process of change involved in the relations between individuals and contexts—both descriptive and explanatory research must be conducted within the actual ecology of people's lives.

In the case of explanatory studies, such investigations by their very nature constitute intervention research. The role of the developmental researcher conducting explanatory research is to understand the ways in which variations in person-context relations account for the character of human developmental trajectories, life paths that are enacted in the "natural laboratory" of the "real world." Therefore, to gain understanding of how theoretically relevant variations in person-context relations may influence developmental trajectories, the researcher may introduce policies and/or programs as, if you will, "experimental manipulations" of the proximal and/or distal natural ecology; evaluations of the outcomes of such interventions become, then, a means to bring data to bear on theoretical issues pertinent to person-context relations and, more specifically, on the plasticity in human development that may exist, or that may be capitalized on, to enhance human life (Lerner, 1988). In other words, a key theoretical issue for explanatory research in human development is the extent to which changes—in the multiple, fused levels of organization comprising human life—can alter the structure and/or function of behavior and development.

Life itself is, of course, an intervention; that is, the accumulation of the specific roles and events a person experiences across life—involving normative age-graded events, normative history-graded events, and non-normative events (Baltes, Reese, & Lipsitt, 1980)—alters each person's developmental trajectory in a manner that would not have occurred had another set of roles and events been experienced. The interindividual differences in intraindividual change that exist as a consequence of these naturally occurring interventions attest to the magnitude of the systematic changes in structure and function—the plasticity—that characterizes human life.

Explanatory research is necessary, however, to understand what variables, from what levels of organization, are involved in particular instances of plasticity that have been seen to exist. Such research is also necessary to determine what instances of plasticity may be created by science or society. In other words, explanatory research is needed to ascertain the extent of human plasticity or, in turn, the limits of plasticity (Baltes, 1987; Lerner, 1984). From a developmental contextual perspective, the conduct of such research requires the scientist to alter the natural ecology of the person or group he or she is studying. Such research may involve either proximal and/or distal variations in the context of human development (Lerner & Ryff, 1978); but, in any case, these manipulations constitute theoretically guided alterations of the roles and events a person or group experiences at, or over, a portion of the life span.

These alterations are indeed, then, interventions: They are planned attempts to alter the system of person-context relations that constitute the basic process of change; they are conducted to ascertain the specific bases of, or to test the limits of, particular instances of human plasticity (Baltes, 1987; Baltes & Baltes, 1980). These interventions are a researcher's attempt to substitute designed person-context relations for naturally occurring ones in an attempt to understand the process of changing person-context relations that provides the basis of human development. In short, then, basic research in human development *is* intervention research.

Accordingly, the cutting edge of theory and research in human development lies in the application of the conceptual and methodological expertise of human development scientists to the natural ontogenetic laboratory of the real world. Multilevel, and hence, multivariate, and longitudinal research methods must be used by scholars from multiple disciplines to derive, from theoretical models of person-context relations, programs of "applied research"; these endeavors must involve the design, delivery, and evaluation of interventions aimed at enhancing—through scientist-introduced variation—the course of human development (Birkel, Lerner, & Smyer, 1989).

This relationism and contextualization has brought to the fore of scientific, intervention, and policy concerns issues pertinent to the functional import of diverse instances of person-context interactions. Examples are studies of the effects of maternal employment on infant, child, and young adolescent development; the importance of quality day care for the immediate and long-term development in children of healthy physical, psychological, and social characteristics; and the effects of marital role strain and marital disruption on the healthy development of children and youth.

Accordingly, as greater study has been made of the actual contexts within which children and parents live, behavioral and social scientists have shown increasing appreciation of the *diversity* of patterns of individual and family development that exist, and that comprise the range of human structural and functional characteristics. Such diversity—involving racial, ethnic, gender, national, and cultural variation—has, to the detriment of the knowledge base in human development, not been a prime concern of empirical analysis (Hagen, Paul, Gibb, & Wolters, 1990).

Yet, there are several reasons why this diversity must become a key focus of concern in the study of the development of children, adolescents, and their families (Lerner, 1991). First, diversity of people and their settings means that one cannot assume that general rules of development either exist for, or apply in the same way to, all children and families. Accordingly, a new research agenda is necessary. This agenda should focus on diversity and context whereas at the same time attending to commonalities of individual development, family changes, and the mutual influences between the two. In other words, diversity should be placed at the fore of our research agenda. Then, with a knowledge of individuality, we can determine empirically parameters of commonality, of interindividual generalizability. Thus, we should no longer make a priori assumptions about the existence of generic developmental laws or of the primacy of such laws, even if they are found to exist, in providing the key information about the life of a given person or group.

Simply stated, integrated multidisciplinary and developmental research devoted to the study of diversity and context must be moved to the fore of scholarly concern. In addition, however, scholars involved in such research must have at least two other concerns, ones deriving from the view that basic, explanatory research in human development is, in its essence, intervention research.

Implications for Policies and Programs

The integrative research promoted by a developmental contextual view of human development must be synthesized with two other foci. Research in human development that is concerned with one or even a few instances of individual and contextual diversity cannot be assumed to be useful for understanding the life course of all people. Similarly, policies and programs derived from such research, or associated with it in the context of a researcher's tests of ideas pertinent to human plasticity, cannot hope to be applicable, or equally appropriate and useful, in all contexts or for all individuals. Accordingly, developmental and individual differences-oriented policy development and program (intervention) design and delivery must be integrated fully with the new research base for which I am calling.

As emphasized in developmental contextualism, the variation in settings within which people live means that studying development in a standard (e.g., a "controlled") environment does not provide information pertinent to the actual (ecologically valid) developing relations between individually distinct people and their specific contexts (e.g., their particular families, schools, or communities). This point underscores the need to conduct research in real-world settings and highlights the ideas that: (a) Policies and programs constitute natural experiments (i.e., planned interventions for people and institutions); and (b) the evaluation of such activities becomes a central focus in the developmental contextual research agenda I have described.

In this view, then, policy and program endeavors do *not* constitute secondary work, or derivative applications, conducted after research evidence has been compiled. Quite to the contrary, policy development and implementation, and program design and delivery, become integral components of the present vision for research; the evaluation component of such policy and intervention work provides critical feedback about the adequacy of the conceptual frame from which this research agenda should derive. This conception of the integration of multidisciplinary research, endeavors centrally aimed at diversity and context, with policies, programs (interventions), and evaluations is illustrated in Fig. 1.1.

To be successful, this developmental, individual differences, and contextual view of research, policy, and programs for children and youth requires not only collaboration across disciplines. Multiprofessional collaboration is also essential. Colleagues in the research, policy, and intervention communities must plan and implement their activities in a synthesized manner to successfully develop and extend this vision. All components of this collabo-

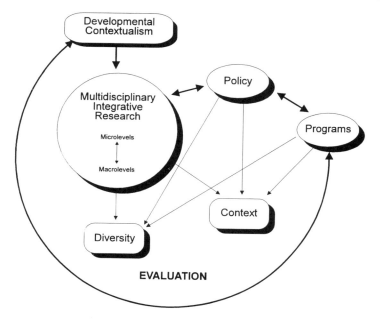

FIG. 1.1. A model of the integration of multilevel, multidisciplinary research, aimed at diversity and context, with policies, programs, and evaluations.

ration must be understood as equally valuable, indeed, as equally essential. The collaborative activities of colleagues in university extension, in service design and delivery, in policy development and analysis, and in academic research are vital to the success of this new agenda for science and service for children, youth, and their contexts (e.g., their families, schools, and communities). Moreover, such collaborative activities must involve the communities within which such work is undertaken. In other words, to enhance its ecological validity, and to provide empowerment and increased capacity among the people we are trying to both understand and serve with our synthetic research and intervention activities, we must work with the community to codefine the nature of our research and program design, delivery, and evaluation endeavors. This viewpoint leads to some observations about directive themes that might organize the future activities of scholars studying children, youth, families, schools, and communities.

Potential Scholarly and Service Themes

Together, the aforementioned facets of developmental contextual-oriented scholarship in the study of children, youth, and contexts suggest several important themes for research, training, and service. First, a developmental, individual-differences perspective is required to understand *both* children and families; this perspective must focus on the relations within the family between parents and children and, as well, on the relations between each family member and the other settings within which he or she functions (e.g., children and day-care settings and parents and the workplace). In addition, the relations among settings must become a focus of developmental analysis as well (Bronfenbrenner, 1979). The compilation of such information will afford a profile of the individual people and relations that comprise a specific family.

Second, the study of children and parents must become broadly contextualized. Variables from multiple levels of organization—ranging from biology and health through social institutions involving education, politics, and the economy—affect people across their lives. It is the array of these variables as they extend across life that can make each person increasingly individually distinct from other in his or her family, social group, cohort, or society (Tobach, 1981).

Moreover, as noted earlier, the contextual and developmental approach to the study of children and their parents must emphasize diversity. There is no one developmental path that is ideal for all people. As such, a key scientific concern of scholars of children, youth, and families must be the understanding of the richness of human life reflected in racial, ethnic, gender, national, and cultural variation. Education, intervention, outreach, and policy endeavors similarly should emphasize the specific patterns of contextual variation associated with the diverse peoples of concern to scholars.

Third, then, because no one discipline or professional area has an experiential or a knowledge base (or a repertoire of methodologies) sufficient to understand this diversity, or the interrelated influences of multiple levels of analysis on children and families, a multidisciplinary and multiprofessional approach to training, research, and service is required. In other words, to study the phenomena and problems of children, youth, and families, as they function and develop in their real-life settings, and to provide effective health, family, and human policies and services, we need interdisciplinary conceptualizations and multiprofessional collaborations.

This integration should be a key facet of the mission of any academic field aimed at advancing science and service for children, youth, and families. The knowledge base that may be generated in activities associated with such a mission may be extended into programs and services for the children and families of a state, of a nation, and—given the proper collaborative arrangements—the world.

CONCLUSIONS

Research must be conducted with an appreciation of the individual differences in human development, differences that arise as a consequence of diverse people's development in distinct families, communities, and sociocultural settings. In turn, policies and programs must be similarly attuned to the diversity of people and context to maximize the chances of meeting the specific needs of particular groups of children and youth. Such programs and policies must be derived appropriately from research predicated on an integrative multidisciplinary view of human development. The evaluation of such applications should provide both societally important information about the success of endeavors aimed at youth enhancement, *and* theoretically invaluable data about the validity of the synthetic, multilevel processes posited in developmental contextualism to characterize human development.

Meeting the challenge represented by the need to merge research with policy, and with intervention design, delivery, and evaluation, will bring the study of children, adolescents, and families to the threshold of a new intellectual era. The linkage between research, policy, and intervention I have envisioned will demonstrate to scientists that the basic processes of human behavior are ones involving the development of relations between individually distinct youth and the specific social institutions they encounter in their particular ecological setting.

This demonstration will be a matter, then, of bringing data to bear on the validity of the developmental contextual conception of basic process and of basic research (Lerner, 1991). Studying changing relations between diverse peoples and contexts alters the core analytic frame in investigations of human development from a personological one to a person-context relational one (Lerner, 1991); this alteration makes the evaluation of the programs and policies aimed at changing developmental patterns of youth a theoretically vital activity, one providing critical empirical feedback about the conceptual usefulness of the ideas of multilevel integration, ideas from which the policies and programs should have been derived.

It is for these reasons then that I have argued that policy and program design, delivery, and evaluation are not "second-class citizens" to basic research. Within the frame of the fused levels of organization that comprise human behavior and development, they constitute necessary *and basic* empirical tests of the core, relational process of life. Accordingly, if we wish to meet the challenge of child and youth development, the activities of colleagues whose expertise lies in policy and program design, delivery, and evaluation are not to be set apart from "basic" scientific activity. The expertise of policy and program professionals must be integrated with that of the researcher, in a fully collaborative enterprise, if we are to make continued progress in the understanding and enhancement of children and youth.

In other words, the knowledge generation-application avenue is not a one-way street. Indeed, just as the practicing physician is often a source of issues that medical scientists then address, colleagues in the policy and program delivery arenas—whose roles emphasize the interface with the individual, family, and community—can provide invaluable feedback both about how the fruits of scholarship are being received and used *and* about new concerns that might be addressed with this scholarship.

In essence, then, the burgeoning high-quality scientific activity in the developmental contextual study of children and adolescents has involved: First, the recognition of the importance of theory and research aimed at elucidating the relations between individually different, developing children and youth and their diverse and changing contexts; *and*, second, the growing appreciation of the necessary linkage among research, policy, and intervention that must exist for the nature of child and youth development—and, more specifically, its individuality and plasticity—to be understood and for the challenges of these periods of life to be best met.

In sum, the developmental contextual view of what constitutes the basic process of human development brings to the fore the cutting-edge importance of a continued empirical focus on individual differences, on contextual variations, and on changing person-context relations. Nothing short of these emphases can be regarded as involving a scientifically adequate developmental analysis of human life. And nothing short of data involving these emphases should be seen as useful for formulating policies and programs suitable for individually different children and youth developing in relation to their specific contexts.

ACKNOWLEDGMENT

The preparation of this chapter was supported in part by NICHD Grant HD23229 to Richard M. Lerner.

REFERENCES

Baltes, P. B. (1987). Theoretical propositions of life-span developmental psychology: On the dynamics between growth and decline. *Developmental Psychology, 23,* 611–626.

Baltes, P. B., & Baltes, M. M. (1980). Plasticity and variability in psychological aging: Methodological and theoretical issues. In G. E. Gurski (Ed.), *Determining the effects of aging on the central nervous system* (pp. 41–60). Berlin: Schering AG.

Baltes, P. B., Reese, H. W., & Lipsitt, L. P. (1980). Life-span developmental psychology. *Annual Review of Psychology, 31,* 65–110.

Baltes, P. B., Reese, H. W., & Nesselroade, J. R. (1977). *Life-span developmental psychology: Introduction to research methods.* Monterey, CA: Brooks/Cole.

Bandura, A. (1978). The self system in reciprocal determinism. *American Psychologist, 33,* 344–358.

Bijou, S. W. (1976). *Child development: The basic stage of early childhood.* Englewood Cliffs, NJ: Prentice-Hall.

Bijou, S. W., & Baer, D. M. (1961). *Child development: A systematic and empirical theory* (Vol. 1). New York: Appleton-Century-Crofts.

Birkel, R., Lerner, R. M., & Smyer, M. A. (1989). Applied developmental psychology as an implementation of a life-span view of human development. *Journal of Applied Developmental Psychology, 10,* 425–445.

Brim, O. G., Jr., & Kagan, J. (Eds.). (1980). *Constancy and change in human development.* Cambridge, MA: Harvard University Press.

Brim, O. G., Jr., & Ryff, C. D. (1980). On the properties of life events. In P. B. Baltes & O. G. Brim, Jr. (Eds.), *Life-span development and behavior* (Vol. 3, pp. 367–388). New York: Academic Press.

Bronfenbrenner, U. (1963). Developmental theory in transition. In H. W. Stevenson (Ed.), *Child psychology: Sixty-second yearbook of the National Society for the Study of Education* (Part 1, pp. 517–542). Chicago: University of Chicago Press.

Bronfenbrenner, U. (1979). *The ecology of human development.* Cambridge, MA: Harvard University Press.

Brooks-Gunn, J. (1987). Pubertal processes and girls' psychological adaptation. In R. M. Lerner & T. T. Foch (Eds.), *Biological-psychosocial interactions in early adolescence: A life-span perspective* (pp. 123–153). Hillsdale, NJ: Lawrence Erlbaum Associates.

Dixon, R. A., & Lerner, R. M. (1988). A history of systems in developmental psychology. In M. H. Bornstein & M. E. Lamb (Eds.), *Developmental psychology* (2nd ed., pp. 3–50). Hillsdale, NJ: Lawrence Erlbaum Associates.

Dixon, R. A., & Nesselroade, J. R. (1983). Pluralism and correlational analysis in developmental psychology: Historical commonalities. In R. M. Lerner (Ed.), *Developmental psychology: Historical and philosophical perspectives* (pp. 113–145). Hillsdale, NJ: Lawrence Erlbaum Associates.

Elder, G. H., Jr. (1974). *Children of the great depression.* Chicago: University of Chicago Press.

Elder, G. H., Jr. (1980). Adolescence in historical perspective. In J. Adelson (Ed.), *Handbook of adolescent psychology* (pp. 3–46). New York: Wiley.

Emmerich, W. (1968). Personality development and concepts of structure. *Child Development, 39,* 671–690.

Erikson, E. H. (1959). Identity and the life-cycle. *Psychological Issues, 1,* 18–164.

Featherman, D. L. (1983). Life-span perspectives in social science research. In P. B. Baltes & O. G. Brim, Jr. (Eds.), *Life-span development and behavior* (Vol. 5, pp. 1–57). New York: Academic Press.

Ford, D. H. (1987). *Humans as self-constructing living systems.* Hillsdale, NJ: Lawrence Erlbaum Associates.

Freud, A. (1969). Adolescence as a developmental disturbance. In G. Caplan & S. Lebovier (Eds.), *Adolescence* (pp. 5–10). New York: Basic Books.

Freud, S. (1954). *Collected works* (Standard ed.). London: Hogarth.

Gesell, A. L. (1946). The ontogenesis of infant behavior. In L. Carmichael (Ed.), *Manual of child psychology* (pp. 295–331). New York: Wiley.

Gottlieb, G. (1970). Conceptions of prenatal behavior. In R. Aronson, E. Tobach, D. S. Lehrman, & J. S. Rosenblatt (Eds.), *Development and evolution of behavior: Essays in memory of T. C. Schneirla* (pp. 111–137). San Francisco: Freeman.

Gottlieb, G. (1976). Conceptions of prenatal development: Behavioral embryology. *Psychological Review, 83,* 215–234.

Gottlieb, G. (1991). Experiential canalization of behavioral development: Theory. *Developmental Psychology, 27,* 4–13.

Hagen, J. W., Paul, B., Gibb, S., & Wolters, C. (1990, March). *Trends in research as reflected by publications in Child Development: 1930–1989.* Paper presented at the Biennial Meeting of the Society for Research on Adolescence, Atlanta.

Hall, G. S. (1904). *Adolescence: Its psychology and its relations to physiology, anthropology, sociology, sex, crime, religion, and education* (Vols. 1 and 2). New York: Appleton.

Hamburger, V. (1957). The concept of development in biology. In D. B. Harris (Ed.), *The concept of development* (pp. 49–58). Minneapolis: University of Minnesota Press.

Harris, D. B. (Ed.). (1957). *The concept of development*. Minneapolis: University of Minnesota Press.

Hetherington, E. M., & Baltes, P. B. (1988). Child psychology and life-span development. In E. M. Hetherington, R. M. Lerner, & M. Perlmutter (Eds.), *Child development in life-span perspective* (pp. 1–19). Hillsdale, NJ: Lawrence Erlbaum Associates.

Jenkins, J. J. (1974). Remember that old theory of memory: Well forget it. *American Psychologist, 29*, 785–795.

Kaplan, B. (1983). A trio of trials. In R. M. Lerner (Ed.), *Developmental psychology: Historical and philosophical perspectives* (pp. 185–239). Hillsdale, NJ: Lawrence Erlbaum Associates.

Kreppner, K., & Lerner, R. M. (1989). *Family systems and life-span development*. Hillsdale, NJ: Lawrence Erlbaum Associates.

Kuhn, T. S. (1970). *The structure of scientific revolutions* (2nd ed.). Chicago: University of Chicago Press.

Kuo, Z. Y. (1967). *The dynamics of behavior development*. New York: Random House.

Lehrman, D. S. (1970). Semantic and conceptual issues in the nature-nurture problem. In L. R. Aronson, E. Tobach, & J. S. Rosenblatt (Eds.), *Development and evolution of behavior: Essays in memory of T. C. Schneirla* (pp. 17–52). San Francisco: Freeman.

Lerner, R. M. (1978). Nature, nurture and dynamic interactionism. *Human Development, 21*, 1–20.

Lerner, R. M. (1982). Children and adolescents as producers of their own development. *Developmental Review, 2*, 342–370.

Lerner, R. M. (1984). *On the nature of human plasticity*. New York: Cambridge University Press.

Lerner, R. M. (1986). *Concepts and theories of human development* (2nd ed.). New York: Random House.

Lerner, R. M. (1988). Personality development: A life-span perspective. In E. M. Hetherington, R. M. Lerner, & M. Perlmutter (Eds.), *Child development in life-span perspective* (pp. 21–46). Hillsdale, NJ: Lawrence Erlbaum Associates.

Lerner, R. M. (1991). Changing organism-context relations as the basic process of development: A developmental contextual perspective. *Developmental Psychology, 27*, 27–32.

Lerner, R. M., & Busch-Rossnagel, N. (1981). Individuals as producers of their development: Conceptual and empirical bases. In R. M. Lerner & N. A. Busch-Rossnagel (Eds.), *Individuals as producers of their development: A life-span perspective* (pp. 1–36). New York: Academic Press.

Lerner, R. M., & Kauffman, M. B. (1985). The concept of development in contextualism. *Developmental Review, 5*, 309–333.

Lerner, R. M., & Lerner, J. V. (1989). Organismic and social contextual bases of development: The sample case of adolescence. In W. Damon (Ed.), *Child development today and tomorrow* (pp. 69–85). San Francisco: Jossey-Bass.

Lerner, R. M., & Ryff, C. (1978). Implementation of the life-span view of human development: The sample case of attachment. In P. B. Baltes (Ed.), *Life-span development and behavior* (Vol. 1, pp. 1–44). New York: Academic Press.

Lerner, R. M., & Spanier, G. B. (1978). A dynamic interactional view of child and family development. In R. M. Lerner & G. B. Spanier (Eds.), *Child influences on marital and family interaction: A life-span perspective* (pp. 1–22). New York: Academic Press.

Lerner, R. M., & Spanier, G. B. (1980). *Adolescent development: A life-span perspective*. New York: McGraw-Hill.

Lerner, R. M., & Tubman, J. (1989). Conceptual issues in studying continuity and discontinuity in personality development across life. *Journal of Personality, 57*, 343–373.

Lewis, M., & Rosenblum, L. A. (Eds.). (1974). *The effect of the infant on its caregivers.* New York: Wiley.

Looft, W. R. (1972). The evolution of developmental psychology: A comparison of handbooks. *Human Development, 15,* 187–201.

Looft, W. R. (1973). Socialization and personality throughout the life span: An examination of contemporary psychological approaches. In P. B. Baltes & K. W. Schaie (Eds.), *Life-span developmental psychology: Personality and socialization* (pp. 25–52). New York: Academic Press.

Magnusson, D., & Allen, V. L. (Eds.). (1983). *Human development: An interactional perspective.* New York: Academic Press.

Maier, N. R. F., & Schneirla, T. C. (1935). *Principles of animal behavior.* New York: McGraw-Hill.

McClearn, G. E. (1981). Evolution and genetic variability. In E. S. Gollin (Ed.), *Developmental plasticity: Behavioral and biological aspects of variations in development* (pp. 3–31). New York: Academic Press.

Musca, T. (Producer), & Menéndez, R. (Director). (1988). *Stand and deliver* [Film]. Burbank, CA: Warner Brothers.

Mussen, P. H., & Kessen, W. (Eds.). (1983). *Handbook of child psychology: Vol. 1. History, theory, and methods.* New York: Wiley.

Nesselroade, J. R., & Baltes, P. B. (1974). Adolescent personality development and historical change: 1970–1972. *Monographs of the Society for Research in Child Development, 39.*

Novikoff, A. B. (1945). The concept of integrative levels of biology. *Science, 62,* 209–215.

Overton, W. F. (1973). On the assumptive base of the nature–nurture controversy: Additive versus interactive conceptions. *Human Development, 16,* 74–89.

Overton, W. F. (1984). World views and their influence on psychological theory and research: Kuhn-Lakatos-Lauden. In H. W. Reese (Ed.), *Advances in child development and behavior* (Vol. 18, pp. 191–225). New York: Academic Press.

Pepper, S. C. (1942). *World hypotheses.* Berkeley: University of California Press.

Petersen, A. C., & Taylor, B. (1980). The biological approach to adolescence: Biological change and psychological adaptation. In J. Adelson (Ed.), *Handbook of adolescent psychology* (pp. 117–155). New York: Wiley.

Piaget, J. (1950). *The psychology of intelligence.* New York: Harcourt Brace.

Reese, H. W., & Overton, W. F. (1970). Models of development and theories of development. In L. R. Goulet & P. B. Baltes (Eds.), *Life-span developmental psychology: Research and theory* (pp. 115–145). New York: Academic Press.

Riegel, K. F. (1975). Toward a dialectical theory of development. *Human Development, 18,* 50–64.

Riegel, K. F. (1976). The dialectics of human development. *American Psychologist, 31,* 689–700.

Rosnow, R., & Georgoudi, M. (Eds.). (1986). *Contextualism and understanding in behavioral research.* New York: Praeger.

Sameroff, A. (1975). Transactional models in early social relations. *Human Development, 18,* 65–79.

Sarbin, T. R. (1977). Contextualism: A world view for modern psychology. In J. K. Cole & A. W. Lundfield (Eds.), *Nebraska Symposium on Motivation, 1976* (pp. 1–41). Lincoln: University of Nebraska Press.

Scarr, S., & McCartney, K. (1983). How people make their own environments: A theory of genotype-environment effects. *Child Development, 54,* 424–435.

Schaie, K. W. (1979). The primary mental abilities in adulthood: An exploration in the development of psychometric intelligence. In P. B. Baltes & O. G. Brim, Jr. (Eds.), *Life-span development and behavior* (Vol. 2, pp. 67–115). New York: Academic Press.

Schneirla, T. C. (1957). The concept of development in comparative psychology. In D. B. Harris (Ed.), *The concept of development* (pp. 78–108). Minneapolis: University of Minnesota Press.

Simmons, R. G., & Blyth, D. A. (1987). *Moving into adolescence: The impact of pubertal change and school context.* Hawthorne, NJ: Aldine.

Simmons, R., Rosenberg, F., & Rosenberg, M. (1973). Disturbance in the self-image at adolescence. *American Sociological Review, 38,* 553–568.

Spiker, C. C., & McCandless, B. R. (1954). The concept of intelligence and the philosophy of science. *Psychological Review, 61,* 255–266.

Thompson, R. A., & Lamb, M. E. (1986). Infant-mother attachment: New directions for theory and research. In P. B. Baltes, D. L. Featherman, & R. M. Lerner (Eds.), *Life-span development and behavior* (Vol. 7, pp. 1–41). Hillsdale, NJ: Lawrence Erlbaum Associates.

Tobach, E. (1981). Evolutionary aspects of the activity of the organism and its development. In R. M. Lerner & N. A. Busch-Rossnagel (Eds.), *Individuals as producers of their development: A life-span perspective* (pp. 37–68). New York: Academic Press.

Tobach, E., & Greenberg, G. (1984). The significance of T. C. Schneirla's contribution to the concept of levels of integration. In G. Greenberg & E. Tobach (Eds.), *Behavioral evolution and integrative levels* (pp. 1–7). Hillsdale, NJ: Lawrence Erlbaum Associates.

von Bertalanffy, L. (1933). *Modern theories of development.* London: Oxford University Press.

White, S. H. (1968). The learning-maturation controversy: Hall to Hull. *Merrill-Palmer Quarterly, 14,* 187–196.

White, S. H. (1970). The learning theory tradition and child psychology. In P. H. Mussen (Ed.), *Carmichael's manual of child psychology* (3rd ed., pp. 657–701). New York: Wiley.

CHAPTER TWO

Accounting for Person–Context Relations and Their Development

Warren Thorngate
Carleton University, Ottawa, Canada

Because easy questions are usually answered before difficult ones, it is a cruel irony of intellectual progress that each new generation of researchers faces a dwindling supply of the former and a constant supply of the rest. I was reminded of the irony in thinking about the topic of this volume, for there are probably no questions more difficult to answer than those associated with describing and explaining the patterns of relations among people and their environments and how these patterns change in time.

Intellectual history is littered with attempts to account for the nature and changes of these patterns. The attempts of biologists and geographers define their subdisciplines of human ecology and social geography. Sociologists and economists pursue their attempts in analyses of individuals in roles and in markets. Psychology has seen its fair share of attempts as well. Notions of proximal development (Vygotsky, 1978), life space (Lewin, 1935), probabilistic function (Brunswik, 1950), behavioral setting (Barker, 1968), adaptation level (Helson, 1964), affordance (Gibson, 1979), and person-by-situation interaction (Mischel, 1968; Wachs & Plomin, 1991) are some of those created in hopes of understanding the changing relations between people and their environments. Developmental psychology has generated an additional set (cf. Bronfenbrenner, 1989; Kindermann & Skinner, 1992; Scarr & McCartney, 1983).

Why have so many accounts of the relations between people and their environments been created? And why do they remain at the periphery of developmental psychology? There seem to be several possible answers to the first question, ranging from academic politics to the definition of complex phenomena as those indescribable from one point of view (cf. Levins, 1966, 1968; Richardson, 1991; Thorngate, 1976a, 1990). Answers to the second question seem to focus on methodological problems. It seems we do not study these interactive phenomena in developmental psychology because we do not know how.

This volume attempts to reduce our ignorance by devising research methods appropriate for the study of changes in person/environment relations. There seem to be two basic strategies for devising these methods. The first is to extend or generalize traditional methods used to study noninteractive phenomena. The second is to create new methods from alternative epistemological and methodological assumptions. I think a good case can be made for trying both. However, I have a strong personal preference to try the second, so I shall leave the first to others.

My preference for devising new methods is largely based on my doubts about the utility of traditional methodologies, even in their noninteractive domains (London & Thorngate, 1981; Thorngate, 1986; see also Hershberger, 1989; Marken, 1988; Powers, 1974, 1989; Runkel, 1990). The kind of data required of traditional methods (almost always measures or counts of variables) are usually inappropriate for the study of interactive phenomena or impossible to obtain. Traditional techniques of aggregation (e.g., calculating averages) across people or environments usually result in misleading summaries of the nature or changes of reciprocal influence. And traditional techniques of variance partitioning are not useful, because the statistical concepts of "residuals" and "interaction effects" bear almost no relationship to the system dynamic concepts of deviation and interaction we are supposed to study. There is, of course, no guarantee that alternative methodologies, including those I outline in this chapter, will lead to methods that tell us much more than our traditional methodology. Yet they may be worth a try.

SOME FIRST PRINCIPLES

Before we examine new methodologies for the study of changes in relations between people and their environments, it is useful to review some first principles. So at the risk of exegesis, permit me to consider briefly a few fundamental questions. What are we trying to do in psychology? Most of us are trying to describe and to explain something about human behavior or experience in terms of variables or constructs within a person, within the environment, or between the two. How do we know when we are done? Most of us trained in traditional scientific methodology believe that developing a description and explanation is the end of our activities; when we have a good account, we are done.

But how do we know when we have a good account? The question vexes all of us who attempt to study the interactions among people and their environments because the usual scientific criteria of generality, accuracy, and parsimony are impossible to attain (Thorngate, 1976a). Sweeping and simple accounts that claim to be general and parsimonious are never very accurate; predictions derived from them tend to be vacuous (e.g., "Things will change") or wrong. Specific and simple accounts (minimodels) that show respectible predictive accuracy fail to generalize beyond their restrictive domains. To increase both generality and accuracy, an account must by necessity become more complex, but it quickly succumbs to the free parameter paradox. Complex accounts, by definition, have more variables or constructs than do simple ones; even a moderately complex account can employ over a dozen of them. Unfortunately, an account with more than three or four variables or constructs becomes logistically impossible to test or to evaluate in any rigorous way. Partial accounts are possible by making a series of simplifying assumptions, often scores of them—many of which are unrealistic or untestable (Levins, 1968). But as their number increases they come to form the bulk of the account, making it largely ad hoc.

Perhaps there is a way to resolve the free parameter paradox, but only if we change our epistemological and methodological assumptions. Four changes are especially important. First, we must learn a lesson from the differences between natural science and natural history. Natural historians in disciplines such as astronomy, geology, paleontology, and ecology make good use of natural science in developing new measurement procedures (e.g., using the Doppler effect, carbon dating, radio telemetry), but they ask different questions than do natural scientists and use different research methods to answer them. Natural historians are usually interested in explaining specific events deemed sufficiently important to warrant the effort. What is the composition of Saturn? Where are the continents drifting? Why are there more species in Costa Rica than in Canada? To answer such questions, the naturalists rarely sample randomly, manipulate variables, or rush to significance tests. Instead, they do detective work, looking and thinking carefully for clues to the answers while forever attempting to improve their measurement devices. The explanations they develop may have general implications, but few naturalists work for the sake of generalization. Theoreticians do that.

The lesson? It seems that the study of relations between people and their environments, and of changes in these relations, is much closer to natural history than to natural science. Accordingly, seeking good accounts of specific relations and their changes should be more useful than seeking generalizations. It is no great feat to examine a set of specific accounts for generalities. But let us refrain from putting the cart before the horse.

As a second change of assumptions, we must realize that at least two good accounts can be found for every interactive phenomenon. Many of us have been trained to believe that one best account exists for whatever we study, and that the purpose of research is to eliminate all but that one. When we study interactive phenomena, however, we can potentially account for them from as many points of view as there are different elements and relations in the interaction. Consider the lesson of ecology: there is no single way to describe or to explain an ecological system (see Levins, 1968). We can account for parts of an ecosystem in terms of energy transfer, parts in terms of population dynamics, parts in terms of life histories, and so on. All are valid, none are complete. The ecologies of people interacting with their environments are sure to have the same epistemological implications. As a result, our explanatory goal as researchers in this area should be to create, develop, and articulate as many good accounts from as many perspectives as possible. This does not imply that anything goes. Most accounts are bad, and many good ones are merely literal or metaphorical translations of others. It is certainly desirable to devise methods for separating the good accounts from the bad ones, and for combining those that say the same thing. At the same time, there is no reason to believe that all the good accounts will be related, and that they will eventually fit together to show us the Big Picture.

A third change in our assumptions concerns the nature and amount of information we gather to explain. Many of us believe that, because science uses numbers, the more we use the more scientific we will be. The deduction is illogical, reflecting a general confusion between quantity and quality and leading us to the error of misplaced precision. In truth, no amount of measurement or statistical manipulation will improve a bad idea. Furthermore, most ideas can be tested without resorting to fancy empirical or statistical procedures. As Darwin, Marx, Freud, Piaget, and others have shown, we can develop very good explanations just by thinking and watching and recording the results in words. Illogical explanations can be eliminated this way. So can those sufficiently clear to be eliminated by a few counterexamples. Most great theoreticians, experimenters, and naturalists in other disciplines keep extensive notebooks or logs for this purpose, but few of us do. In our rush to SPSS we usually overlook the power of careful observation, compulsive description, and skeptical thinking. These are three good habits, and we would benefit from acquiring them, especially if we choose to explain phenomena as resistant to numerical summary as person/environment interactions.

As a final change in our assumptions, remember that descriptions and explanations are not only ends of science; they are also means of communication. Technically, descriptions and explanations are sets of rewrite rules mapping percepts into concepts, concepts into percepts, or concepts into other concepts—a translation from what we see to what we say, what we say to what we see, or what we say to what we mean. Explanations differ from descriptions only by addressing the question "Why?" Both come in a wide variety of forms. Descriptions, for example, may be general or specific, detailed or sketchy, verbal or statistical, and so on. Explanations may be categorical or contingent, structural or functional, mechanistic or teleological, static or dynamic, reductionist or contextualist, analytical or analogical, and have disciplinary qualifiers such as economic or sociological, cognitive, behavioral, or humanistic. Their variety is not the result of some necessary relation between the form of an account and the nature of the phenomenon accounted. Instead, the variety reflects large individual differences in preferences for accounts—preferences that become important when communicating ours to other people (Thorngate, 1990; Thorngate & Plouffe, 1987).

It is one thing to build a better account and quite another to sell it. Unless we believe that our accounts should be secret, we should eventually consider how they are communicated to others and what the effects will be. Perhaps there was once reason to believe that scientific accounts would sell themselves simply because we had given them some laboratory seal of approval. The belief no longer seems justified. Particularly as we produce multiple accounts from various perspectives on the relations between people and their environments, we provide the consumer with an increasing variety of choice—often as supplements to the consumer's own accounts. There is no law of nature or legislation forcing people to consume our accounts just because we argue they are beautiful or true. Although consumers seem to have no strong preferences for accounts of, say, particle physics or RISC processor design, most do have preferences for accounts of their own behavior, and for the behavior of others. For example, most people prefer teleological explanations of the behavior of others; they expect a reason, motive, or purpose to answer "Why?" As for themselves or loved ones, most people prefer personal explanations of their accomplishments and circumstantial explanations of their errors. These preferences are difficult to change. It takes 4 or more years of university training, for example, to rid students in cognitive psychology of interest in popular explanatory concepts such as emotion, habit, and will.

Although it may be desirable to be ecumenical about accounts of relations and their changes, we must be aware of at least two possible consequences. First, many people may not understand them. Second, they may not care. Consider the lesson of a discipline dying of its own weight: literary criticism. Each generation of literary critics tends to produce another layer of criticism, each striving for more profundity while becoming more insular and obscure. There are now far more words of criticism than of literature, and almost no one reads the stuff. Life has more interesting challenges than pondering yet another angle on Chaucer. If we are to avoid a similar trajectory, we must be considerate of our audiences. In practical terms this means communicating in a clear, simple, and interesting way.

The most useful way to approach the study of relations between people and their environments and how they change is to (a) consider it a matter of history, (b) develop multiple perspectives and explanations, (c) make more use of careful observation and verbal description, and (d) know our audience. Changing our methodological and epistemological assumptions in these ways would put us in an intellectual domain somewhere between the sciences and the humanitites. It is not uncharted territory. Many research methods and styles have been developed there, and in the past few decades some have been greatly perfected. Case histories (Feagin, Orum, & Sjoberg, 1991), content and qualitative analyses (e.g., Miles & Huberman, 1984; Rosengren, 1981), and observation and interview techniques (e.g., Mishler, 1986; Stubbs, 1984), for example, now help to generate respectible accounts in Sociology, Political Science, Social Geography, Women's Studies, and other disciplines.

Many of these methods may be useful to us. Still, we are faced with unique problems trying to describe and to explain person/environment relations and their development. Let us now consider how we might approach solutions to some of them.

SOME SIMPLE METHODS FOR DEVELOPING AND TESTING ACCOUNTS

The task we set for ourselves is to account for people, their environments, changes in people, changes in their environments, the relations between changes in people and changes in their environments, and changes in the relations between changes in people and changes in their environments. It is a daunting task, in part because we are not yet very sophisticated about describing environments or explaining their relations with people. We tend to think of an environment as a stimulus soup full of causes of behavior. Our listing of environmental ingredients is usually rather Aristotelean, more phenotypic than genotypic, often confusing relations with properties or elements (e.g., considering the relations mother and father as properties, and the relations familiarity and hostility as elements, of an environment). Our distinctions between environmental soups are usually conveyed by simple terms such as home, school, work, or party, or by simple judgments such as hostile or friendly, predictable or unpredictable, rich or poor in stimuli. As a result, many of us believe that our accounting task will be accomplished by making an increasingly long list of observed behavior/environment contingencies, such as "Males aged 7 to 9 and raised in poor families tend to become more aggressive at school than at home, but females aged 4 to 7 and raised in middle-class families tend to become more aggessive at home than at school."

I think such a list of contingencies would be unsatisfying for at least three reasons. First, it would be useless. Second, it would be boring. Third, it would not explain why the contingencies occurred. Perhaps if all else fails, we may be forced to resort to such a list. Until then, let us try something else.

What are the alternatives? Of the many we might pursue, the most fruitful are those that begin with the construction or adaptation of a perspective (like Brunswik's conceptual framework) to guide us in selecting what we observe in people and in their environments, and in judging what relations and changes we should try to explain. It is no small challenge to construct a conceptal framework, but perhaps we can meet it by considering a few that now exist in other areas and that may be adapted to address developmental concerns.

The Perspective of Purpose

In a series of provocative discussions, William Powers (e.g., 1974, 1989) and others (e.g., Hershberger, 1989; Marken, 1988; Runkel, 1990) sketch a perspective on the study of changes in person/environment interactions that are well suited to developmental interests. Known as *Control Theory*, the perspective is constructed from four basic concepts: *situation, perception, behavior*, and *purpose*. Their relations are easily summarized: The purpose of behavior is to control perception or, more specifically, to reduce the perceived difference between what one is motivated to obtain and what is provided by one's situation. Such a difference can be reduced in two general ways: by changing one's motivation or purpose, and by changing one's perception of the situation. The perception of the situation, in turn, can be changed by either altering the situation or by looking at it from another point of view.

To date, most work arising from Control Theory has focused on analyzing a simple behavior (e.g., a joystick movement) that changes some aspect of an experimental situation (e.g., a tracking task) to suit a single purpose conveyed by experimental instructions (e.g., "Please try to keep the red dot in the center of the computer screen."). Even so, the work has important methodological implications. For example, Control Theory assumes that situation/behavior or person/environment relations are the manifestations of perception and purpose. Control theorists would thus suggest that our accounts of development should be accounts of changes in perceptions and purposes rather than accounts of changes in the person/environment relations. This is equivalent to suggesting that we account for genotypic differences rather than phenotypic differences (see Thorngate, 1975).

Because control theorists assume that person/environment relations are mediated by perception and purpose, they would also warn us against looking for perceptions or purposes in situation/behavior correlations. Often, for example, one's purpose is to keep constant a feature of an environment by manifesting behaviors that compensate for changes in the feature. Thus, I may open or shut windows, open or close drapes, light or douse a fire, adjust a thermostat, and so forth to keep the room temperature constant.

Because the temperature normally changes over night and day without my intervention, my behavior would be highly correlated with the darkness of the sky. But my behavior would not covary with temperature simply because the temperature does not vary when my purpose is fulfilled. My purpose in this case would be revealed by a lack of covariation; even high covariation would be incidental.

To a control theorist, the major purpose of gathering information about person/environment relations is to infer percepts and purposes. Control theorists suggest variations of classic ecological and diagnostic methods for gathering this information. First, give a person a purpose, place the person in an environment, and watch what he or she disturbs; alternatively, disturb the environment a person is in and observe how the person behaves. Next, look for unique patterns. If a given purpose leads to disturbances or behaviors that others do not, then the disturbances or behaviors become good diagnostic cues; by observing them we can then infer their purpose. And if such inferences are made over time, we can begin to see any developmental trajectory.

I do not think Control Theory is complete. It currently does not seem to address where purposes come from (except to say that "low-level" purposes come from "high-level" ones) or why they change. Multiple and conflicting purposes are acknowledged, but only to suggest how the observation of behavior/environment relations can sometimes tell us how the conflicts are resolved. There is little discussion of the possibility that purposes are stimulated by the environment or relations with the environment, and little discussion of what happens to purposes once they are fulfilled. In addition, Control Theory does not address issues of ability, instead tacitly assuming that if one has a purpose, then one has the knowledge, skill, and power to fulfill it. By including these additional concepts in Control Theory, it becomes both more realistic and less elegant (Thorngate, 1976a). Because people make mistakes, we cannot immediately infer a purpose from a behavior/environment relation. And because people may lack the skill or power to serve a purpose, the absence of a behavior/environment relation may not imply the absence of the purpose.

Still, Control Theory does remind us of the importance of a perspective in directing research. It also reminds us that people do have purposes and do manipulate the environment to suit them, and that by studying the effects of people on environments we may develop some insight into reciprocal person/environment relations.

The Perspective of Familiarity

One of the most interesting aspects of relations between people and their environments is that so many relations are boring. They are boring largely because the environments have predictable contingencies that people learn and habituate to through repetition. Indeed, our brains seem wired to detect and to learn these contingencies quickly; our faculties of pattern recognition and long-term memory are a perfect match for predictable environments. In addition, the environments often help us by providing so many correlated cues that we need only to attend to a few to predict what will happen and to respond adaptively, thus leaving most of our attention for more interesting things. To make life even easier, many environments are also benign or resilient. We can make mistakes without suffering too many bad consequences, while the environments quickly recover from our errors. Such are the advantages of familiar environments (Thorngate, 1976b, 1979), and by considering the relational concept of familiarity, we may be able to provide a respectible account of human development.

The account may go something like this. We are born into a world in which almost nothing is familiar. With luck, however, our home environment soon becomes familiar—so familiar that we become bored with it and curious about others. Each new one excites our exploration and our fear, and when the latter exceeds the former, we seek our familiar environments to calm down. Exploring two and more environments allows us to compare them, to assess their similarities and differences. We begin to make finer distinctions: "Home and not home" becomes "home, school, and new places" becomes "kitchen, living room, school, playground, and elsewhere." As we explore more, we find what is familiar to each and to all. The first environments become prototypes. Later we adjust them, learning that we cannot survive by treating each environment as completely new or as identical to all others.

As with all conceptual perspectives, many of the ideas in this one are untestable, but they can at least direct us to examine aspects of person/environment relations that we might otherwise ignore. It may be difficult to estimate the familiarity of environments in small children because they may be unable to answer our questions about it, and we may be unable to describe their worlds. However, most older children could help us by describing environments they have known in their own language, and by answering questions about what each reminds them of.

The Perspective of Time

It seems natural that developmental psychologists would be interested in time; after all, that is when development happens. But by concentrating on developmental sequences, we tend to overlook some other potentially useful concepts of time. One of these is the concept of time expenditures suggested by two curious English phrases: "paying" attention and "spending" time. These economic metaphors may be useful, for they allow us to view person/environment relations and their changes as aspects of an attentional or temporal economy and to make use of methods developed to study them (see Thorngate, 1988a, 1990).

The few economists and others who study how people spend their time are fond of recording *time budgets*, lists of activities, locations, and time (e.g., see Juster & Stafford, 1985; McGrath, 1988). Table 2.1 provides a sample time budget of Fred, a hypothetical 8-year-old living in Ottawa, Canada.

Such lists alone can be instructive for what they do and do not contain. For example, the prominance of television over homework (354 minutes vs. 23) might have implications for what is learned about consuming versus producing information (e.g., see Postman, 1986).

The lists can also be instructive in comparison with those of other people. For example, consider in Table 2.2 a sample time budget of Marta, a hypothetical 8-year-old from a barrio outside Santiago, Chile. No television, fewer meals, less school, more work and homework. Also, far more time with others. Surely these differences have implications for what is developed in each person and what is not.

Time budget variations within the same person at different ages may be equally revealing. In Table 2.3, for example, consider again Fred at age 24. Most of the environment has changed as have the person's relations with it. Television time, for example, drops from 354 minutes to 20. Contact with family members drops from 264 minutes to 4. Times increase with car, work, drinks, and roommate. We may wish to ask control theorists to infer what developments in purpose or perception are reflected in these changes.

People often confront environments that require choices among alternative ways to spend their time. Often their choices affect the environments they subsequently confront. If we observe people in these situations, we can sometimes deduce important conclusions about their values and priorities and over time note how their values and priorities may change. Watching interruptions can be especially useful. For example, if a child doing her homework can be interrupted by a younger brother, a call for food, an urge

TABLE 2.1
Sample Time Budget of Fred, Age 8, Living in Ottawa, Canada

Activity	Location	Duration
eat breakfast	in kitchen with mother	27 minutes
watch television	living room with sister	34 minutes
pack lunch bucket	kitchen with mother	12 minutes
go to school	bus with students	18 minutes
attend five classes	school with teachers & students	360 minutes
go home	bus with students	20 minutes
watch television	basement alone	200 minutes
dinner	kitchen with family	39 minutes
homework	bedroom alone	23 minutes
watch television	basement with mother & father	120 minutes
sleep	bedroom alone	480 minutes

TABLE 2.2
Sample Time Budget of Marta, Age 8, Living outside Santiago, Chile

Activity	Location	Duration
clean chicken coop	street alone	23 minutes
walk to school	streets with 4 sisters & 5 brothers	45 minutes
attend three classes	school with teacher & students	180 minutes
walk to work	streets with 2 brothers & 3 sisters	45 minutes
work	car wash with fellow workers	360 minutes
jump ride home	back bumper of bus	40 minutes
dinner	kitchen with family	60 minutes
homework	kitchen with family	130 minutes
sleep	bedroom with family	480 minutes

to nap, or most household noises, we would deduce that homework is low on her list of priorities. If she awakes from a nap for dinner and if the brother and the noises cannot interrupt her while she eats, more priorities would be revealed. Many people set priorities by urgencies or deadlines, allowing lots of little emergencies to interrupt a few important tasks. Such tendencies can be revealed by examining "to do" lists for what is done and undone, and by examining how the do and done lists (reflecting changes in person/environment relations) change over years.

The Perspective of Proliferation

The perspectives of purpose, familiarity, and time all consider that the relation between a person and the environment is determined by characteristics of each. We must not overlook, however, that characteristics of an environment may be determined by "larger forces" including the forces of culture, econom-

TABLE 2.3
Sample Time Budget of Fred, Age 24, Living in Ottawa, Canada

Activity	Location	Duration
eat breakfast	dining room with roommate	9 minutes
pack briefcase	kitchen alone	4 minutes
drive to work	car alone	37 minutes
work	grocery store with customers	480 minutes
drive home	car with carpool	45 minutes
drinks	living room with roommate	67 minutes
dinner	kitchen with roommate	23 minutes
read for course	study alone	200 minutes
call parents	living room alone	4 minutes
television	living room with roommate	20 minutes
sleep	bedroom with roommate	480 minutes

ics, and history. Many of these forces are manifested as aspects of proliferation; when something in an environment multiplies, things change. For example, many environments are shared, and when they become crowded, their nature and their relations with the people in them may change dramatically.

To illustrate, consider what can happen to inner-city housing over time. For some time, it is desirable to live downtown, influencing many people to live there, which causes crowding and an increased rate of decay. The crowding and decay usually influence rich people to move out, increasing the buyer's market for the inner city and lowering property values there. Lower property values in turn attract more people with less money, increasing the crowding and decay rate again. As the cycle continues the environment declines, and children there face a very different environment than children of previous generations. Similar changes can occur to good, affordable, uncrowded schools that soon become bad because people learn they are good and crowd them with their children, or they become unaffordable because there is more demand than supply.

Barbara Carroll and I have spent many years studying a similar form of proliferation that affects the environment of every competitive child. Consider the following. The proud parents of 10-year-old Mary note that she seems to have a natural gift for swimming and enroll her in a local swimming program. Soon her coach discovers her talent and encourages her to compete in a local swim meet. She does and wins with little effort. After a few more wins in local competitions, she becomes a big fish in a small pond. Thus rewarded for her talent, she decides to enter regional meets. Here she discovers that many competitors are talented, and after a few losses realizes that she can now win only by training more.

More training produces more wins. But at the Provincial meets Mary discovers that every competitor is talented and every competitor trains hard. Thinking even more training will give her a winning edge, she reduces her school load, moves to another city to work with a professional trainer, and spends almost all her waking hours in the pool. She is now 12 years old.

A few losses at the Provincials are devastating. Now training almost all her waking hours, Mary tries other strategies. She lifts weights. She convinces her parents to hire a sports psychologist. Knowing nothing else, she devotes herself totally to her only source of reward. Her parents continue to invest thousands of dollars to her performance. And it works. At age 14 Mary wins the Provincials and now trains for the Nationals.

But at the National swim meet Mary notices that every competitor is talented, every competitor trains hard, every competitor lifts weights and consults a sports psychologist. Except for drugs, there is nothing more she can do. The race will be won or lost by no more than 3 or 4 hundredths of a second, a blink of an eye. And it will be determined not by talent, not by training, not by motivation but by chance. Mary will have devoted much of her development to enter a situation where her fate will be determined at random. In doing so she will experience the mathematics of situational change that explain why the best person rarely wins (Thorngate & Carroll, 1987, 1991).

Things get worse, as illustrated by the Principle of Invidious Selection (Thorngate, 1988b). Consider an educational example of the co-relation between the evolution of environments and development. People of my generation were told that a BA was a ticket to a wonderful job because it gave us something called *competitive advantage* over those without the degree. For reasons I am embarassed to reveal, we believed it, and for a short time it was true. The next generation also believed it, and far more received BAs, only to discover that because it was common it had lost its competitive advantage. Competitive advantage shifted to the MA just long enough to prompt the lucrative expansion of university graduate programs. Yet in one more generation and for the same reason, the MA lost its competitive advantage. People of the next generation needed a PhD just to have the same kind of chance as Mary.

We are now at the point where a PhD has lost much of its competitive advantage, and it is fun to speculate what will replace it. Another degree? A co-op program certificate? Relevant volunteer experience? Or will it be the original source of competitive advantage that education was supposed to supplant: social and political connections? I vote for connections, in which case we will have come full circle after drastically transforming the educational environment and expectations of children.

There are perhaps more moral than methodological lessons to be learned from the perspective of proliferation. But it should at least make us aware of the possibility that environments have their own developmental trajectories, and that a person's adaptation to these trajectories can be a major determinant of the person's own development.

CONCLUSION

The perspectives just outlined are only four of several from which interesting accounts may be created of the development of person/environment relations and their changes. Other perspectives come from research in areas such as communication, social networks, social dilemmas, political economy, systems engineering, even library science. I have no strong reason to believe that the four I mentioned will be especially useful to developmental psychologists interested in changing environments and person/environment relations. Indeed, it is likely that the best perspectives and the accounts derived from them will be built by developmental psychologists themselves and not merely adapted from others.

Once again, however, the number and variety of possible perspectives points to the conclusion that no single one can adequately account for the complexity of person/environment relations and their changes. In view of this conclusion, I am surprised by the paucity of perspectives of human development that have been articulated or explored. Perhaps this reflects a paucity of developmental psychologists. On the other hand, a single epony-mous perspective of cognitive development (Piagetian) seems to cover at least half the pages of developmental books and journals. It may answer the easy questions, but perhaps the time has come to build more perspectives to answer what is left.

As noted earlier, it is no easy task to build a perspective or to develop an account from it. Other disciplines, however, can instruct us who should do it if not how. All other sciences I know have room for both empiricists (lookers) and rationalists (thinkers). The two groups usually do not like each other, but there is general recognition that the rationalists earn their keep by generating many perspectives and accounts, some of which are empirically useful. Psychology, at least in North America, has been domi-nated by empiricists and has been hostile to rationalists. This can be seen in our textbooks that characterize the discipline as a series of experiments rather than a series of ideas. Perhaps the time has come to let some rationalists grow, especially in developmental psychology. Otherwise our discipline will continue to generate lists of contingencies, truths with no stories, for a dwindling audience.

ACKNOWLEDGMENTS

My thanks go to Barbara Carroll for teaching me what developmental psy-chologists do, and to Thomas Kindermann for giving me sagacious editorial advice.

REFERENCES

Barker, R. (1968). *Ecological psychology: Concepts and methods for studying the environment of human behavior.* Stanford, CA: Stanford University Press.

Bronfenbrenner, U. (1989). Ecological systems theory. In R. Vasta (Ed.), *Annals of child devel-opment* (pp. 187–249). Greenwich, CT: JAI.

Brunswik, E. (1950). *The conceptual framework of psychology.* Chicago: University of Chicago Press.

Feagin, J., Orum, A., & Sjoberg, G. (Eds.). (1991). *A case for the case study.* Chapel Hill: University of North Carolina Press.

Gibson, J. J. (1979). *The ecological approach to visual perception.* Boston: Houghton Mifflin.

Helson, H. (1964). *Adaptation-level theory.* New York: Harper & Row.

Hershberger, W. (Ed.). (1989). *Volitional action: Conation and control.* Amsterdam: Elsevier/North-Holland.

Juster, F. T., & Stafford, F. (Eds.). (1985). *Time, goods, and well-being.* Ann Arbor: Institute for Social Research, University of Michigan.

Kindermann, T., & Skinner, E. (1992). Modelling environmental development: Individual and contextual trajectories. In J. Asendorpf & J. Valsiner (Eds.), *Stability and change in development* (pp. 155–190). Newbury Park, CA: Sage.

Levins, R. (1966). The strategy of model building in population biology. *American Scientist, 54,* 421–431.

Levins, R. (1968). *Evolution in changing environments.* Princeton, NJ: Princeton University Press.

Lewin, K. (1935). *A dynamic theory of personality.* New York: McGraw-Hill.

London, I., & Thorngate, W. (1981). Divergent amplification and social behavior: Some methodological considerations. *Psychological Reports, 48,* 203–228.

Marken, R. (1988). The nature of behavior: Control as fact and theory. *Behavioral Science, 33,* 196–206.

McGrath, J. (Ed.). (1988). *The social psychology of time.* Newbury Park, CA: Sage.

Miles, M., & Huberman, A. M. (1984). *Qualitative data analysis.* Beverly Hills, CA: Sage.

Mischel, W. (1968). *Personality and assessment.* New York: Wiley.

Mishler, E. G. (1986). *Research interviewing: Context and narrative.* Cambridge, MA: Harvard University Press.

Postman, N. (1986). *Amusing ourselves to death. Public discourse in the age of show business.* New York: Penguin.

Powers, W. (1974). Quantitative analysis of purposive systems: Some spadework at the foundations of scientific psychology. *Psychological Review, 85,* 417–435.

Powers, W. (1989). *Living control systems: Selected papers of William T. Powers.* Gravel Switch, KY: Control Systems Group, Inc.

Richardson, G. (1991). *Feedback thought in social science and systems theory.* Philadelphia: University of Pennsylvania Press.

Rosengren, K. E. (1981). *Advances in content analysis.* Beverly Hills, CA: Sage.

Runkel, P. (1990). *Casting nets and testing specimens: Two grand methods of psychology.* New York: Praeger.

Scarr, S., & McCartney, K. (1983). How people make their own environments: A theory of genotype/environmental effects. *Child Development, 54,* 424–435.

Stubbs, M. (1984). *Discourse analysis: The sociolinguistic analysis of natural language.* Chicago: University of Chicago Press.

Thorngate, W. (1975). Process invariance: Another red herring. *Personality and Social Psychology Bulletin, 1,* 485–488.

Thorngate, W. (1976a). Possible limits on a science of social behaviour. In L. Strickland, F. Aboud, & K. Gergen (Eds.), *Social psychology in transition* (pp. 121–139). New York: Plenum.

Thorngate, W. (1976b). Must we always think before we act? *Personality and Social Psychology Bulletin, 2,* 31–35.

Thorngate, W. (1979). Memory, cognition, and social performance. In L. Strickland (Ed.), *Soviet and Western perspectives in social psychology* (pp. 289–316). Oxford: Pergamon.

Thorngate, W. (1986). The production, detection, and explanation of behavioral patterns. In J. Valsiner (Ed.), *The individual subject and scientific psychology* (pp. 71–93). New York: Plenum.

Thorngate, W. (1988a). On paying attention. In W. Baker, L. Mos, H. Rappard, & H. Stam (Eds.), *Recent trends in theoretical psychology* (pp. 247–264). New York: Springer-Verlag.

Thorngate, W. (1988b). On the evolution of adjudicated contests and the principle of invidious selection. *Journal of Behavioral Decision Making, 1,* 5–16.

Thorngate, W. (1990). The economy of attention and the development of psychology. *Canadian Psychology, 21,* 62–70.

Thorngate, W. & Carroll, B. (1987). Why the best person rarely wins: Some embarrassing facts about contests. *Simulation and Games, 18,* 299–320.

Thorngate, W., & Carroll, B. (1991). Tests versus contests: A theory of adjudication. In W. Baker, M. Hyland, R. van Hezewijk, & S. Terwee (Eds.), *Recent trends in theoretical psychology* (Vol. 2, pp. 431–438). New York: Springer-Verlag.

Thorngate, W., & Plouffe, L. (1987). The consumption of psychological knowledge. In H. Stam, T. Rogers, & K. Gergen (Eds.), *Metapsychology: The analysis of psychological theory* (pp. 61–92). New York: Hemisphere.

Vygotsky, L., (1978). *Mind in society: The development of higher mental processes.* Cambridge, MA: Harvard University Press.

Wachs, T., & Plomin, R. (Eds.). (1991). *Conceptualization and measurement of organism-environment interaction.* Washington, DC: American Psychological Association.

CHAPTER THREE

Processes of Development, and Search for Their Logic: An Introduction to Herbst's Co-Genetic Logic

Jaan Valsiner
University of North Carolina at Chapel Hill

Development of ideas transcends life and death of the creators of those ideas. It was by coincidence (during an occasional meeting with Ragnar Rommetveit) that I got to know of the late David Herbst's intellectual efforts. What followed was occasional correspondence with David, which ended when the message of his untimely death reached me. Persons die, but ideas remain, and this chapter (together with the publication of Herbst's paper that was originally not meant for a volume on developmental thinking in psychology) should both pay tribute to the author who is no longer with us and preserve his intellectual contribution to the understanding of the world.

As I show later, Herbst's contribution to the search for logic of change processes in the 1980s is a fitting endeavor within a long history of similar efforts in developmental psychology. The latter discipline has of course been vulnerable to the socially constructed fashions in its methodological core (see Gigerenzer et al., 1989). One of the curious results of the social reconstruction of developmental psychology is the disappearance of the focus on development from that discipline (Benigni & Valsiner, 1985), and the replacement of the focus on logic of developmental processes (which was part of scientific discourse at the turn of this century) by statistical aggregation of empirical data—loosely connected with model-fitting efforts.

From the viewpoint of the history of developmental psychology, Herbst's efforts to develop basic apparatus of co-genetic logic constitute a promising alternative to the impasse of nondevelopmental methodology of present-day developmental psychology (Asendorpf & Valsiner, 1992). The prevailing inductive-statistical mindset of psychologists has led them to look at developing persons and their contexts as separate *and segregated* entities (by "measuring" them separately from each other). In that operation of measurement, the *very nature of developmental processes*—the dynamic interchange between person and context—has been *eliminated from the data derivation process* from the very beginning of the researcher's work. No matter what sophisticated methods are later used to recapture the mystical "interaction" between person and context, the actual reality of development has become irreversibly lost (Kindermann & Valsiner, 1989; Valsiner, 1987, 1991).

Hence the need for alternative formal systems to replace the statistical world view as consensually constructed "scientific method" in developmental psychology. In the history of psychology, we can observe a variety of ways of arriving at knowledge (Danziger, 1990), only some of which entailed quantification. It could probably be adequate to state that psychological phenomena—and especially those of development (seen as transformation of structural organization; Basov, 1991)—usually can be viewed as nominal scale phenomena (or, in few cases, as ordinal scale phenomena). The issue of formal relationships between the nominal-scale phenomena, and especially those of their transformation into others in irreversible time (Valsiner, 1993), constitute the central unsolved problem of understanding development.

PARADOXES OF HISTORY: PSYCHOLOGY VERSUS BIOLOGY

It is a paradox of history of psychology that developmental psychology is part of psychology at all. Almost all of developmental psychology's theoretical background is derived from different developmentally oriented branches of biology (embryology, evolutionary theory, comparative physiology with behavioral manifestations; see Cairns, 1983; Gottlieb, 1992). The majority of leading figures in the history of developmental psychology were oriented toward biology in either their thinking and/or empirical work: C. Lloyd Morgan, James Mark Baldwin, Jean Piaget, Heinz Werner, Zing-Yang Kuo, Theodor Schneirla. In contrast, the contributions by researchers whose starting ground has been interest in child psychology as such have been limited to specific issues.

LOGIC, CHEMISTRY, AND DEVELOPMENT: A DIFFICULT SYNTHESIS

If the ideal of scientific rigor at the turn of the century was logic, then the reconciliation of interest in the openness of development and the fixedness of logical systems was not an easy task. Neither was the use of the other available scientific model—that of chemistry—for psychology of the mental processes. Interestingly, it may be the thought model of chemical synthesis (rather than logic) that could have fitted developmental thinking (and yet it was not developed further). Thus, Thomas Brown argued in 1820 in his *Lectures on the philosophy of the human mind* (see Woodworth, 1948):

> As in chemistry it often happens that the qualities of the separate ingredients of a compound body are not recognizable by us in the apparently different qualities of the compound itself—so in this spontaneous *chemistry of the mind*, the compound sentiment that results from the association of former feelings has in many cases . . . little resemblance to these constituents. (pp. 43–44)

Wundt's further emphasis on the "chemistry of the mind" was of course without a developmental focus. Nevertheless, the chemistry of the mind label could have easily led to the study of developmental-psychological synthesis of new "mental compounds" in person-context relations. Yet, the developmentalists at the turn of the century tried to emulate logical rigor instead. The major theoretician with that goal in mind was Baldwin, whose complex trilogy, *Thought and Things* (Baldwin, 1906, 1908, 1911), still awaits careful analysis. Presently, Baldwin's efforts to construct a system of genetic logic that could serve as methodology for the study of development is of interest.

BALDWIN'S TIME AND CONTEXT: DEVELOPING AMERICAN PSYCHOLOGY

Baldwin's life course maps well upon the sensitive period in the development of psychology in North America. The new discipline was being established on the North American continent, based on the sociomoral value system of the society that itself was in a turmoil. The rapid industrialization and urbanization of the U.S. society in the last decades of the 19th century created both the fertile grounds and the limits for the establishment of psychology in the New World (Dolby, 1977). Baldwin (1894) has given a concise participant observer's account of the context in which American psychology emerged:

> In America the influences which have tended to control psychological opinion have been mainly theological on one side and educational on the other. The absence of great native systems of speculative thought has prevented at once the rationalistic invasions into theology which characterized the German development, and the attempts at psychological interpretation which furnished a supposed basis of fact to the idealistic systems. In Germany various 'philosophies of nature' sought to find even in objective science support for theoretical world-dialectic: and psychology fared even worse, since it is, *par excellence*, the theatre for the exploitation of universal hypotheses. But in America men did not speculate much: and the ones who did were theologians. So naturally psychologists were theologians too. (p. 364)

Baldwin's life, work, and fate is in some sense a good example of the social processes of the American society, internalized by an ambitious young man, and externalized in the form of all the variety of activities in which he was involved. Like many American men of the 1880s who later became psychologists, Baldwin at one time was not far away from a career as a clergyman. Similarly to others of his cohort, he made the fashionable educational trip to Germany (1884–1885; spending a semester in Leipzig in Wundt's laboratory, another in Berlin with Paulsen, and a third in Freiburg with Stumpf). However, differently from his fellow countrymen whose fascination during their trips to Germany was with the technical organization of experiments in Wundt's laboratory, Baldwin's main intellectual benefit from the study trip was the introduction to Spinoza's philosophy in Berlin (see Baldwin, 1926, chap. 3; also 1902, chap. 2). It is worth noting that interest in Spinoza's world view constitutes one of the background similarities between Baldwin and Vygotsky—the latter's lifelong fascination with Spinoza is well known (Van der Veer & Valsiner, 1991). Baldwin's intellectual relations developed a clearly Francophilic focus from the 1890s onward.

From his developmental standpoint, Baldwin translated the question of existence of volition *from an ontological issue into the question of its ontogenetic emergence.* That kind of a translation is predicated upon the author's consistent developmental view of the world. Many a developmentalist adheres to a time perspective that entails *past-to-present* focus of the emergence (i.e., a retrospective view). His answer to this question is in his analysis of different kinds of imitation. Few—Baldwin as well as Vygotsky among them—have taken an explicitly *present-to-future*-oriented stance, as is well explained by Baldwin (1895) as he addressed the issue of adaptation:

> Considering the state of an organism at any moment, with its readiness to act in an appropriate fashion—say a child's imitation of a movement—the appropriateness of its action may be construed in either of two ways: either *retrospectively* or *prospectively.* By construing it retrospectively, I mean that an organism performs its appropriate function when it does what it has done before—what it is suited to do, however it may have come to be so suited. The child imitates my movement because his apparatus is ready for this movement. This is Habit; it proceeds by repetition. But when we come to ask how it got to be suited to do this function *the first time,* or how it can come to do a new function *from now on*—how the child manages to imitate a new movement, one which he has never made before—this is the prospective reference, and this question we must now try to answer. (p. 171)

It is this prospective developmental orientation that made it possible for Baldwin to join with Morgan (1896) and Osborn (1896) in suggesting an alternative theoretical model for evolutionary thought that attempted to overcome the artficially exaggerated "darwinist" versus "lamarckian" fights of evolutionists. His notion of "organic selection" was based on the idea that selection at the species level operates upon individual organisms after the latter have proceeded to generate new forms of adaptations. Furthermore, Baldwin's ideas served as a relevant input for Bergson's philosophy of creative evolution, whose role in the history of developmental science should not be underestimated (Valsiner, 1993).

BALDWIN'S GENETIC LOGIC AND ITS IMPLICATIONS

It was clear to Baldwin (1930) that developmental science (or, as he termed it, *genetic science*) could not develop using the inferential tools of nondevelopmental sciences. Thus, he understood the futility of the transfer of quantitative methodology to psychology:

> The ... quantitative method, brought over into psychology from the exact sciences, physics and chemistry, must be discarded; for its ideal consisted in reducing the more complex to the more simple, the whole into its parts, the later-evolved to the earlier-existent, thus denying or eliminating just the factor which constituted or revealed what was truly genetic. Newer modes of manifestation cannot be stated in atomic terms without doing violence to the more synthetic modes which observation reveals. (p. 7)

Likewise, Baldwin did not find much value in the behaviorist ways of analyses of "objective" phenomena, criticizing that orientation for its elimination of consciousness from consideration (Baldwin, 1930, p. 29). Needless to add, in both of these evaluations (made after his active work in psychology had ended more than a decade previously), Baldwin's criticism paralleled that of Vygotsky (see Van der Veer & Valsiner, 1991). Both of these thinkers used the same general argument (i.e., the nonreducibility of the properties of a molecule, say, water, into its atomary components—a defense of the view of "analysis-into-units") in their methodological claims in favor of the study of psychological synthesis. However, Baldwin (1906) in his productive years had gone further, pointing to the uselessness of importing the nondevelopmental notions of causality into the new "genetic science":

> We must be free from all constructions drawn from the strictly a-genetic sciences in which the causal sequence is the typical one. The birth of a new mode in the psychic life is a *"progression" from an earlier set of conditions, not the effect of these conditions viewed as cause*; and this is equally true of any new genetic mode, just so far as the series in which it appears is really genetic at all. (p. 29; italics added)

Baldwin formulated four "axioms" of genetic science (1902, p. 323; 1906, p. 20), which fortified the irreducibility of the developmentally more complex phenomena to their preceding (less complex) counterparts. However, from the standpoint of "genetic logic" as a basic methodology of developmental science, his two "postulates of method" are of more immediate importance (Baldwin 1906):

> *First.* The first or negative postulate: *the logic of genesis is not expressed in convertible propositions.* Genetically, A = (that is, becomes, for which the sign = is now used) B; but it does not follow that B = (becomes, =) A.

> *Second.* The second or positive postulate: that series of events is truly genetic which cannot be constructed before it has happened, and which cannot be exhausted backwards, after it has happened. (p. 21).

Interpretation of Baldwin's "Postulates." The first postulate indeed specifies the realm of possible relations that are allowable among the formulae of "genetic logic"—namely, each proposition includes a temporal directionality vector. It is the second postulate that seems more problematic, as it possesses an agnostic flavor. If a developmental phenomenon cannot be explained before it takes place, nor afterwards, then when and how can the genetic science explain anything? It seems appropriate to interpret the second postulate as an imperative for the study of developmental events as those unfold (i.e., concurrently). This interpretation maintains the productivity of the "genetic science."

Baldwin complemented the postulates with a series of "canons of genetic logic" (see Table 3.1).

From Table 3.1 it is possible to gain further understanding what Baldwin had in mind with his program of logic. His fight for the preservation of developmental *processes* is evident in the case of each canon: Instead of viewing an event as without predecessors, he insists upon the continuity with previous states (Canon 1), whereas the continuity entails constant transformation of the state of the event (Canon 7). This state of affairs is brought about by irreversibility of developmental processes (Canon 2), and that entails transformation of the qualitative reorganization of the events (synthesis, Canon 3). Finally, all the uniqueness of developmental psychic events is context bound: Hence, Baldwin demands that scientific analysis maintain the linkages with context (Canon 4) and not be transposed to another context (Canon 5). For a contemporary sociocultural developmentalist, all these canons may look very familiar, as our talk of our time returns constantly to themes of "context-dependency," "continuity/discontinuity" in development, and to the irreversibility of development.

BALDWIN'S CANONS, AND BEYOND

There exists somewhat illusionary comfort in thinking that Baldwin's canons fortify our present-day quests for novel methodology in the study of development. This becomes evident if we address the issue of how Baldwin developed

TABLE 3.1
James Mark Baldwin's Canons of Genetic Logic, and Their "Fallacies"
(Concentrated from Baldwin, 1906, pp. 22–24)

Canon	Fallacy
1. **Canon of Continuity:** All psychic process is continuous.	Discontinuity: treating any psychic event as **de novo**, or as arising in a discontinuous series.
2. **Canon of Progression:** All psychic process is genetic, not a-genetic, expressed by the formula A → B (A becomes B) whether or not it is ever true that B → (becomes) A.	Treating a psychic event as compounded or made up or caused by other psychic events (e.g., sensation of purple viewed as made up of sensations blue and red, or as caused by them).
3. **Canon of Quality:** Every psychic event is qualitatively different from, not equal to, the next antecedent and the next succeeding event and also from its own earlier or later case.	Equality: treating any two psychic events as equal, or any one as identical with itself when repeated; fixity of meaning of terms and of substitution of one experience for another.
4. **Canon of Modal Relevancy**: No psychic event can be taken out of its own mode and treated as belonging in or with events of another mode.	Modal Confusion: treating an event or meaning of one mode as remaining what it was, when taken up in the synthesis of another mode.
5. **Canon of Modal Unity:** No psychic event or meaning can be treated as being what it is except as in the entire context of the mode in which it arises.	Modal Division: treating an event or a meaning as a static and separable unit.
6. **Canon of Actuality:** No psychic event is present unless it be actual (corollary from this Canon requires us to identify first the clear and unambiguous case).	Implication: treating something as implicitly or potentially present when it is not actual (e.g., finding implicit logical process in the prelogical modes; or "potential self" in the impersonal modes).
7. **Canon of Revision:** No psychic event or meaning is to be treated as original or unrevised except in its first appearance, because its reappearance may be in a mode in which it is essentially revised.	Consistency: holding the psychic process to any consistency except what it shows (e.g., holding reflective meanings to reference they had had before taken up in the revision of reflection).

his imperatives further (into productive methodology). The unfortunate answer to this question is that he did not—after declaring the relevance of genetic science, he continued his general philosophical system building (ending in the absolute synthesis of everything human, in case of Pancalism). Canons of "genetic logic" were not developed further as a formalized logical system. However, even more discomforting would be a corollary to this posed question: Why are we (in the 1980s and 1990s) escaping from efforts to solve the problems of developmentally adequate methodology of research, to the comfort of following general declarations of the sociocultural thinking giants of the past? It is probably the case that our own sociocultural theories and methodologies are not much developed since the turn of the century.

It is quite possible that Baldwin's general direction of intellectual pursuits at about the time of formulating the canons of genetic logic was already such that further productive development of that logic was impossible. On the side of declaration of his developmental perspective, the canons are of course clearly powerful. However, if we examine them from a standpoint of how Baldwin could have moved beyond these canons in the direction of their elaborations, conceptual complications begin to emerge.

Perhaps the most puzzling of the canons in this respect is that of Actuality (#6), because it is here where Baldwin's metatheoretical imperatives seem to turn against his own developmental claims. If we interpret Canon 6 as merely a conservative stance against researcher's "reading into" the given event "hidden competencies" that cannot be proven or analyzed other than by axiomatic admission, then this canon may be productive. But to study exactly the developmental transformations of one event into another (rather than treat the next one as *rootlessly* de novo; see fallacy of Canon 1), some analysis of the connections between the presently actual and the not-yet-actual (but possible in the nearest future) is inevitable. If, by following Canon of Actuality, we proceed to study only those forms that can be viewed as already actually present, then our developmental account is reduced to the description of time sequences of already finished forms. This would make the actual processes of emergence of novel forms undetectable by our research efforts and would therefore render the positive foci of other canons unproductive.

Furthermore, Baldwin's emphasis on the preservation of context (as in Canons 4 and 5) seems to proceed along a route on which many of our contemporary "contextualist approaches" have become methodologically derailed. Namely, the imperative of preservation of context of the given event, without theoretical language of how to conceptualize that preservation in general (i.e., in an abstract form), leads necessarily to the study of endless versions of particular events together with their particular contexts (see the issue of "context specificity" in contemporary comparative-cultural psychology; Winegar & Valsiner, 1992). Indeed, Baldwin's imperatives can work here at the level of empirical descriptions, but that of course is no substitute for the lack of progress in the general context-inclusive "genetic science" as Baldwin envisaged it.

FROM BALDWIN TO HERBST: DEVELOPMENTAL NATURE OF CO-GENETIC LOGIC

Herbst's co-genetic logic can be viewed as an effort similar to Baldwin's, only perhaps starting from the side of context-oriented thinking in modern-day sciences. His emphasis on the *triadic units* that emerge when distinctions are being made is the foundation for any context-dependent developmental formalization. Developmental psychology's usual problem has been the lack of understanding that its analytic units need to reflect not just the state of the developing organism and its environment but the process that relates them (Markova, 1990). As was already pointed out by Baldwin, the traditional quantitative methodology that operates on the basis of the axiom of additive elementarism (Valsiner, 1987) does not fit for the explanation of development. Herbst's elegant designation of triadic units that emerge in the process of making distinctions (differentiation) provides a novel solution to the issue of developmental context-inclusive analysis units. *Process networks* that follow from viewing the triadic units in their dynamics allow for the holistic (yet exact) description of the dynamic mechanisms that maintain and develop the system. However, in his chapter in this volume, Herbst reaches only the relevant issue—transactional relationships between process networks (see the Appendix to chap. 4)—without elaborating those in co-genetic logical terms. Of course, Herbst's subtitle ("An elementary introduction to co-genetic logic") explains the limited coverage. Nevertheless, the very perspective of co-genetic logic—even in its elementary form—serves as a fruitful starting point for developmental thinking. For example, Herbst's elementary co-genetic process network structures may make it possible to turn Werner's (1957) *orthogenetic principle* (i.e., the proposition that development takes place through differentiation, articulation, and hierarchical integration) into a more elaborated deductive system. It could then become linked with empirical inductive observations of development in terms of logical propositions. Furthermore, the ethos of the developmental systems theory (Ford & Lerner, 1992; see also Lerner, chap. 1 in this volume) or theoretical efforts to conceptualize development via relationships (Fogel, 1993) can be expanded in their formal core.

In the more fundamental domain of science, Herbst's co-genetic logic sets the stage for formalization of the *internal relations* (as opposed to external relations—posited in classical logic) within developing systems, and between those and their environments. This natural-philosophical view has been inherent in developmental theorizing over a long time (Markova, 1983, 1987) and yet has remained ill-defined (or defocused by all too frequent use of the label *dialectical* in conjunction with intrasystemic relations). Herbst's contribution is thus a pioneering one in this field—even if he did not chart out his historical antecedents (for that, see Markova, 1990; Rommetveit, 1990). It is hoped that Herbst's contribution will lead other thinkers to move on from where he had to stop—in the difficult construction of new ideas and toward an adequate formalization of the logic of development.

REFERENCES

Asendorpf, J. B., & Valsiner, J. (Eds.). (1992). *Stability and change in development: A study of methodological reasoning.* Newbury Park, CA: Sage.

Baldwin, J. M. (1894). Psychology past and present. *Psychological Review, 1,* 363–391.

Baldwin, J. M. (1895). *Mental development in the child and the race.* New York: Macmillan.

Baldwin, J. M. (1902). *Fragments in philosophy and science.* New York: Scribner's.

Baldwin, J. M. (1906). *Thought and things: A study of the development and meaning of thought, or genetic logic. Vol. 1. Functional logic, or genetic theory of knowledge.* London: Swan Sonnenschein.

Baldwin, J. M. (1908). *Thought and things: A study of the development and meaning of thought, or genetic logic. Vol. 2. Experimental logic, or genetic theory of thought.* London: Swan Sonnenschein.

Baldwin, J. M. (1911). *Thought and things: A study of the development and meaning of thought, or genetic logic. Vol 3. Interest and art being real logic.* London: Swan Sonnenschein.

Baldwin, J. M. (1926). *Between two wars 1861–1921* (Vols. 1 & 2). Boston: Stratford.

Baldwin, J. M. (1930). James Mark Baldwin. In C. Murchison (Ed.), *A history of psychology in autobiography* (Vol. 1, pp. 1–30). New York: Russell & Russell.

Basov, M. (1991). The organization of processes of behavior. In J. Valsiner & R. Van der Veer (Eds.), *Structuring of conduct in activity settings: The forgotten contributions of Mikhail Basov* (Part 1). *Soviet Psychology, 29,* 5, 14–83.

Benigni, L., & Valsiner, J. (1985). Developmental psychology without the study of processes of development? *Newsletter of the International Society for the Study of Behavioral Development,* No. 1, pp. 1–3.

Cairns, R. B. (1983). The emergence of developmental psychology. In W. Kessen (Ed.), *Handbook of child psychology. 4th ed. Vol. 1. History, theory and methods* (pp. 41–102). New York: Wiley.

Danziger, K. (1990). *Constructing the subject.* Cambridge, England: Cambridge University Press.

Dolby, R. G. A. (1977). The transmission of two new scientific disciplines from Europe to North America in the late 19th century. *Annals of Science, 34,* 287–310.

Fogel, A. (1993). *Developing through relationships.* Chicago: University of Chicago Press.

Ford, D. H., & Lerner, R. M. (1992). *Developmental systems theory.* Newbury Park, CA: Sage.

Gigerenzer, G., Swijtink, Z., Porter, T., Daston, L., Beatty, J. & Krüger, L. (1989). *The empire of chance.* Cambridge, England: Cambridge University Press.

Gottlieb, G. (1992). *Individual development & evolution: The genesis of novel behavior.* New York: Oxford University Press.

Kindermann, T., & Valsiner, J. (1989). Research strategies in culture-inclusive developmental psychology. In J. Valsiner (Ed.), *Child development in cultural context* (pp. 13–50). Toronto: Hogrefe & Huber.

Markova, I. (1983). The origin of the social psychology of language in German expressivism. *British Journal of Social Psychology, 22,* 315–325.

Markova, I. (1987). On the interaction of opposites in psychological processes. *Journal for the Theory of Social Behaviour, 17,* 279–299.

Markova, I. (1990). A three-step process as a unit of analysis in dialogue. In I. Markova & K. Foppa (Eds.), *The dynamics of dialogue* (pp. 129–146). Hemel Hempstead: Harvester Press.

Morgan, C. L. (1896). On modification and variation. *Science, 4* (No. 99), 733–740.

Osborn, H. F. (1896). Ontogenetic and phylogenetic variation. *Science, 4* (No. 100), 786–789.

Rommetveit, R. (1990). On axiomatic features of a dialogical approach to language and mind. In I. Markova & K. Foppa (Eds.), *The dynamics of dialogue.* Hemel Hempstead: Harvester Press.

Valsiner, J. (1987). *Culture and the development of children's action.* Chichester, UK: Wiley.

Valsiner, J. (1991). Integration of theory and methodology in psychology: The legacy of Joachim Wohlwill. In L. Mos & P. van Geert (Eds.), *Annals of theoretical psychology* (Vol. 7, pp. 161–175). New York: Plenum.

Valsiner, J. (1993, July). *Irreversibility of time and the construction of historical developmental psychology.* Paper presented at the XII Biennial Meetings of the International Society for the Study of Behavioural Development, Recife, Pernambuco, Brazil.

Van der Veer, R., & Valsiner, J. (1991). *Understanding Vygotsky: A quest for synthesis.* Oxford: Basil Blackwell.

Werner, H. (1957).The concept of development from a comparative and organismic point of view. In D. B. Harris (Ed.), *The concept of development* (pp. 125–147). Minneapolis: University of Minnesota Press.

Winegar, L. T., & Valsiner, J. (1992). Re-contextualizing context: Analysis of metadata and some further elaborations. In L. T. Winegar & J. Valsiner (Eds.), *Children's development within social context. Vol. 2. Research and methodology* (pp. 249–266). Hillsdale, NJ: Lawrence Erlbaum Associates.

Woodworth, R. S. (1948). *Contemporary schools of psychology* (rev. ed.). New York: Ronald.

CHAPTER FOUR

What Happens When We Make a Distinction: An Elementary Introduction to Co-Genetic Logic

David P. Herbst*

Work Research Institute, Oslo, Norway

This chapter does not attempt to give an account of all the implications of a contextual logic, as far as we have been able to explore them. The aim is to bring the reader to the point where he or she can do his or her own exploring.

As far as the methods are concerned, they are simpler in practice than the addition and multiplication tables that we learned by rote in our first year at school, scarcely perhaps understanding what we were doing. The point of departure is the world before there was any subject or objects. Or more correctly, the time before there was any time.

When a distinction is made, a boundary comes into being together with the inside and the outside of a form. What is generated in this way is a triadic co-genetic unit consisting of the inside and outside and the distinction made that is represented by the boundary. At this stage, we have nothing more than a form in an empty space (see Fig. 4.1).

In its most general form what has become generated in this way is a unit consisting of not less than three elements, which we denote by $[n, m, p]$. In this case, the primary distinction that generates the form (the inside) together with the empty space (the outside), and the boundary separating and distinguishing inside and outside, is only one particular realization of the primary distinction, which was first formulated by Spencer-Brown (1969) in a different way. A triadic unit has the following four properties:

1. *It is Co-genetic*
The three elements that are generated come into being together.

---

*Author deceased.

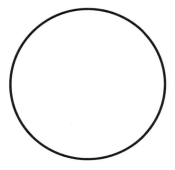

FIG. 4.1. The form of the primary Distinction.

2. *It is Nonseparable*

We cannot take the components apart. And also, we cannot have them initially apart and then put them together. This has a number of implications, because what we have here is not a modular or mechanical structure, and it also does not correspond to the assumptions of Boolean algebra, classical logic, or set theory.

3. *It is Nonreducible*

There cannot be less than three components. If any one component, the boundary, the inside, or the outside is taken away, then all three components disappear together. What results then is the primary state that is nondenotable and nondescribable and for which we use the symbol Ø. It is not nothingness, because nothingness does not come into being except in contrast to and in relationship to a form. The nonreducible property is the converse of the co-genetic property that says that all three components come into being together.

4. *It is Contextual*

None of the components have individually definable characteristics. In fact, they have no intrinsic characteristics that belong to them. This is because they are not separable, so they are not able to carry and display any characteristics individually and by themselves. In the triadic unit $[n, m, p]$ the components are individually undefined, but each is definable in terms of the two others. Thus if we wish to define the boundary we can do so in terms of the inside and outside as that which is crossed by moving from the inside to the outside. If n denotes the inside and m the outside, then p denotes the operation of crossing.

There are at this stage a number of implications: (a) What is generated is a functioning unit; (b) at least one of the components functions as an operation and the other two as dual possible states; (c) the two possible states n and m are not yet at this stage distinguishable in terms of their characteristics; (d) because each component is definable in terms of the

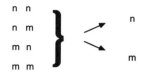

FIG. 4.2. The operational unit.

others, it is sufficient to retain no more than two, which we denote by n and m.

It may be somewhat misleading to talk about components or elements that form part of the traditional language of modular thinking. Often, we assume when we use these terms that everything that exists can be taken apart into constituent elements or built up from individual elements. There are demonstrably conditions where this is the case. However, there are also conditions where this is not the case.

For suppose we say "I am hungry." Can we separate the "I" from the "hungry" and then put them together again? Or, if we have a wife and a husband, do we first and independently have a wife and a husband, and then link them together by marriage?

If we take the triadic unit as our starting point, then a better way of thinking about the components is to conceive them as nodes of a network. For when the network disappears, so also do the nodes. This in fact corresponds to what is derivable as the next step from the contextual principle. When we formulated this principle, we assumed implicitly that we can define pairs and individual elements. However, to begin with we have only three, and not yet either two or one.

We started off with the notion of a primary distinction that generated the triad. What we can do next is to make a distinction within the distinction as follows: $[n, m, p]$. In whichever way we do this, we obtain a pair together with a single element.

The Definitional Triad thus takes the form: [single element, pair, pair defines element]. What we arrive at in this way are four possible pairs that each define or have as their outcome one of two possible elements, as shown in Fig. 4.2.

Characteristics of Contextual Process Networks

Let us look at an example of an operational unit in which each pair of elements leads to one of two possible outcomes:

$$n\ n = n$$
$$n\ m = m \qquad \text{Operational}$$
$$m\ n = m \qquad \text{Unit [2a]}$$
$$m\ m = n$$

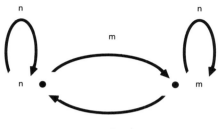

FIG. 4.3. The operational unit generates the process network [2a].

We read $n\,n = n$ as follows. If we start with the state n and apply the operation n, then the outcome is n. However, if we instead apply the operation m, then the outcome is m. How this operational unit functions becomes much more comprehensible if we map it out (see Fig. 4.3). As before, if we start off with n and apply n, we come back to n. However, if we apply m, then we obtain a transition to m.

We see immediately that under every condition, in this particular case, if we apply n and continue doing so, then the form or state is maintained in existence. However, whenever m is applied, this results in an inversion of states. In this case, then, n functions as an *Identity Maintaining Operator*, and m as an *Inversion Operator*.

We note that the symbols n and m have no predefined or intrinsic properties. Within the operational unit, both can function, or be interpreted, as states or operations. Within a given process network, they then acquire specific identifiable characteristics, and once this stage is reached, they become applicable.

A concrete example that I present here comes from Socrates. And the reason for this is that the earliest account in the Western World of what we now call the primary distinction and its consequences goes back to, for the most part forgotten, fragments of the teaching of Socrates and Plato. An account of these can be found in Beth (1955).

Socrates in the hours before his death discussed the nature of death and of birth. He starts off with the analogy of going to sleep and then again waking up. What he points out is that if there was only a transition from being awake to sleeping, then eventually we would all be asleep. So there also has to be a transition from sleep to the waking state. The Operational Unit has the form:

$$
\begin{array}{llll}
\text{Wake Wake} & = \text{Wake} & n\,n & = n \\
\text{Wake Sleep} & = \text{Sleep} & n\,m & = m \\
\text{Sleep Wake} & = \text{Wake} & m\,n & = n \\
\text{Sleep Sleep} & = \text{Sleep} & m\,m & = m
\end{array}
$$

Now when we map this out in the form of a process network, we arrive at Fig. 4.4.

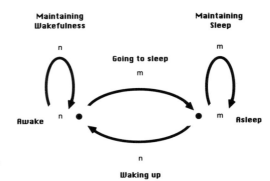

FIG. 4.4. The sleep-wake inversion
cycle. Network [2b].

Every symmetrical pattern *nn* and *mm* maintains the existing state. Every asymmetrical pattern *nm* and *mn* leads to a transition. Or, we can say that in this case an operation applied to itself is an identity-maintaining operator, whereas an operator applied to the dual state is an inversion operator. Within this contextual structure, awake and asleep become distinguishable as asymmetrical and qualitatively different states.

The difference between the two networks that we are looking at is that in the case of [2a], the process algebra is commutative: $n\ m = m\ n$. In the case of [2b], it is not commutative: $n\ m \neq m\ n$.

Let us consider, as an example for [2a], that we have a sphere on which we make a circumnavigating line. Having made the distinction, we now have two hemispheres that came into being together, and thus two distinguishable locations. We denote these locations by *n* and *m*, or the other way around, because it makes no difference. Given no more than the distinction, the hemispheres are different, but not distinguishable in terms of their characteristics.

Having marked the distinction, we now find ourselves in either region, so we call the one where we are *n* = *stay*, and the other *m* = *transit*. If we now start with the location where we are staying *n*, and apply the operation *m*, transit, then we come to *m*. We are now in location *m* and apply the operation *n*, stay, and then remain in the location *m*. So, in this case, the condition $n\ m = m\ n$ is satisfied (see Fig. 4.5).

Suppose now that we impose the condition that starting at any point we pass through every process link just once to get back to the point of departure. In this case, we obtain a Hamiltonian circuit, which can only take the form of an alternating sequence of operations, *n m n m* or *m n m n*.

The network now functions like a pendulum that, when we start it off with some displacement, moves to the other side, stops momentarily, and then moves in the reverse direction. The network is completely symmetrical, so we would expect that it cannot be used to distinguish between one direction or another. Surprisingly, however, the Hamiltonian circuit distin-

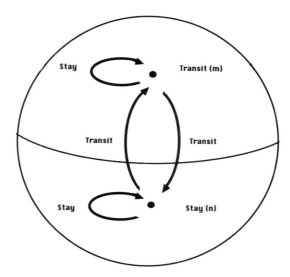

FIG. 4.5. Transit between two regions on a sphere. Process network [2a].

guishes between clockwise and counterclockwise directions, or between left and right.

If we map the Hamiltonian circuit in the way shown in Fig. 4.6, then starting at n and applying m, the process goes in a clockwise direction to return to the point of departure. However, if we start with the operation n, then it goes in the opposite counterclockwise direction.

Having looked at these examples, the transition between hemispheres and the path of a pendulum, we might expect that the process structure should provide some elementary base for counting, keeping in mind that we have not yet reached the stage where we can formulate a number system. What we can do, and what also George Boole looked at to begin with, is to see how our elementary operations such as + and − work.

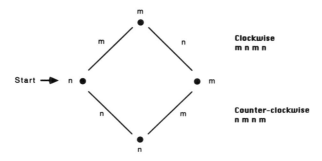

FIG. 4.6. The direction distinguishing Hamiltonian circuit of network [2a].

If, in our Operational Unit, we put $n = +$, and $m = -$, then this gives the following operational unit:

$$
\begin{array}{ccc}
+ & + & = + \\
+ & - & = - \\
- & + & = - \\
- & - & = +
\end{array}
$$

This is correct, if we read each line as denoting multiplications. In this case, "+" functions as the identity maintaining operation, and "−" functions as the inversion operator. In all its simplicity, however, there is something more to it. The operational unit distinguishes between events that are similar and events that are dissimilar.

Whenever we have a pair of similar elements of events, say + + or − −, then the outcome is +. However, if we have a set of dissimilar elements, + − or − +, the outcome is −. This is also the case if we continue the pairwise sequence in any case. Thus $(+ -) (+ -) (+ -) \ldots = (-)$.

We can here safely disregard Leibniz's pseudo-paradox, which shows that the series $+ 1 - 1 + 1 - 1 + 1 \ldots$, read either as multiplication or as addition and subtraction, can have no determinable outcome, because this disregards the pairwise inversion of the process structure. This illustrates one of the traps in which it is possible to fall, if one treats arithmetical problems as problems in pure number theory. Although we are still at the pre-numerate stage, it turns out that we can distinguish between what later will become recognizable as odd and even numbers.

Let us put the inversion sequence in its general process form as shown in Fig. 4.7. There, we apply the inversing operation over and over again. With the first inversion, a mismatch is obtained, and with the next, a self-matching of the initial state, which whenever it occurs, will correspond to an even number. Thus, this becomes recognized as an event that has recurred.

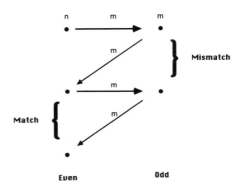

FIG. 4.7. The inversion sequence.

In closing this part of the discussion, I show briefly how the triadic unit representation and its consequences are related to Spencer-Brown's original formulation of the primary distinction. (A schematic overview of our exploration can be found in the Appendix.)

In the Spencer-Brown logic the point of departure is a set of axioms as follows:

$$\neg \ \neg \ = \ \neg \qquad \dots\dots\dots\dots \ (1)$$

$$\neg\!\neg \ = \qquad \dots\dots\dots\dots \ (2)$$

There are just two symbols. $\neg$ denotes the creation of the boundary by the act of crossing it, and thus the creation of the primary distinction. The absence of a symbol denotes an empty space.

The first axiom states that if the distinction is made and then made again, this is the same as making the distinction. Formally, this corresponds to Boole's first axiom, which has the form: $x\,x = x$. However, the interpretation is quite different here, because no notion of a class or set of objects is taken as given. Boole assumes to begin with the existence of discrete, identifiable objects. Spencer-Brown starts at the point before anything identifiable as a subject or object has come into being.

The second axiom is said to state that if the boundary is crossed and then re-crossed, which is possible only in the reverse direction, then this eliminates the boundary and we return to the state before any distinctions existed. The sequence of inversions in Equation 2 has the same structure as the dual of process network [2a]. The equation in this case does not represent the primary distinction that needs to be formulated as an initial distinction creating co-genetically two dual states.

We note something quite remarkable in Spencer-Brown's formulation. The act of creation is an act of negation. It is a negation of the original state, and it is through the act of negation that a finite, bounded, and segmented world is produced. Hence, it is only by the negation of the negation that we are able to return to the original state, that is the same as the state that we left and also not. For it is said that the man who has done the outward journey and later returned is no longer the same as he was before he made his journey.

The Ten Process Networks

Up to the middle of the 1970s, the process networks that had been identified and studied were those that correspond in their form to the Boolean operations, "and," "or," and "negation," together with the Sheffer stroke operation. These are known to be sufficient to derive Boolean logic and set theory (cf. chap. 7 on behavior logic in Herbst, 1976). No further progress was made until 10 years later when Paal Rasmussen (1986) showed in a three-page note that there are in fact 16 possible process networks that correspond to the 16 so-called Boolean binary connectives and surmised that at least some of these might have interesting properties.

This opened the door to take a new look at the problem. It turned out that there are in fact nine structurally different (binary) process networks together with a tenth, which has no transition links and thus consists of nothing more than discrete process elements. Each of these were found to have interpretible properties. At least one case demonstrates the possibility of switching between the subject and the object perspective. In every case, both a physical and a psychological interpretation can be found.

Given the interpretative analysis so far, the reader may perhaps find it of interest to explore some of the other cases before reading my interpretation (Herbst, 1987). Table 4.1 gives the 16 Operational Units together with the corresponding Binary Boolean Connectives. Figure 4.8 shows the 10 process structures. Each process structure can be represented by the outcome column in the operational unit. Thus, network [2a] is completely represented in the form (n, m, m, n). The process networks are classifiable in terms of the number of transition links. [4] denotes the network with two different inversion operations, but no state in which it can maintain itself. [0] denotes the zero-network that has no transition links.

At this stage the implications of the primary distinction as we pursue them may have no end. So, in closing, I would like to consider some fundamental implications to the validity of alternative theories of the world. Of particular interest is the [0] network that appears in the form of discrete enduring and identical process elements. What takes form at this stage corresponds in its structure to the Democritian universe of atoms and in the more modern form to the assumption basis of class logic and set theory. We note also that in the modern formulation the elements are formulated as identity maintaining, but only in the formal tautological sense. Here we see that each element is constituted as an identity-maintaining process. No matter which operation is applied, the element maintains itself in existence. This, however, implies also that under certain conditions the structure will break down and become metamorphosed into potentially any one of the other process networks.

What we can see now is that the atomistic state is no more than the zero level of structure in which the world can manifest itself. This means that theories that are established on the preassumption of discrete atomic elements cannot have validity beyond the range in which these conditions are met. This, however, is also the case for any other process network.

For instance, network [2c] can be elaborated to correspond to an ergodic or entropy process that ends inevitably in a stable trapping state. Now if,

TABLE 4.1

The Possible Outcome States Define the Ten Process Networks, Which are Classified by the Number of Transition Links (see Fig. 4.7). The Corresponding Binary Connectives are Shown.

State and Operation	[0]	[1]	[1]	[2]	[2]	[2]	[2]	[2]	[3]	[3]	[3]
	a	â	b	ƀ	a	â	b	c	d	ā	a	b	ƀ
n n	n	n	n	n	n	m	n	n	m	m	m	n	m
n n	n	m	n	n	m	n	m	n	n	m	m	n	m
m m	m	m	m	m	n	n	m	n	m	m	n	n	n
m m	m	m	n	n	m	m	m	m	m	m	n	n	n
Binary Connective	**p**	**p ∧ q**	**p ← q**		**p ↔ q**	**q**	**~q**	**∅**	**1**		**p ↑ q**	**p → q**	**p**
		p ∨ q	**p ← q**		**p ≥ q**						**p ↓ q**	**p → q**	
Spencer-Brown Calculus		⌐⌐ (⌐⌐)			⌐⌐ (=⌐⌐)								

76

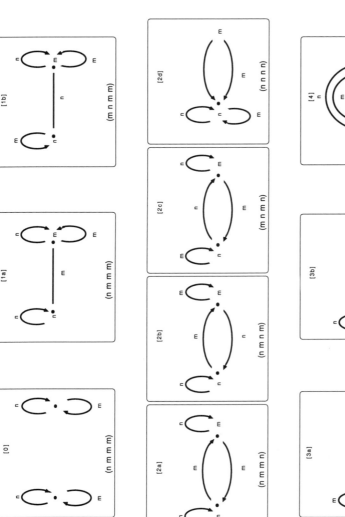
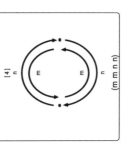
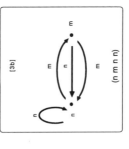
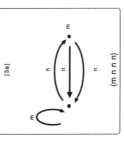

FIG. 4.8. The ten process networks.

as we do, we encounter this type of process, we cannot assume that it is eternally and universally operative, because with a transformation of the process structure it ceases and becomes converted into some other structural form. In fact, each process structure turns out to provide a valid and possible theory of the world. However, the validity of a theory cannot be extended beyond the conditions that maintain the existence of a given process structure.

Put in the most simple way, the fact that a theory is demonstrably valid does not imply that it is valid universally, nor does it necessarily exclude or negate the validity of other theories. In fact, any theory or philosophy based on a particular process structure is valid only as long as the conditions for the manifestation of this structure are maintained. At this point we come to two general conclusions:

1. Any theory that is based on pre-specified conditions can have local validity, but not universal validity.
2. It is demonstrable that starting with non-Boolean axioms, class and set logic are derivable as a special case. However, there is no demonstrable route by which the axioms of a Boolean or set logic can be used to derive a contextual logic.

REFERENCES

Beth, E. W. (1955). *Foundations of mathematics.* Amsterdam: North-Holland.
Boole, G. (1951). *The laws of thought on which are founded the mathematical theories of logic and probabilities.* New York: Dover.
Herbst, D. P. (1976). *Alternatives to Hierarchies.* Leiden, The Netherlands: Nijhoff.
Herbst, D. P. (1987). Co-genetic logic: The ten process networks. *Work Research Institute Documentations, 1,* Oslo, Norway.
Plato (1954). *The last days of Socrates.* New York: Penguin.
Rasmussen, P. (1986). *Short note on binary connectives.* Unpublished manuscript, Department of Psychology, University of Oslo, Norway.
Spencer-Brown, L. (1969). *Laws of form.* London: Allen & Unwin.

Appendix

Map of the Present State of Exploration

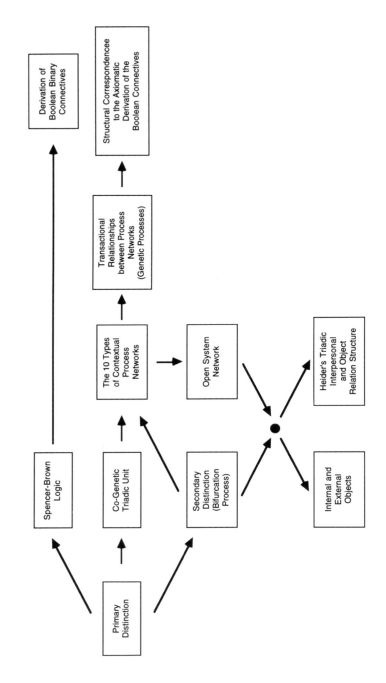

PART TWO

EMPIRICAL APPROACHES TO THE STUDY OF DEVELOPING PERSON–CONTEXT RELATIONS

Understanding the Economic Framework: Children's and Adolescents' Conceptions of Economic Inequality

Annette Claar
Technical University of Darmstadt,
Darmstadt, Germany

In past research on the development of concepts about cultural phenomena, for example in domains such as politics, economics, or religion, only occasionally the cultural context in which such concepts are developed by individuals has been included in the research. In this chapter, it is argued that to account for the adaptive function of conceptual construction, the inclusion of context is a prerequisite for both an adequate theoretical framework and empirical reconstruction. The adaptational character of concept development becomes most evident when a context itself is in the process of considerable transformation, and when individuals attempt to understand, evaluate, and cope with these changing conditions. One example in the present time are the political, economic, and social changes taking place in many countries from the former Eastern bloc. The context-inclusive view of concept development is illustrated by findings from a research project on economic concept development, which is currently carried out with children and adolescents from East and West Germany in the course of the political and economic reunion. This chapter deals with the findings on descriptions, explanations, and evaluations of economic inequality at the time when the German reunion was just in its beginning.

CULTURE AS AN OBJECT OF COGNITIVE DEVELOPMENT

In the analysis of individual development within cultural context, the emergence of culture-specific action patterns, cognitive structures, value systems, and other psychological features is considered useful or even necessary for the individual to successfully adapt to the conditions of his or her specific culture (e.g., Berry, 1976; Dasen, 1975). The acquisition of certain competencies and values enables a person to orient in the environment, to act in it in more or less adequate ways, and to a certain degree even to select and modify the context according to one's own needs and goals. In principle, the human environment has to be conceptualized as culturally organized, and the individuals learn to relate to these cultural contexts in ways that are prestructured by their culture (Eckensberger, 1990; Valsiner, 1987, 1989).

As one important part of these successful adaptations, cognitive structures are developed that are directly concerned with one's own culture as an object. Thus, cultural organization and cultural meaning systems do become a content of a person's developing cognitions. From early on, children elaborate an increasingly differentiated and integrated understanding of the numerous phenomena that are typical and significant for their sociocultural context. Even more, as development proceeds, experiences with other, more or less foreign cultures may be included to enrich the basic cultural knowledge structures. A process of intercultural comparison and a reflection of cultural conditions may commence.

If the human ecology is viewed as basically a cultural environment, it could be argued that just about any cognition of a human individual is concerned with his or her cultural context. At least if we understand the expression "cognition about cultural context" in a wider sense, this position seems plausible. However, it is advocated here that some phenomena may be considered more relevant than others to characterize the organization of a culture. Such a selection of variables is exactly what is done by scientists, who are interested in identifying the most critical variables of cultural contexts (e.g., to analyze their interrelation with some aspect of individual development). In a less systematic fashion, something similar is done by any individual who is trying to understand the characteristics of his or her own culture, perhaps in comparison to other cultures. As an early example for the scientific perspective, Kroeber and Kluckhohn (1952), in their important work on the concept of culture, differentiated between reality culture (material objects, techniques, economy), value culture (world views, religion, ideological systems), and social culture (family, kinship, social organization) as three important domains of culture. More recently, in a comprehensive discussion of the concept of culture in the human sciences, Krewer (1990) pointed to the necessity of selecting appropriate domains of human activity for the analysis of cultural meaning systems and their transmission in individual development. Krewer (1990) also made clear, however, that different theoretical approaches in cultural anthropology and psychology will emphasize different domains and target phenomena.

This rather fundamental discussion will not be entered here by any attempt to define or to enumerate the cultural domains that may be most meaningful.

Rather, one specific domain will be selected to analyze some aspects in the transmission of cultural meaning systems in the development of children and adolescents. The discussion concentrates on the domain of economics, a field that is selected for three reasons: First, this domain entails the provision of the necessary means of life in a society through goal-directed and organized ways of production and distribution of goods and services. In this respect economics may be considered to be one of the most central domains of culturally structured meaning systems. Second, this meaning system provides guidelines for individuals' actions to participate in shaping the path of their own development. Third, children's understanding of economic phenomena has been an area of growing interest in developmental psychology during the last decade (e.g., Berti & Bombi, 1988; Furnham & Stacey, 1991; Furth, 1980; Sonuga-Barke & Webley, 1993).

The Development of Economic Understanding in Childhood and Adolescence

In recent years, a number of empirical studies has been carried out in this field. They provide a considerable range of examples to analyze the development of concepts about the cultural organization of a person's environment.

The cognitions children develop about the economic system in their culture may be concerned with different levels of organization. At the one extreme, they might deal with the immediate surrounding and the concrete experiences of an individual child; at the other extreme, they may refer to the culture and its organization as a whole, perhaps even in comparison with other cultures. Besides being more or less closely related to the immediate experience of the individual, such levels of cultural organization are increasingly comprehensive and require different degrees of generality and abstractness for an adequate description. To distinguish various levels of the cultural context that may be an object of an individual's cognition, it might be helpful to refer to Bronfenbrenner's (1979) description of the human ecosystem. In general, we might characterize children's culture-related conceptual development as dealing with phenomena of their micro-, meso-, exo-, and macrosystems.

Although using a different theoretical framework and terminology than suggested by Bronfenbrenner, Furth introduced a tentative sequence of conceptual stages in the understanding of society that summarizes the development of children's thinking in a similar way (1978, 1980; Furth, Baur, & Smith, 1976; see also Berti & Bombi, 1988; Danziger, 1958). During the preschool and early elementary school years, children's social and economic concepts are typically concerned with their everyday experiences. Children elaborate conceptual reconstructions of the various objects and events they encounter within their microsystems. For example, children may observe a doctor, a salesperson, or a teacher in their immediate surrounding taking specific social roles, or they may watch the exchange of money and merchandise during shopping. Many studies have been undertaken to reconstruct the developmental sequences along which the elaboration of such very specific social and economic concepts typically takes place; to name but a few examples, there are studies about children's understanding of various social roles (Berti, 1981; Emler, Ohana, & Moscovici, 1987), about the concept of money and its use in buying (Berti & Bombi, 1981; Strauss, 1952), the reasons for price differences (Berti & Bombi, 1988; Burris, 1983; Claar, 1990), or the perception of social inequality (Baldus & Tribe, 1978; Jahoda, 1959; Leahy, 1981, 1983).

Starting out from their yet available cognitive structures, children are actively trying to make sense of their experiences. Especially in the early stages, the concepts and scripts that they elaborate are of a very concrete nature. Also, the early concepts are of a more prototypical kind, and less generalized, differentiated, and integrated than the concepts that will be elaborated later in development. In many instances, the children's explanations are quite imaginative and idiosyncratic, and they do not have to be correct from an adult point of view at all. According to an anecdotical example reported to us by the father of a 3-year-old boy, his child enthusiastically interpreted a cash automat as a money-making machine. The boy found it natural to make and to take as much money as one would desire. Another boy showed vast disappointment when, in the course of opening his very first savings account, he had to leave the content of his money box at the bank. He had been informed that he would get a savings box and colored pencils, and he enjoyed the coins being counted by a machine, but leaving the money at the bank had not been part of his expectations. Many inadequate conceptualizations of this kind can be explained as unwarranted generalizations of already available concepts (e.g., Burris, 1983; Jahoda, 1981), as a lack of coordination of given conceptual parts (Claar, 1989; Jahoda, 1979), or at least partly as missing background information about processes and interrelations that are beyond the child's personal experience (Berti & Bombi, 1989).

During the elementary school years, children expand their field of interest toward more distant phenomena that are not as readily observable. Parental explanations, school lessons, and mass media presumably play an important role in the transformation of economic knowledge. However, children do not simply accumulate the information that is given. Rather, they interpret any incoming message on the basis of their yet available logical and conceptual structures. In their search for plausible explanations, they actively elaborate their own naive theories. While doing so, they increasingly include objects and events that are not observable in their own microsystems, and they successively integrate their initially limited conceptual structures into a larger system. Following Bronfenbrenner, these improvements can be understood as a conceptualization of economics on a meso- and exosystemic level. Again, children's elaboration of such background understanding can nicely be demonstrated for the field of economics: Children elaborate their assumptions about the origin of merchandise in the shop (e.g., Berti & Bombi, 1989; Burris, 1983; Danziger, 1958), about the origin of the payment for the workers (Berti & Bombi, 1980, 1988; Danziger, 1958), or what is done with the saver's money in the bank (Claar, 1989; Jahoda, 1981; Wong, 1989). Also, they connect their initially rather isolated concepts of the shop, paid work, the factory, the bank, and so on into a more or less coherent system of the economy as a whole (Berti & Bombi, 1989; Berti, Bombi, & De Beni, 1986; Furth, 1980; Jahoda, 1979).

Eventually, a conceptualization of economics evolves that may be characterized as a macrosystem perspective. However, there is almost no empirical evidence on the development of thinking about the economic system as a whole. Presumably this level of economic thinking does require a certain degree of understanding of a number of economic subsystems and their interrelations, but a thorough or complete understanding does not seem to be a prerequisite. Rather, macroeconomic thinking probably begins somewhat later than thinking in terms of meso- and exosystems, and develops simultaneously with further conceptual integrations of various microsystems.

It has to be underlined that a person can think about the economic macrosystem in ways that show different levels of elaboration. An adult observer should not be deceived by a subject who is using conventional verbal expressions. In our interviews, even children at an early elementary school age occasionally mentioned such words as "medium of exchange," or "market economy," but the use of such conventional verbal terms may actually involve quite different degrees of conceptual differentiation, integration, and abstractness on the side of the individual. As an example, in our interviews we found a third-grade boy mentioning "the market economy." However, from further explanations given by this child it became obvious that he was thinking of a concrete market place where fruit and vegetables are sold.

The difficulties that even many seventh-grade children experience with abstract terms of this type are nicely demonstrated in a study by Berti (1991) on the understanding of socialism and capitalism. Even after having worked through special texts about this topic at school, the children "showed an extremely limited understanding of the functioning of capitalist and socialist economies and of the differences between the two types of systems" (p. 419).

In general, during concept development, children's understanding of economics and economic terms does become increasingly similar to the conventional word meanings in their society. However, the conceptual structures of an individual always remain ideosyncratic to a certain degree (Seiler & Wannenmacher, 1983). This is due to three reasons. First, the specific combination of experiences, observations, and available information in the personal history of each individual forms a variable basis of conceptual construction. Second, keep in mind that the developing individual is not confronted with just one form of adult understanding, but that often there are different and sometimes competing views about economic matters that prevail even in the adult world. An individual who is confronted with such heterogeneous and even contradictive informational offers has to select and elaborate his or her own interpretation. And third, the ideosyncratic character of concepts is due to the constructive nature of concept development in general. When we look at the details, each individual relates the various aspects of one or more (economic) phenomena in a slightly different way.

Usually, when researchers attempt to reconstruct the typical age-related concepts, and, in a second step, developmental sequences, they abstract from such differences. With their task in mind, the numerous ideosyncratic aspects of each specific person's understanding appear as disrupting the general picture they are trying to delineate. Due to the necessary process of abstraction, the various ideosyncratic nuances of each concept usually receive little or no attention. However, it should be kept in mind that these ideosyncrasies exist, and that they are an expression of the human capacity to understand and relate phenomena in different and new ways. This is why individuals—whereas they continue to strive for more adaptive and adequate explanations for how things work—become able to go beyond conventional conceptualizations that exist beforehand in their culture.

Economic Understanding in Different Cultural Contexts

If we consider economics as a genuinely cultural phenomenon, it seems inevitable to include the specific cultural context into the analysis of individual's economic concept development. One way to do this is via cross-cultural comparisons, especially between cultures that are differently structured with respect to economics. Thus, research questions of the following type do become relevant: How does economic concept development differ for subjects growing up in different types of cultures (e.g., in first versus third world countries, or in rural as compared to industrialized societies)? What difference does it make for a child to be raised in a society with a planned versus a market economy? What are the consequences of strong religious traditions (e.g., poverty as an expression of God's providence, or individual prosperity as a sign of divine benevolence; see Waines, 1984), or tribal traditions (e.g., reciprocal responsibility in a group)?

Along the same lines, it is important to look at relevant variation between contexts within a society. There might be important regional differences (e.g., between predominantly agricultural and industrial, or between economically prospering and declining regions). Also, we know little about the consequences of specific opportunities and limitations that are present in a person's immediate microsystems. What is the role of children's active participation in various economic activities (working, buying and selling, saving), or the effect of parental variables such as (un)employment, spending behavior or economics-oriented education practices, or educational goals (Sonuga-Barke & Webley, 1993; Ward, Wackman, & Wartella, 1977). As yet, we have very little information about the interrelations of such context variables and the course and rate of individual development, at least when it comes to economic understanding and to children's actions within economic frameworks.

Up to now, there are only few comparative or context-inclusive studies. Most of them were conducted with children and adolescents from different countries, as was the case in Jahoda's studies about the concept of shop profit in England, Scotland, and Zimbabwe (Jahoda, 1979, 1983), or in a number of studies on the concept of banking, carried out in Hong Kong, Scotland, and the United States (Jahoda, 1981; Ng, 1983; Wong, 1989; also see Leiser, Roland-Lévy, & Sévon, 1990). These studies have all been interested in the relative rate of developmental progress across time, and not in possible differences with respect to typical paths of development. Thus, the underlying assumption was that cultural conditions can accelerate or impede developmental progress along a given developmental sequence.

Most relevant for our current purpose are studies that focus on children's immediate experiences. Jahoda (1983) was able to identify children's active participation in buying and selling as a specific variable in the everyday life of Zimbabwean children that promotes an early understanding of profit. Similarly, the research by Berti and Bombi (1989) with children from urban industrial and mountain village regions and by Carraher, Carraher, and Schliemann (1985; Carraher & Schliemann, 1988; also Saxe, 1991) with Brazilian children who make their living as candy sellers in the streets underlines the significance of immediate and context-specific experience.

Another branch of research that is of interest here focused on individual's understanding and evaluation of economic inequality. In a number of studies (Burgard, Cheyne, & Jahoda, 1989; Emler & Dickinson, 1985; Leahy, 1981, 1983), children's concepts of economic inequality were related to variables of the family environment, especially to aspects that are tied to the family's socioeconomic status. We return to some findings from these studies later in this chapter.

Cultural Transformation and Economic Concept Development

A special situation is given when a cultural context itself is experiencing a process of fundamental and sometimes rapid transformation. Typical examples may be the transformation from traditional or tribal communities into increasingly urban and industrialized societies, or the transformations that are currently taking place in the countries that formerly belonged to the Eastern bloc. All in all, many countries or regions in the world are affected by such changes. In many cases, at least some of the old political and economic structures do persist, while new forms of organization are developing. Old and new structures may exist simultaneously for some time, and in many cases severe contradictions between new and old structures arise.

What effect does it make for an individual's economic development to live in a country with fundamental changes of its economic macrostructure (e.g., in a rapidly developing economy, or perhaps in a society with economic breakdown, as compared to conditions of comparatively little economic change)? What are the effects of the current economic transformations in Eastern Europe for the developing individual?

As yet very little is known about what these kinds of transformations mean for the economic understanding, action patterns, and value systems of an individual. Besides the economic hardship that comes about under such circumstances for many people, we have to expect that formerly well-established and reliable action schemes and conventional ways of explaining and predicting economic reality become inefficient. For example, traditional social roles become problematic, ways of managing personal economic resources (saving, spending) turn out to be inadequate, and former ways of making a living become less valued economically. At the same time, new economic phenomena develop and formerly unknown opportunities may arise. Thus, the acquisition of a new occupational training, starting a new job, or the possibility to participate in some new kind of business may be a challenge to the individual.

These examples point to the necessity to analyze the interrelation of active individuals in a changing (economic) context from a developmental perspective. Both the objective consequences of a specific economic transformation and the meaning that an individual will attribute to these circumstances are related to age. For example, the devaluation of a specific occupational qualification on the labor market will mean something different to a 30- than to a 50-year-old individual. Furthermore, individuals might develop new cognitive competences and action patterns in response to the changing conditions. Gaining access to the enormous quantity and variety of merchandise in a market economy after a life under planned economy conditions will be experienced and dealt with quite differently by adolescents, middle-aged adults, or elderly persons.

ECONOMIC CONCEPT DEVELOPMENT IN FORMER EAST AND WEST GERMANY: AN EMPIRICAL INVESTIGATION

At the present time, in the course of its reunion Germany is experiencing such a period of fundamental and rapid political, social, and economic change. The East German population is more dramatically affected than are people in West Germany. Presumably, the transformations have serious consequences for individuals in all periods of the life cycle, and they will affect, among other things, their understanding, action patterns, and values related to the economic domain. At the same time, economic actions, understanding, and values of the people in both parts of Germany will influence the course and the velocity of the historical transformation. In a way, history has provided psychology with an experiment on the developing individual in a changing cultural context. In the following, the most important historical data and the present situation are outlined to inform the reader about the cultural background of our study, which is presented afterwards.

The Political, Social, and Economic Transformations in Germany

After World War II, Germany was divided into two parts, the German Democratic Republic (East Germany), and the Federal Republic of Germany (West Germany). In the following, these two parts took different courses of political, social, and economic development. Economically seen, one part of Germany was organized as a planned, the other as a social market economy system. During the Cold War and even during the time of Detente, access from one part to the other was quite difficult for most ordinary people. Only when the border between the East and the West was opened in November of 1989, free travelling became possible. For people from Eastern Germany this included the possibility to work in the West and to buy in West German shops with West German currency. A preliminary economic union between the two parts of Germany was established in July of 1990, and the official political reunion of Germany followed in October of the same year. These historical data mark the beginning of a process, during which the economic system of the former German Democratic Republic (East) is being transformed from a planned into a social market economy. At the same time, the two German economies are becoming integrated into one. This process is still going on, and in the regions of former East Germany it involves a breakdown of many factories and trade organizations, significant changes in the levels of incomes and prices, and a high rate of unemployment. In this respect, it is especially the Eastern part of Germany that is undergoing rapid and fundamental changes. The people in the Western part of Germany are mainly affected by the fact that social security contributions and taxes are being increased to finance the economic transformation. Also, due to the growing deficit spending in the Federal budget, people were temporarily confronted with an increased rate of inflation, which in turn was a negative factor in the macroeconomic situation of worldwide economic recession.

The public opinion about these events has, by and large, changed considerably over time. Initially, in the fall of 1989, there was widespread enthusiasm about the political reunion, especially about the new political freedoms, about personal freedoms such as the possibility of largely unrestricted travelling, and about economic freedoms, including the access to the enormous variety of merchandise supply in a market economy. At that time, only few people gave warnings that the transformation would take considerably more time, cost much more money, and involve many more economic and social conflicts than was claimed, especially by the responsible politicians. During the past four years, many of the pessimistic predictions have come true, and feelings of disappointment and future fears have spread in the East, whereas in the West dissatisfaction with raised taxes and increased welfare contributions is growing.

This unusual political and economic situation is the background of our research on economic concept development with children and adolescents from both parts of Germany. The study is concerned with the development of various basic economic concepts in two different cultural contexts (e.g., money, prices, profit, work, banks, economic inequality). In one of these contexts, rapid and fundamental economic, social, and political transformations are taking place, whereas there is relative stability in the other.

Development of Conceptions
About Economic Inequality

In the following part of this chapter, I will focus on the part of our study that is concerned with our subjects' understanding and evaluation of economic inequality. The topic of economic inequality is of fundamental importance in the course of the German reunion, as especially in Eastern Germany many people experience significant changes in income. Most people's standard of living has improved; but at the same time there are many who have lost their jobs and at least some of their income. Thus, the concept of economic inequality might be especially sensitive for examining individual reactions and coping efforts in response to the fundamental transformations of the East German society.

Furthermore, children's and adolescents' understanding of economic inequality is not only an interesting object of children's cognition. It is potentially relevant for their personal future time perspective and actions. A child expecting that personal effort and a good education are effective means to get rich might be motivated differently than a child attributing prosperity to luck or to inheritance within the familiy. Thus, economic concept development may be seen as part of a more general framework of economic and professional socialization.

In the next section I describe some results from earlier studies on children's and adolescents' conceptualizations of economic inequality. These previous findings might provide some information about the kind of differences we have to expect for our subjects in the two parts of Germany, and about typical age differences. Afterwards, the hypotheses and the procedure of our study are presented.

Findings From Previous Studies

Results from earlier research on children's and adolescents' descriptions, explanations, and evaluations of economic inequality, by and large, point to consistent age differences and to some relations with parental socioeconomic status.

In his very comprehensive and detailed study on the description and explanation of economic inequality between the ages of 6 and 17, Leahy (1981, 1983) found an age-related decrease in the use of peripheral descriptors (external qualities, money and possessions, surroundings), whereas psychological and sociocentric categories such as life chances, prestige, and power became more frequent with age. This developmental trend from very concrete external attributes to more abstract and psychological descriptions is typical for concept development in general, and for person concepts in particular (Livesley & Bromley, 1973; Secord & Peevers, 1974). With respect to rich and poor people, this seems to be confirmed in recent, yet unpublished, studies by Enesco et al. (1992) in Spain, and by Vila (1992) in Mexico.

When asked about their explanations and evaluations of poverty and wealth, younger children in Leahy's (1983; also see Danziger, 1958) study typically gave definitional answers ("They are poor, because they have no money."). Also, many were uncertain about what might be proper explanations and evaluations ("Don't know."). In late childhood, equality is proposed quite often, but this category does become less frequent again in later adolescence. Compared to the younger age groups, the oldest subjects were the ones who presented both fatalistic views and equity-based conceptions most often. According to principles of equity, resources should be distributed depending on merit, acquired by contributions such as work, effort, education, and intelligence (Leahy, 1983). Similarly, in their study on income estimates, Emler and Dickinson (1985) found an increase of equity propositions with age; a subsequent suggestion of equal incomes was more likely to be rejected by older subjects than by younger ones (also see Burgard, Cheyne, & Jahoda, 1989).

In these studies, the developmental context in which these views are being constructed has been included primarily by taking the socioeconomic status of the children and their families into account. Some interesting findings have resulted from these studies. Adolescents from working-class backgrounds showed a preference for societal explanations, whereas individualistic explanations for poverty were more popular in middle-class adolescents (Furnham, 1982). In Leahy's study, lower class subjects in their descriptions more often referred to the better life chances of the rich, and they were more likely to consider negative consequences of insufficient economic resources for the poor (Leahy, 1981, 1983). Along the same lines, Waines (1984) reported observations from an Egyptian sample that only children from the disadvantaged groups pointed to the complete destitution of some poor people. According to Leahy (1983), lower class children were more likely than other groups to consider work as a possibility to improve their own life conditions. Also, older adolescents from this group expected resistance against social change more frequently than others, and more often they denied that they wanted to get rich themselves.

In comparison, upper middle-class subjects were more likely to explain poverty by referring to equity variables. They perceived a change in individual values as the starting point for social change (Leahy, 1983). Egyptian middle-class children much more than their lower class peers emphasized the importance of a good education (Waines, 1984).

In agreement with these results, Emler and Dickinson (1985) reported a preference for equity among children from economically more prosperous backgrounds. In their study, middle-class children differentiated more clearly between four types of jobs in their estimates of incomes, and they were less likely to agree upon a suggestion of equal payment for all. Emler and Dickinson explained their results in terms of social representations that are specific to socioeconomic status. They suspected that these status-specific representations are transmitted to children, among other things, by the parental value system and the respective information with which parents provide their children. Emler and Dickinson (1985) did not, however, assess these parental variables empirically to test their relation to children's judgments.

They were included in a replication study by Burgard, Cheyne, and Jahoda (1989), but a relationship between parental and child judgments was not confirmed. Also contrary to Emler and Dickinson's results, children's income estimates were found to be associated with age, but not with social status. Older children more adequately differentiated between the different occupations than younger ones. Above that, children's evaluations of income differences were neither related to age nor to social class. In their discussion of these contradictive results, the authors suspect that class differences might be less pronounced in Germany than in England, and that discrepant findings might thus be attributable to greater differences in social representations between groups in England, and within groups in Germany. Furthermore, Burgard et al. (1989) came to the important conclusion that their own cognitive-developmental view of concept construction, and the position of Emler and Dickinson (i.e., regarding concept acquisition as a transmission of social representations), are by no means contradictive. Rather, both aspects have to be taken into account in an adequate analysis of the precise conditions and mechanisms that characterize the process in which (e.g., status-specific) social representations are transmitted during concept development.

The empirical findings seem to indicate that subjects construct their conceptualizations of poverty and wealth in a way that permits a justification and explanation of their own material status. By doing so, an individual can avoid possible dissonances, which might otherwise affect self-esteem or the personal value system. The results from a longitudinal study reported by Gurney (1981) on adolescents' attributions of the causes of unemployment also point in this direction. Four months after leaving school, those who had found jobs in the meantime had shifted toward more internal causal attributions, whereas the group of still unemployed adolescents showed a nonsignificant trend toward more external attributions. The author suspects this tendency to become more extreme after a longer period of unemployment, and to result in negative consequences for self-esteem.

Judgments About Economic Inequality in Eastern and Western Germany

What can we learn from these findings on the relation between children's own socioeconomic status and their conceptualizations of economic inequality about the possible differences that we have to expect for subjects in the two parts of Germany? Keep in mind that all of these data were collected in contexts with a comparatively low degree of transformation. Subjects probably did not anticipate any fundamental changes in the socioeconomic structure or of their own material status for the near future.

A generalization is not easily possible. At first glance, we may note that people in the Western part of Germany are on average comparatively prosperous, whereas economic resources for most people in the East are still more limited. Insofar, one might expect a more widespread proposition of the equity principle in the West, whereas people in Eastern Germany would be more likely to favor an equal distribution. This would also be consistent with the political ideologies that have been prominent in two parts of Germany from World War II on. In Eastern Germany, the socialist ideology had proposed a rather egalitarian distribution of resources, whereas the ideology of capitalist West Germany was and still is much more in favor of equity and achievement principles.

But there are other and perhaps more important variables that might have an opposite effect on people's judgments. An important factor is the position an individual takes toward one's own society, that is, the evaluations of the political and economic system the person is living in, and the hopes and fears that are associated with the personal future time perspective. In particular, judgments about economic inequality may be influenced by the anticipated macroeconomic situation and by the kind of consequences that are foreseen for the personal living conditions.

What were the predominant expectations of the East German and West German population at the time our study was started? Spring and summer of 1990 were the last months during which the German Democratic Republic existed. The old system was highly rejected by large parts of the East German population. At the same time, the Federal Republic of Germany and a market economy were mostly considered attractive. Economically seen, the reunion seemed to promise the possibiliy that everyone could participate in the affluence of the Western societies. People in the East had no experience with a competitive economy, and a vast majority probably was quite optimistic that they personally would be successful. Under these conditions, people are likely to favor principles of equity.

Some people, even at that time, were sceptical and predicted severe negative side effects. For an unpredictable period of transformation, increasing prices, unemployment, and professional dequalification would have to be expected for many people in the East. Despite such warnings, however, the public opinion about the political and economic situation was, by and large, quite optimistic.

Taking a political position that is favorable of the reunion and developing a positive kind of personal future time perspective would seem to increase the likelihood of judgments based on equity principles in individuals from former East Germany. This effect would be contrary to the expected influences of the degree of relative affluence versus scarcity, and of the past political ideologies in the formerly independent parts of Germany. All in all, we expected these factors to balance out, so that the subjects in our East Berlin sample would support equity principles of resource distribution as frequently as subjects in the Western sample.

With respect to the description of poor and rich people, we assumed that the subjects in our Western sample would draw a far more extreme picture than the subjects from East Berlin. In the past, the extreme poles of the income distribution in former East Germany have been clearly less apart than in the West German society. We expected children's and adolescents' descriptions of the conditions and attributes of rich and poor people to be influenced by the observations and experiences they have been able to make in their respective contexts.

Furthermore, in their explanations of becoming rich or poor, we expected the typical opportunities and risks of a market economy, such as owning a company, or losing one's job, to be mentioned more often in the Western sample. For the Eastern sample, a more frequent reference to well-paid jobs and to positions in the state and party apparatus seemed probable.

Consistent with the age effects found in previous studies (Emler & Dickinson, 1985; Leahy, 1983), our youngest subjects were expected to be either insecure about the proper type of distribution, or to favor an allocation of economic wealth based on individual need or equality, whereas the older subjects would be more likely to propose equity principles.

Method and Findings of the Present Empirical Study

Method. The study is designed longitudinally, with two points of measurement in 1990 and 1991 and in 1992 and 1993. With our Eastern sample, located in East Berlin, the first interviews took place in the spring of 1990, which was soon after the opening of the border and before any economic or political union had been established. The second implementation of interviews was carried out in the summer and fall of 1992, that is, 28 months later. Interviews in the West German city of Darmstadt were first administered in the winter of 1990-1991 and are currently repeated (spring and summer of 1993). Thus, the data presented in this chapter are limited to the first point of measurement.

Subjects' understanding of economic inequality was assessed by means of semistructured interviews, containing a number of standardized questions and some flexible additional questions that depended on previous specifications. Questions were directed at descriptions of "poor" and "rich," explanations of the causes of poverty and wealth, and as a more evaluative aspect, a judgment of what would be the proper distribution of economic resources. The questionaire on economic inequality is listed in detail in Table 5.1.

Subjects were 167 children and adolescents (East Germany: $n = 75$; West Germany: $n = 92$) between the ages of 8 and 15 years, and attending third, fifth, seventh, and ninth grade at the time of the first interview. Both samples were equivalent with regard to distribution of gender and school achievement, and in both cultures, about 20 children were in each age group. In the presentation of results, however, this number is reduced in some instances due to occasional problems during the interview procedure (e.g., tape recording problems, insufficient clarification of topic in interview).

The transcribed interviews were coded according to five category systems, in which different answer types to each of the following five aspects of economic inequality were specified: (a) descriptions of poverty, (b) descriptions of wealth, (c) explanations of poverty, (d) explanations of wealth, and (e) evaluation. The type of categories that have been used, including some examples, are named in the section of interview results.

For determining interrater reliability, 20% of all interviews, about evenly distributed across ages and cultural contexts, were coded by a second rater. Interrater reliabilities for the five category systems on economic inequality (Cohen's kappa) were between k = .86 and k = .92.

Because many subjects gave multiple answers to the questions about the description and explanation of poverty and wealth, each answer category pertaining to these four questions was analyzed separately.[1] In the course

---

[1]Answer categories that were found in less than 5% of both the Eastern and the Western sample were omitted from further analysis.

TABLE 5.1
Interview on the Description, Explanation,
and Evaluation of Economic Inequality

Description:
1   What do you think, when is a person poor?   2   What do you think, when is a person rich?
Explanation:
3   How did the poor people get poor?   4   How did the rich people get rich?
Evaluation:
5   Would it be possible that everybody gets the same share? How should it be done? (or) Why is it not possible? Do you think that would be good or would it not be so good? (Standardized countersuggestions:) (if "unequal":) But aren't there also people, who have worked a lot and tried hard, and are still poor, isn't that unjust? (if "equality":) But if everybody gets the same amount anyway, are people going to make an effort in what they do?

of analysis, a combination of the four age groups into two groups (3rd and 5th grade versus 7th and 9th grade) turned out to be necessary, as the number of cells had to be kept small.

For each category, a logit analysis was carried out, which is a special variant of the general loglinear model. In general, the strategy in loglinear analysis is to calculate the fit between a theoretical model and the data via maximum-likelihood statistics. The special advantage of logit analysis is the possibility to treat age, cultural context, and gender as independent variables, and to test main and interaction effects on the frequency distributions in children's answer types (the dependent variables). According to Knoke and Burke (1980), a model with a probability level of $p > .10$ is acceptable. Besides the overall fit of a model, the size and significance of single (main or interaction) effects can be calculated. Single effects are determined as the difference between likelihood-ratio chi^2 values for the models with versus without the respective effect. Accordingly, degrees of freedom result from the difference between degrees of freedom of the two models.

Results. In the following, results are presented for the description (poor-rich) of economic inequality first, followed by findings for explanations (poor-rich), and evaluative judgments. For each category, the chi^2-values of main or interaction effects are presented in Tables 5.2 to 5.6, including the respective degrees of freedom and levels of significance. Also, the overall fit of the accepted model is reported, including all effects that have been found to be significant for the distribution of an answer category.

The findings for children's *descriptions of poor people* are listed in Table 5.2.[2] Younger subjects more frequently than adolescents simply referred to the amount of money a person possesses ("someone who has [almost] no money"). This kind of description has previously been found especially in younger children (Danziger, 1958; Leahy, 1981). Although it is certainly accurate in general, it gives little extra information as to the living conditions or qualities of poor people.

With respect to the other answer types, there are some main effects for developmental context. First, a main effect of context was found for an extreme fashion to characterize poverty, namely, describing that basic economic needs are not or are barely satisfied. For example, subjects state that a poor person cannot buy enough food or has to wear old and shabby clothes. This type of answer was overrepresented in the Western sample. A less extreme description to characterize poor people is to state that they own no or only few nice or spare things. This type of answer was given more frequently by Eastern subjects. Also, the statement "there are no really poor people around here" was made almost exclusively by children and adolescents from the Eastern context (19 out of 21 cases). Furthermore, all subjects who gave descriptions of poor people by making a reference to the other part of Germany came from the Eastern sample. When asked about poverty in general, these children and adolescents from East Berlin spontaneously referred to the Western socioeconomic context for description.[3] This pattern of various context-related answer distributions confirmed our expectation that children and adolescents from Eastern Germany, in the spring and early summer months of 1990, painted a clearly less dramatic picture of poverty than their Western German peers.

Contrary to previous studies (Livesley & Bromley, 1973; Secord & Peevers, 1974), psychological descriptions were infrequent altogether, and there was no increase with age. This is probably due to a slightly different emphasis in the interview. In the present investigation, emphasis has been not so much on a description of the person than on the criteria as to when a person is poor (or rich) or not. This way of posing the questions may be less prone to elicit psychological descriptions.

Compared to the description of poverty, the *descriptions of rich people* are characterized by clearly fewer relationships with age, context, or gender. Table 5.3 presents an overview.

---

[2]Some answers such as "unemployment," "saving lots of money," or "owning a factory" may be considered both descriptive and explanatory. To count answers of this type only once, it was decided to omit them in the section on descriptions of poor people and to include them in the section on explanations of poverty. The same procedure was chosen for descriptions of rich people and explanations of wealth.

[3]In the analysis presented here, this type of answer was not further coded with respect to content of the statement, as we wanted to keep them apart from a subject's descriptions of poverty or wealth in one's own cultural context.

TABLE 5.2

Description of Poverty (What do you Think, When is a Person Poor?)[a]

Category	Effect, Cells with High f_o [b]	LR-$Cb\chi^2$/df/p of Single Effect	Overall Model Fit:[c] LR-$Cb\chi^2$/df/p
(Almost) No money (f_o = 82)	Age (younger S's)	14.19 / 1 / <.001	10.01 / 6 / .12
Basic needs barely/not satisfied (f_o = 77)	Context (Western S's)	17.73 / 1 / <.001	2.44 / 6 / .88
Own only few nice or spare things (f_o = 29)	Context (Eastern S's)	7.12 / 1 / <.01	2.43 / 6 / .88
Psychological description (f_o = 10)	(No significant main or interaction effects)		10.10 / 7 / .18
No really poor people around here (f_o = 21)	Context (Eastern S's)	23.85 / 1 / <.001	5.97 / 6 / .43
Eastern S's refer to West / Western S's to East (f_o = 12)	Context (Eastern S's)	21.39 / 5 / <.001	.76 / 2 / .68
Reference to 3rd world countries (f_o = 12)	(No significant main or interaction effects)		7.74 / 7 / .35

[a]N = 157.
[b]Observed frequencies.
[c]Including all specified significant effects.

TABLE 5.3
Description of Wealth (What do you Think, When is a Person Rich?)[a]

Category	Effect, Cells with High f_o[b]	LR-Cht^2/df/p of Single Effect	Overall Model Fit:[c] LR-Cht^2/df/p
(Very) Much money ($f_o = 95$)	(No significant main or interaction effects)		8.91 / 7 / .26
Can afford (almost) everything ($f_o = 53$)	(No significant main or interaction effects)		1.43 / 7 / .99
Can afford nicer/better things ($f_o = 42$)	(No significant main or interaction effects)		4.08 / 7 / .77
Psychological description ($f_o = 14$)	(No significant main or interaction effects)		8.80 / 7 / .27
No really rich people around here ($f_o = 14$)	Context (Eastern S's)	18.16 / 1 / <.001	3.55 / 6 / .74
Eastern S's refer to West / Western S's to East ($f_o = 8$)	Context (Eastern S's)	14.61 / 5 / <.05	1.26 / 2 / .53

[a]$N = 151$.
[b]Observed frequencies.
[c]Including all specified significant effects.

Similar to the description of poor people, a significant main effect of culture is found for the statement "there are no really rich people around here," which was presented by subjects from the East in 14 out 15 of cases. Also, 8 subjects from Eastern Germany characterized rich people by reference to the Western part of Germany. No differences were found with respect to the extreme characterization "rich people can afford almost anything," and for the less extreme description "rich people can afford nicer/better things."

Compared to the description of poor people, differences between the two contexts were less pronounced for the description of wealth. This result was unexpected, as we had assumed that both ends of the poverty–wealth dimension, being rich and being poor, would be described more extremely in the West, and less extremely in the East. The present findings seem plausible, however, when the fact is taken into consideration that Western images of wealth and prosperity have been spread by mass media (especially TV) in Eastern Germany for a long time even before the border was opened. For information and images of extreme poverty, this might have been much less the case.

Which *explanations* for poverty and wealth did our subjects present? For *explanations of poverty*, the results are summarized in Table 5.4. The most frequent of all answers was reference to unemployment. The distribution of this category showed no relation with age, context, or gender.

Significant age differences were found for explanations in terms of a bad job, and poor education/professional training. Both of these types of answers were stated by older subjects more often. In Leahy's (1983) study, they had been considered as equity variables. Other typical equity categories, however, showed no relation to age (lack of motivation, no effort) or were too infrequent to be further analyzed (intelligence).

The fatalistic view of ascribing poverty to fate or bad luck was also found to be related to age. Again similar to Leahy's (1983) findings, this answer becomes more frequent with increasing age. From the younger children, nine gave naive explanations such as "poor people have no money to pay for a new job" or "the bank did not give them a loan." This kind of answer was too infrequent, however, to permit the specification of a logit model with sufficient fit (see Table 5.4).

Explanations in terms of exploitation were typically given in the Eastern sample. Above a main effect of context, an age x context interaction effect was found. Answers referring to exploitation were most frequently given by younger Eastern subjects who referred, for example, to "a king, taking all the food from the peasant, and giving almost no money." An explanation for these findings that suggests itself is that the answers of the Eastern subjects reflect the influences of the educational system in a socialist country. Interestingly enough, these influences decrease by the time of adolescence. Children, in their younger years, adopt the views they were presented in

TABLE 5.4

Explanations of Poverty (How did the Poor People get Poor?)[a]

Category	Effect, Cells with High f_o[b]	LR-Chi2/df/p of Single Effect	Overall Model Fit:[c] LR-Chi^2/df/p
Unemployment (f_o = 98)	(No significant main or interaction effects)		8.05 / 7 / .33
Bad job (f_o = 63)	Age (older S's)	11.82 / 1 / <.001	
	Age × context × gender	3.82 / 1 / <.05	8.35 / 5 / .14
No / poor education (f_o = 29)	Age (older S's)	7.45 / 1 / <.01	2.02 / 6 / .92
Lack of motivation, no effort (f_o = 48)	(No significant main or interaction effects)		3.54 / 7 / .83
Psychological problems (f_o = 29)	(No significant main or interaction effects)		7.31 / 7 / .40
Poor family (no inheritance, many children) (f_o = 30)	(No significant main or interaction effects)		7.95 / 7 / .34
Use of money (f_o = 63)	(No significant main or interaction effects)		12.14 / 7 / .10
Loss of invested capital (company, stock market) (f_o = 9)	Age × context × gender	8.33 / 1 / <.01	8.13 / 6 / .23
Exploitation (f_o = 17)	Context (Eastern S's)	11.25 / 1 / <.001	
	Age × context (Eastern younger S's)	6.25 / 1 / <.02	5.81 / 5 / .33
Fate, bad luck (f_o = 13)	Age (older S's)	7.51 / 1 / <.01	5.75 / 6 / .45
Catastrophy (fire, war) (f_o = 15)	Age × context (Western younger S's)	5.96 / 1 / <.02	4.32 / 6 / .63
Naive explanations (f_o = 9)	(trend: younger S's / no significant effects)		7.19 / 7 / .41

[a]N = 167.
[b]Observed frequencies.
[c]Including all specified significant effects.

103

kindergarten and elementary school but do not retain them in their later years. In contrast, younger children in the West more often referred to specific catastrophies such as a fire, burglary, or even war. Apart from these differences in the mentioning of exploitation and specific catastrophies, note that the similarities between the two cultural contexts prevail over the differences for most answer patterns.

With respect to *explanations of wealth*, the results of the statistical analysis are given in Table 5.5. Older subjects more often than younger ones referred to effort and achievement, which are typical equity criteria. With respect to another equity argument, the answer "much, hard, good work," frequency distributions differed in the two contexts. In the East, older subjects were more likely than younger ones to explain wealth in terms of work, whereas in the Western sample this type of explanation decreased with age. Two other equity-type arguments, professional qualification and advancement, and education, showed no relation with age or context.

Two kinds of arguments referring to the social structure increased with age. Adolescents were more likely to regard access to a special social position (king, minister), and coming from a rich family background, and inheriting family money as a way to become rich. Also, adolescents frequently mentioned the possibility of investing money, for example at the stock market, a strategy only rarely suggested by children. Furthermore, older subjects more often considered illegal methods as ways to become rich. This might reflect an increasingly fatalistic view of adolescents on the acquisiton of wealth. Above a main effect of age, a context by gender interaction effect was found for this category. Boys in the Eastern sample and girls in the Western sample mentioned illegal methods more often than others.

All in all, previous findings that the use of equity arguments in the explanation of both poverty and wealth will increase during adolescence were confirmed for some but not for all explanations that may be subsumed under this principle. Age differences were found for some equity explanations of poverty (bad jobs, no/poor education) and of wealth (effort and achievement). Also, an increase of fatalistic explanations during adolescence, as has been described in the literature (Leahy, 1983), is supported by our own data in that explanations of fate/bad luck prevailed for poverty, and of illegal methods for wealth.

Differences between the two cultural contexts were found in the reference to saving, or a renunciation of consumption, and mentioning of the possibility to invest money, for example at the stock market. Both categories were mentioned more frequently by Western subjects. In contrast, explaining wealth by exploitation, although infrequent altogether, was found exclusively for younger children in the Eastern sample. Again, similarities between the two contexts are more salient than the few differences. For example, being the owner of a shop or a company, which is certainly a typical strategy in a

TABLE 5.5
Explanations of Wealth (How did the Rich People get Rich?)[a]

Category	Effect, Cells with High f_o[b]	LR-Chi2/df/p of Single Effect	Overall Model Fit:[c] LR-Chi2/df/p
Much/hard/good work ($f_o = 70$)	Age × context (older Eastern and younger Western S's)	4.05 / 1 / <.05	11.87 / 6 / .07 (insufficient fit)
Qualification, professional advancement ($f_o = 41$)	(No significant main or interaction effects)		4.84 / 7 / .68
Position (king, minister) ($f_o = 17$)	Age (older S's)	5.69 / 1 / <.05	2.91 / 6 / .82
Education ($f_o = 15$)	(No significant main or interaction effects)		9.14 / 7 / .24
Effort, achievement ($f_o = 13$)	Age (older S's)	11.91 / 1 / <.001	5.33 / 6 / .50
Saving ($f_o = 41$)	Context (Western S's)	6.95 / 1 / <.01	2.54 / 6 / .87
Rich family, inheritance ($f_o = 66$)	Age (older S's)	24.01 / 1 / <.001	6.81 / 6 / .34
Owner of company, shop/capitalist ($f_o = 53$)	(No significant main or interaction effects)		11.04 / 7 / .14
Invest money, e.g., at stock market ($f_o = 15$)	Age (older S's)	14.75 / 1 / <.001	
	Context (Western S's) (Eastern younger S's)	4.85 / 1 / <.05	4.98 / 5 / .42
Exploitation ($f_o = 7$)	(No significant main or interaction effects)	(insufficient fit, small frequencies)	
Luck ($f_o = 42$)	Age (older S's)	6.35 / 1 / <.02	13.57 / 7 / .06
Illegal methods ($f_o = 12$)	Context × gender (Eastern boys, Western girls)	4.63 / 1 / <.05	4.16 / 5 / .53

[a] $N = 165$.
[b] Observed frequencies.
[c] Including all specified significant effects.

market economy, was equally likely to be mentioned by Eastern and Western subjects.

The presentation of results is concluded with the findings for our subjects' *evaluations* of what would be a proper distribution of economic resources. In contrast to the previous analyses, each subject was assigned only one answer category. This permitted a simultaneous statistical examination of the different answer types. Three kinds of judgments were frequent. The first is a conceptualization we have labeled "impracticable" ($n = 20$); these children stated that real equality is impossible, as everybody would have to do the same thing at the same time (do the same kind of work, buy the same kind of thing, spend the same amount of money, and thus go to the bank at the same time) to maintain equality. Thus, the idea of equality is played through in a very meticulous way and is consequently rejected for practical reasons. These children did not suggest any specific alternative (e.g., they did not favor equity). The second type of judgment proposes equality, suggesting that everybody should get (about) the same share of resources ($n = 45$). For a few subjects, this included the necessity to control lazy people so they "will do their share of work." According to the third type of judgment, equity, everybody should get a share, according to his or her personal input (e.g., in effort, education, or responsibility; $n = 84$). Some other, very infrequent answers, such as "don't know" ($n = 4$), "according to need" ($n = 1$), "there is not enough money" ($n = 3$), "some people want more than others" ($n = 7$), were omitted from further analysis.

The logit analysis revealed a significant main effect of age and a significant age by context interaction (overall model fit: chi^2 = 13.72; df = 10; p = .19; N = 149). The distribution of judgments in the four age groups is presented in Fig. 5.1.

Not surprisingly, the evaluation of an equal distribution as "impracticable" was primarily found in younger subjects. As these children do not come to a positive solution of the distribution problem, this answer type might resemble the answer "I don't know" in Leahy's (1983) study, where it has been one of the more frequent answers in first-grade children.

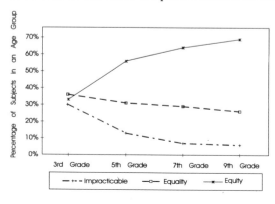

FIG. 5.1. Judgments about the proper kind of distribution of economic resources: Proportions of subjects from each age group.

Children and adolescents proposing "equality" were about evenly distributed over the age groups, with a slightly increased probability in third and fifth graders. Older subjects were more likely to propose the equity position (age effect: chi^2 = 9.16; df = 2; p < .02). Thus, age trends reported from earlier studies (Burgard, Cheyne, & Jahoda, 1989; Emler & Dickinson, 1985; Leahy, 1983), suggesting high frequencies of equality judgments in middle childhood and an increase of equity propositions in adolescence, were confirmed by the present data.

Furthermore, a significant interaction of age and context contributed to the distribution of frequencies (chi^2 = 6.23; df = 2; p < .05; see Fig. 5.2). This was due to the fact that the age effect as described earlier was more typical for the Western sample, whereas in the Eastern sample the younger subjects were more likely to argue according to equity considerations than their Western peers. At the same time, fewer of the younger subjects in the East supported an equal distribution.

So the equity principle, which may be considered as typical for the ideology of Western market economies, was not supported more often in the Western sample. On the contrary, there was even a nonsignificant trend of more frequent equity propositions in the Eastern sample. We assume that the children and adolescents from East Berlin were influenced by the widespread dissatisfaction with the East German planned economy, which was still established when they were interviewed during the first half of 1990. At the same time, they were influenced by general hopes and expectations about the West German market economy coming ahead. This is clearly demonstrated in an interview statement by one of the adolescents from East Berlin. In response to the question whether everyone might get the same amount of resources, he said: "That's what they've tried here, for 40 years, . . . nobody's seen an incentive, . . . everyone tried to work as little as possible."

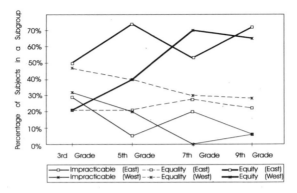

FIG. 5.2. Judgments about the proper kind of distribution of economic resources in former East and West Germany: Proportions of subjects from each age group.

How can we explain that the East German children proposed equity more often than their Western peers, whereas adolescents from the two contexts did not differ in their judgments? We assume that the children in the Eastern sample proposed the equity principle so frequently, because they were strongly influenced by the general political and economic climate described previously. In contrast to that, for the adolescents in the East, this effect of general optimism is counterbalanced by another influence. Adolescents are much closer than children to entering their own work life; under the present conditions of dramatic macroeconomic transformations, the course of their professional career is uncertain at best. Hence, they may be affected by expectations of unemployment or fears of having to accept a job that they do not like or that is low paid. Only recently, Palentien, Pollmer, and Hurrelmann (1993) presented empirical evidence showing that East German adolescents, who go through a training of apprentices, are increasingly insecure about their professional future the closer the end of their training gets. Perhaps, the data of our East German adolescents reflect a balance of optimism, on the one side, and their fears, on the other side, to be on the losers' side in the distribution of economic resources in the society.

ECONOMIC CHANGE AND INDIVIDUAL DEVELOPMENT

From 1990 to the present time, both the economic situation and people's attitudes have changed considerably. In the course of the economic transformation of East Germany to a market economy, many companies have laid off large numbers of their personnel or have been closed down altogether. Many other people are working short time or are threatened with unemployment. Under these economic circumstances, the general optimism of many in the East has given way to more pessimistic expectations and to a certain degree of dissatisfaction with the political management of the economic transformation. Children and adolescents are not spared by these political, social, and economic processes, and in many cases their own families might be directly affected. As our data showed, subjects from different age groups may even react differently to the changes in their developmental context.

Thus, the data presented in this chapter most likely are specific for the early phase of the German reunion; it is assumed that the findings would differ for other periods of this historical process. To reconstruct how individual development interacts with changes in life conditions and developmental contexts, we are presently repeating the interviews of 1990 after a 28-month interval.[4] We expect that children's and adolescents' descriptions, explanations, and evaluations of economic inequality will have changed

---

[4]The 1992–1993 study is a joint project, carried out in collaboration with Herbert Hagendorf, Birgit Sá, Stephan Fischer, and Uwe Pekrul, Humboldt University at Berlin.

considerably by the time of the second interview. Furthermore, we assume that children's and adolescents' understanding will be related not only to changes in the political and economic macrosystem but also to the situation in their immediate family context. Therefore, parents are now included in the study and interviewed about their interpretation of basic economic phenomena and about the economic situation of the family.

Because unemployment has increased in Eastern Germany, and because income differences both within Eastern Germany and between Eastern and Western Germany are experienced more sharply, it seems plausible that the subjects from our Eastern sample will experience the phenomena of poverty and wealth more dramatically than at the time of the first interview. Eastern subjects might catch up with their Western peers or become even more extreme in their descriptions of being poor or rich. Also, a decrease in equity positions is assumed for Eastern children and adolescents. Especially those subjects whose families are going through a period of economic hardship are expected to describe, explain, and evaluate economic inequality in a way similar as that reported by Emler and Dickinson (1985), Furnham (1982), Leahy (1981, 1983), and others for children from families with a disadvantaged social status. Children from economically more successful backgrounds are expected to argue similarly to children from upper middle and middle class in these previous studies.

Adaptive Functions of Concept Development

The construction of economic concepts, similar to other concepts directed at the cultural context, enables the individual to classify, to relate, and to predict economic phenomena both in the immediate everyday surrounding and in society as a whole. In constructing an understanding of economic phenomena, the individual does react to present and to anticipated economic circumstances in a way that permits coping with them in a more or less adequate way. Economic inequality is one example to demonstrate this view. In the beginning of the economic transformation in East Germany, the decline of the largely unliked and in many respects ineffective political system, together with the expectation (but not yet reality) of a market economy, created an atmosphere of sheer unlimited economic opportunities. In such a situation, the proposition of equity principles for society in general is in accordance with the perception of a subject's own possibilities to influence one's fate. If the individual is successful, internal control attributions and self-esteem are enhanced. The subject assumes that success was due to his or her own effort and achievement, and efforts are more likely to be continued in the future (Gurney, 1981).

In contrast, when the economic opportunities deteriorate, it would be counterproductive to maintain that "everyone is the architect of his or her own future." In such a situation, it seems more adequate to try whatever opportunities exist, but for the case of failure to have an external control attribution at hand. The possibility to attribute unemployment and economic hardship to the limited circumstances, and to hold that chances are not distributed equally, will help to maintain a positive self-image and an action readiness for the time when a better opportunity comes ahead. Thus, the individuals construct representations of the economic context in a way representing reality adequately enough, but at the same time in a way to allow the individual to maintain both self-esteem and further action motivation—at least for some period of time.

In this way, concept development is not a purely cognitive affair but is throughly interrelated with emotional and motivational aspects and with an individual's actions. Conceptual construction serves the individual's adaptation to a specific culture, and, if necessary, to a changing cultural environment.

ACKNOWLEDGMENTS

I would like to acknowledge the support of Karin Goede, Angelika König, and Claudia Thörmer, who assisted in the collection and analysis of the data presented in this chapter. Also, I am grateful to Bernd Schmitz for his methodological advice, and to Jeanette Roos for her valuable comments on an earlier version of this paper.

REFERENCES

Baldus, B., & Tribe, V. (1978). The development of perceptions and evaluations of social inequality among public school children. *Canadian Review of Sociology and Anthropology*, *15*, 50–60.

Berry, J. W. (1976). *Human ecology and cognitive style: Comparative studies in cultural and psychological adaptation.* New York: Wiley.

Berti, A. E. (1981). The "boss": Its conceptual development in children. *The Italian Journal of Psychology*, *8*(2), 111–120.

Berti, A. E. (1991). Capitalism and socialism: How 7th graders understand and misunderstand the information presented in their geography textbooks. *European Journal of Psychology of Education*, *IV*(4), 411–421.

Berti, A. E., & Bombi, A. S. (1980). Chi paga la gente? [Who pays the people?]. *Giornale Italiano di Psicologia*, *8*, 249–266.

Berti, A. E., & Bombi, A. S. (1981). The development of the concept of money and its value: A longitudinal study. *Child Development*, *52*, 1179–1182.

Berti, A. E., & Bombi, A. S. (1988). *The child's construction of economics.* Cambridge, England: Cambridge University Press.

Berti, A. E., & Bombi, A. S. (1989). Environmental differences in understanding production and distribution. In J. Valsiner (Ed.), *Child development in cultural context* (pp. 247–271). Toronto: Hogrefe & Huber.

Berti, A. E., Bombi, A. S., & De Beni, R. (1986). The development of economic notions: Single sequences or separate acquisitions? *Journal of Economic Psychology*, 7, 415–424.

Bronfenbrenner, U. (1979). *The ecology of human development*. Cambridge, MA: Harvard University Press.

Burgard, P., Cheyne, W. M., & Jahoda, G. (1989). Children's representations of economic inequality: A replication. *British Journal of Developmental Psychology*, 7, 275–287.

Burris, V. (1983). Stages in the development of economic concepts. *Human Relations*, 36, 791–812.

Carraher, T. N., Carraher, D. W., & Schliemann, A. D. (1985). Mathematics in the streets and schools. *British Journal of Developmental Psychology*, 3, 21–29.

Carraher, T. N., & Schliemann, A. D. (1988, December). Using money to teach about the decimal system. *Arithmetic Teacher*, 42–43.

Claar, A. (1989, July). *Concept construction by integration of previously independent conceptual subsystems: The bank*. Poster presented at the 1st European Congress of Psychology, Amsterdam.

Claar, A. (1990, August). *Stages and developmental transition in concept construction: The concept of price in children and adolescents*. Poster presented at the 4th European Conference on Developmental Psychology, Stirling, Scotland.

Danziger, K. (1958). Children's earliest conceptions of economic relationships (Australia). *The Journal of Social Psychology*, 47, 231–240.

Dasen, P. R. (1975). Concrete operational development in three cultures. *Journal of Cross-Cultural Psychology*, 6(2), 156–172.

Eckensberger, L. H. (1990). From cross-cultural psychology to cultural psychology. *The Quarterly Newsletter of the Laboratory of Comparative Human Cognition*, 12(1), 37–52.

Emler, N., & Dickinson, J. (1985). Children's representation of economic inequalities: The effects of social class. *British Journal of Development Psychology*, 3, 191–198.

Emler, N., Ohana, J., & Moscovici, S. (1987). Children's beliefs about institutional roles: A cross-national study of representations of the teacher's role. *British Journal of Developmental Psychology*, 57, 26–37.

Enesco, I., Delval, J., Villuendas, D., Navarro, A., Sierra, P. & Soto, P. (1992, September). *The construction of social knowledge on children's ideas about social mobility*. Poster presented at the 5th European Conference on Developmental Psychology, Seville, Spain.

Furnham, A. (1982). The perception of poverty among adolescents. *Journal of Adolescence*, 5, 135–147.

Furnham, A., & Stacey, B. (1991). *Young people's understanding of society*. London: Routledge.

Furth, H. G. (1978). Young children's understanding of society. In H. McGurk (Ed.), *Issues in childhood social development* (pp. 228–256). London: Methuen.

Furth, H. G. (1980). *The world of grown-ups. Children's conceptions of society*. New York: Elsevier.

Furth, H. G., Baur, M., & Smith, J. E. (1976). Children's conception of social institutions: A Piagetian framework. *Human Development*, 19, 351–374.

Gurney, R. M. (1981). Leaving school, facing unemployment, and making attributions about the causes of unemployment. *Journal of Vocational Behavior*, 18, 79–91.

Jahoda, G. (1959). Development of the perception of social differences in children from 6 to 10. *British Journal of Psychology*, 50, 159–175.

Jahoda, G. (1979). The construction of economic reality by some Glaswegian children. *European Journal of Social Psychology*, 9, 115–127.

Jahoda, G. (1981). The development of thinking about economic institutions: The bank. *Cahiers de Psychologie Cognitive*, 1, 55–73.

Jahoda, G. (1983). European "lag" in the development of an economic concept: A study in Zimbabwe. *British Journal of Developmental Psychology*, 1, 113–120.

Knoke, D., & Burke, P. J. (1980). *Log-linear models*. Newbury Park, CA: Sage.

Krewer, B. (1990). Psyche and culture—can a culture-free psychology take into account the essential features of the species "homo sapiens"? *The Quarterly Newsletter of the Laboratory of Comparative Human Cognition, 12*(1), 24–37.

Kroeber, A. L., & Kluckhohn, C. (1952). *Culture—a critical review of concepts and definitions.* Cambridge, England: Vintage.

Leahy, R. L. (1981). The development of the conception of economic inequality: I. Descriptions and comparisons of rich and poor people. *Child Development, 52,* 523–532.

Leahy, R. L. (1983). Development of the conception of economic inequality: II. Explanations, justifications, and concepts of social mobility and change. *Developmental Psychology, 19,* 111–125.

Leiser, D., Roland-Lévy, Ch., & Sévon, G. (1990). Economic socialization (special issue). *Journal of Economic Psychology, 11,* 4.

Livesley, W. H., & Bromley, D. B. (1973). *Person perception in childhood and adolescence.* London: Wiley.

Ng, S. H. (1983). Children's ideas about the bank and shop profit: Developmental stages and influence of cognitive contrast and conflict. *Journal of Economic Psychology, 4,* 209–221.

Palentien, Ch., Pollmer, K., & Hurrelmann, K. (1993, June). Ausbildungs- und Zukunftsperspektiven ostdeutscher Jugendlicher nach der politischen Vereinigung Deutschlands [Occupational and future time perspectives of East German adolescents after the political reunion of Germany]. *Aus Politik und Zeitgeschichte. Beilage zur Wochenzeitung das Parlament.* Bonn: Bundeszentrale für politische Bildung.

Saxe, G. B. (1991). *Culture and cognitive development: Studies in mathematical understanding.* Hillsdale, NJ: Lawrence Erlbaum Associates.

Secord, P. F., & Peevers, B. H. (1974). The development of person concepts. In Th. Mischel (Ed.), *Understanding other persons* (pp. 117–142). Oxford: Basil Blackwell.

Seiler, Th. B., & Wannenmacher, W. (1983). How can we assess meaning and investigate meaning development: Theoretical and methodological considerations from an epistemological point of view. In Th. B. Seiler & W. Wannenmacher (Eds.), *Concept development and the development of word meaning* (pp. 320–339). Berlin: Springer.

Sonuga-Barke, E. J. S., & Webley, P. (1993). *Children's saving: A study in the development of economic behaviour.* Hove, UK: Lawrence Erlbaum Associates.

Strauss, S. (1952). The development and transformation of monetary meanings in the child. *American Sociological Review, 17,* 275–286.

Valsiner, J. (1987). *Culture and the development of children's action.* Chichester: Wiley.

Valsiner, J. (Ed.). (1989). *Child development in cultural context.* Toronto: Hogrefe & Huber.

Vila, I. M. (1992, September). *Comprehension of social organization notions in Mexican children and adolescents from three different sociocultural contexts: urban, rural, and urban slums.* Poster presented at the 5th European Conference on Developmental Psychology, Seville, Spain.

Waines, N. O. (1984). Development of economic concepts among Egyptian children. *Journal of Cross-Cultural Psychology, 15,* 47–64.

Ward, S., Wackman, D. B., & Wartella, E. (1977). *How children learn to buy: The development of consumer information-processing skills.* Newbury Park, CA: Sage.

Wong, M.-H. (1989). Children's acquisition of economic knowledge: Understanding banking in Hong Kong and U.S.A. In J. Valsiner (Ed.), *Child development in cultural context* (pp. 225–246). Toronto: Hogrefe & Huber.

CHAPTER SIX

Person–Context Relations as Developmental Conditions for Empathy and Prosocial Action: A Cross-Cultural Analysis

Gisela Trommsdorff
University of Konstanz, Germany

Empathy and prosocial behavior constitute aspects of child-context relations. They are influenced by the environment of the developing child, and they influence the child's relation to his or her environment. The child's most intimate environment are the caretakers, whereas on a macrolevel the cultural environment and the sociopolitical system are operating. These environments are interconnected and affect the child-context relation, and thereby the child's development.

This chapter is based on a larger study that entails investigations at several levels of complexity in person-context relations. The focus is on the macro-contextual influences that cultural environments may have on empathy and prosocial action in social interactions. In specific, within a frame of macro-cultural comparisons, behavioral observations and self-reports are used for microanalyses of contextual influences on children's empathy and prosocial actions.

Assume here that the child's prosocial action—an altruistic motivated person-context relation—occurs on the basis of certain emotions, especially on the basis of empathic feelings with other people. Traditionally, the understanding of the determinants of prosocial behavior is based on studies that have focused almost exclusively on adults. Consequently, cognitive aspects have been the center of attention, and little effort has been paid to examining emotional aspects. However, for young children, it appears questionable whether the study of empathy can rely solely on a cognitive framework. Thus, there are doubts as to whether the specific emotional qualities of prosocial behavior and empathy can be disregarded at early ages. As recent studies have shown, even infants demonstrate "prosocial" behavior when observing a person in distress (Radke-Yarrow & Zahn-Waxler, 1984). This may be a result of emotional contagion—a precondition of empathy. The general question raised here is about how and in which way a child's interactions with his or her environment affect that child's emotional and prosocial development. More specifically, what are their interactional effects on the relations between emotional processes like empathy and distress, on the one hand, and other elements of the prosocial action system, on the other hand? The focus of this study is on empathy as the *emotional experience* of the other person's inner state.

In this chapter, first the concepts of empathy and prosocial behavior as aspects of child-context relations are discussed. Then questions of their development in general and in certain cultural environments are dealt with. This is followed by a brief description of our cross-cultural studies, the methods used, and some results. Special attention is paid to discussing the extent to which the determinants of empathy and prosocial action need to be studied within a framework of developing person-context relations.

EMOTIONAL REACTIONS AND PROSOCIAL BEHAVIOR

Emotional Reactions

In the following, we focus on the role of specific emotions for prosocial behavior. It is assumed that certain emotional reactions, especially empathy, may occur when observing a person in need.

Empathy is part of certain person-context relations. Empathy—the feeling with the other person's inner state (according to Eisenberg, 1986, "sympathy")—is assumed to activate altruistic behavior. Theoretically, empathic feelings and consequent prosocial actions will depend on the quality of people's relationships with their social partners. In turn, empathy and empathy-related social behaviors will affect the quality of the relationship among interactional partners. Accordingly, reciprocal influences are assumed to exist between a person's empathic response and his or her behavior on the one hand, and the specific context in which these social interactions take place on the other hand.

Most studies on empathy have focused on the activating role of empathy for prosocial behavior. According to Hoffman (1981), empathy implies the anticipated joy when the needs of the other person have been fulfilled ("empathic joy"). Thus, empathy may trigger an altruistic motivation (Batson et al., 1989; Eisenberg, McCreath, & Ahn, 1988). However, so far the results on the relations between empathy and prosocial behavior in children are very inconsistent (for a review see Eisenberg & Miller, 1987).

The confusing and inconclusive empirical results with respect to empathy and prosocial behavior depend partly on the definition of the concepts. The concept of *empathy* (Mitleid) was already discussed in the 18th and 19th centuries by German philosophers. Immanuel Kant (1724–1804), Arthur Schopenhauer (1788–1860), or Friedrich Wilhelm Nietzsche (1844–1900) were interested in the function of empathy for moral action. Kant considered empathy as a mood but not a virtue. Nietzsche went even further. For him, empathy was a weakness and a danger for mankind leaving no room for the "Superhuman" (Übermensch). In contrast, Schopenhauer viewed empathy as the only basis for justice and human behavior. He regarded as moral behavior only actions based on empathy. Schopenhauer conceived empathy as a motivation inducing moral action.

In early psychology, empathy ("Einfühlung") was seen by Lipps (1903, 1907) as an emotion that arose in the observer when perceiving the expression of another person. Titchener (1908), a student of Wundt, introduced the concept of empathy into the American experimental psychology. Lipps had conceptualized "Einfühlung" as imitation (by facial feedback) of the other person's emotion. Accordingly, empathy was seen as an unconscious involuntary process equivalent to drives and instinctive processes (cf. Lipps, 1907). This conception was criticized by subsequent studies because it did not differentiate between the self and the other person. In contrast to Lipps, empathy was later conceived of as a process of perceiving the other person's emotions as belonging to oneself and understanding the other person's emotions "as if" one were this person or as if one's own emotions were part of the other person (e.g., Rogers, 1959).

In contrast to the emotion-focused conceptualization of empathy, the cognitive-oriented psychology conceived of empathy as a purely cognitive reaction like perspective taking or role taking. According to this view, empathy could occur only after the relevant cognitive functions have developed (e.g., reduction of egocentrism). Recently, the emotional quality of empathy has been brought back by Hoffman's (1983; 1984) influential work focusing on the *developmental* processes of empathy. A developmental view distinguishes among several forms of emotional and other reactions when perceiving emotional expressions of another person:

1. An unconscious process of *emotional contagion* occurs when the observer does not differentiate between the self and the other person; here one's own emotions and the emotions of the other person are fused. Children (in the first 2 years of life) who have not yet developed person permanence and a concept of the self demonstrate such emotional reactions. (Eisenberg, 1986, uses the term *empathy* here.)

2. Cognitive perspective taking is a cognitive process by which the inner state of the other person is taken into account while emotional reactions need not occur. Children must have reached the stage of cognitive development of decentrism to demonstrate this reaction.

3. Personal *distress* is usually defined as an aversive vicarious emotional reaction. According to Eisenberg (1986), "personal distress" is "a negative, self-oriented concern in reaction to another's emotional state" (p. 31). Batson, Fultz, and Schoenrade (1987) conceived of "personal distress" as self-oriented emotions characterized by upset, discomfort, and anxiety. It is implicitly assumed that this emotional reaction can occur at an early developmental age when a self-other differentiation is developed. However, only little research has been carried out with respect to this emotional reaction. Therefore, it is unclear how distress develops and whether it will decrease in the course of individual development.

4. Eisenberg (1986) stated that *empathy* is conceived of as "an emotion that is not identical to the other's emotion, but is congruent with the other's emotional state and his or her welfare" (p. 31). For this emotional state, Eisenberg (1986) used the term *sympathy*, and Hoffman (1984) used the term *sympathetic distress*. These definitions are not consistently used by specific authors (e.g., Eisenberg has changed her definitions over the years). In this study the concept of empathy is used for these emotional processes.

The conceptualization of empathy (sympathy; sympathetic concern) introduces another problem in view of the fact that we conceive of empathy as an emotion. This emotion, however, has a special quality different from other emotions insofar as basic interpersonal processes are entering into this emotion. The partially vicarious emotional reaction includes a conception of the self and of the other person as sharing certain emotions while at the same time differentiating between one's own and the other person's emotions.

To summarize, empathy seems to be a prototypical case in the study of person-context relations: Elements of empathy imply on the one hand a cognitive understanding of one's context, and on the other hand a congruence of feeling with one's context (the other person).

Prosocial Behavior

Prosocial behavior could similarly be seen as a prototypical case for actions that are directed toward context inasmuch as the behavior is directed toward fulfilling the needs of an interaction partner. One of its primary functions is to make the other person feel better. This understanding of prosocial behavior is in line with the definitions of Eisenberg (1982) or Staub (1986), who conceived of prosocial behavior as voluntary acts to benefit another person. Our interest is in the role that specific emotions, such as empathy, may have for prosocial behavior to occur.

Interestingly, empirical studies have so far mostly ignored both—the possible role of emotions in prosocial behavior and the fact that prosocial behavior is a part of social interaction constituting a special case of person-context relations. Furthermore, studies on prosocial behavior have focused mainly on adults, ignoring developmental conditions. Also, very few observational studies of actual prosocial behavior exist. Another problem is that these studies usually do not differentiate between different qualities of prosocial behavior. This is obviously another deficit because prosocial behavior can differ in intensity and investment of individual resources: Just verbal comforting or giving advice is not as costly as sharing or sacrificing someone's property to the person in need.

Because most studies on prosocial behavior have used only verbal reports about intentions to help, or prosocial attitudes, they have traditionally been restricted to the cognitive domain; they focus mostly on cognitive processes such as the relevance of social norms, or reward-cost calculations. However, before such cognitive processes can operate, children must undergo a certain cognitive development. Young children—although they are not yet cognitively advanced (in the first year of life)—nevertheless show positive social behavior that is similar to cognitively based prosocial behavior such as sharing or caring (Radke-Yarrow & Zahn-Waxler, 1984). Such findings lead to the question of whether certain emotions may be relevant for prosocial behavior to occur, at least in early development and childhood.

Relations Between Emotional Reactions and Prosocial Behavior

In his studies on the development of prosocial and moral behavior, Hoffman (1982, 1983) explicitly dealt with the role of emotions, especially empathy, in prosocial behavior. His work has stimulated a number of empirical studies on the relation between empathy and prosocial behavior in children. Those results, however, were quite inconsistent (Eisenberg & Miller, 1987, for a review). One of the reasons for these inconsistencies with respect to the role of empathy presumably is the lack of differentiation between different emotions involved in the activation of prosocial behavior. Beside empathy, other emotional reactions like distress and guilt feelings may be relevant, as Hoffman (1983) pointed out.

Hoffman (1983) viewed distress as a self-oriented emotional reaction inducing the desire to end one's discomfort by reducing the distress of the other person. Distress motivates helping to feel better oneself ("negative state relief model"; Cialdini et al., 1987). Distress has mostly been considered an egoistic emotional reaction whereas empathy ("sympathy") has been considered an altruistic emotional reaction. If this is correct, prosocial behavior can be based on different emotions and motivations—in the case of distress on egoistic and in the case of empathy on altruistic motivation. As a matter of fact, in their studies on adults Batson and Oleson (1991) provided empirical support for empathy evoking an altruistic motivation.

However, why should distress necessarily induce an egoistic motivation? In the case of distress, egoistic and altruistic concerns may be mixed. On the one hand, one feels with the other person and wants to re-establish his or her well-being; on the other hand, one feels irritated by the other's distress and wants to re-establish one's own well-being. The question thus is which one becomes the dominant goal. When distress is oriented to the other person, we should expect an other-oriented, altruistic motivation to help. However, the prosocial action may be blocked by one's helplessness: One does not know which kind of help induces the other person's well-being. In the case of egoism-based distress, the goal is to reduce one's own distress by either helping the other person or by not helping at all but "leaving the field" (e.g., distracting oneself). Therefore, different qualities of distress should be differentiated to clarify whether distress activates altruistic or egoistic motivation, and whether this leads to prosocial behavior or not. Accordingly, empirical studies on the emotional reaction of a child to another person's distress should differentiate between qualitatively different emotions such as empathy ("sympathy"), empathy-based altruistic distress, and egoistic distress. Otherwise, different emotional reactions are confounded, and their possible distinctive relations to prosocial behavior are ignored.

Prosocial behavior is therefore differentiated with respect to its altruistic and egoistic *motivational basis*. Prosocial behavior that is altruistically motivated takes place to benefit another person (or other people; cf. Staub, 1986, p. 136); egoistically motivated prosocial behavior serves the person's own interests (although it is prosocial; Karylowski, 1987). The relations between emotional reactions and these motives have so far not been clarified.

Summary of Deficits in Studies on Relations Between Emotional Reactions and Prosocial Behavior

The inconsistencies of findings on the relation between empathy and prosocial behavior in children are presumably based on the following theoretical and methodological shortcomings in most studies. Main theoretical problems are *a neglect of the developmental process* of the relation between the child and his or her context. Most studies are restricted to adults. In case of studies on children when the focus is on developmental age and individual personality constructs, a static approach is usually taken. These studies fail to take into account that empathy and prosocial behavior are aspects of a developing relationship between an individual and his or her context.

Therefore, the study of the development of empathy and prosocial behavior should be embedded in a person-context relational framework, where cognitive and interactional processes are considered as well as emotional characteristics. However, in more recent studies in which emotions were taken into account, the interactive processes were neglected. Furthermore, in these studies emotional reactions and prosocial behavior were not differentiated according to specific functional qualities. Mostly "positive" emotions such as empathy were taken into account, omitting "negative" emotions such as guilt and distress, even though the possible role of such "negative" emotions for prosocial behavior has been theoretically discussed by Hoffman (1983, 1984). Only recently, distress was studied as an emotion that hinders prosocial behavior (egoistic concern) or that induces egoistic prosocial motivation. However, the emotional and motivational basis of prosocial behavior was not classified. The theoretical question has so far not been taken into account, that prosocial behavior may be based on both, on empathic feelings and on distress. In case of distress, there may be different emotional bases confounded that evoke altruistic versus egoistic motivation.

To summarize, Theoretical problems are:

- a neglect of the children's developmental process;
- a neglect of the socialization context in which the child grows up;
- a lack of differentiation between different emotional reactions;
- a lack of differentiation between different motivational qualities of prosocial behavior.

Methodologically, there are major measurement problems:

- There is a lack of effort to study natural emotions in interactions (instead, the presentation of tapes, stories, or other artificial stimuli prevail).
- Typically, verbal measurements are taken of emotional reactions and prosocial behavior (measuring intentions) using self-reports or reports by teachers or parents. Especially for children, the validity of self-reports must be questioned.
- There is a lack of differentiation between different qualities of emotional antecedents (empathy and different kinds of distress) and different kinds of prosocial behavior.

DEVELOPMENT OF EMPATHY
AND PROSOCIAL BEHAVIOR

Developmental Concerns

Most studies on empathy and prosocial behavior have ignored the fact that prosocial actions are aspects of the child-context relation and therefore are embedded in real social interactions that may change during the process of development. A developmental approach is necessary to understand the actual prosocial action process including the role of emotions (empathy, distress) for prosocial behavior and to understand the development of interindividual differences in the development of the prosocial motive and action system. We take the situation-specific prosocial behavior as an indicator of the individual motive system and thus of the quality of person-context relations.

Here, we reach methodological frontiers and new tasks of developmental psychology. It seems promising to tackle questions about the pathways of cultural transmission processes by studying differences and similarities of processes across different cultures, perhaps within a life-span perspective of human development. In our own studies on the development of empathy and prosocial motivation, a longitudinal approach is pursued, focusing on social interactions between children and their social environment in different cultural contexts.

Our studies are based on the assumption that the person develops and acts in a certain cultural environment that affects all levels of the person's context. These aspects include one's physical and social environment, as well as his or her everyday socialization contexts, parental goals, and parent's naive theories about development and social behavior. Furthermore, these influences exist from childhood onward throughout the entire life span, but specifics of how their influence occurs may change, and these influences are reciprocal in nature: The child's development is affected by his environment while, at the same time, the environment is affected by the child.

On a larger scale, the social and political conditions in which children grow up also need to be considered. However, from a psychological point of view, the global system variables must be "translated" into relevant psychological conditions. Examples for these conditions are (implicit and explicit) social norms and expectations that are experienced when people act within a social role, or social values that are commonly shared in a culture and transmitted (through positive or negative social sanctions). These elements of the cultural context affect the person's development, including empathy and prosocial motives. Thus, while macrocontextual influences are operating, the specifics of such influences, the processes of transmission, and the outcomes of such processes will also depend on the individual (e.g. his or her disposition, affiliations with reference groups, or his or her current developmental stage). Nevertheless, these influences will also have a strong cultural basis that may be comparable across individuals within a given culture.

Overall, a strong interrelation is expected between people's broader cultural environment, their immediate socialization context, and their actions within a given culture. Consequently, the occurrence of empathy, the pathway of its development, and the effects of empathic feelings on a person's behavior are expected to be influenced by the given cultural context, whereas that person's empathy and empathy-related behavior should, in turn, affect that person's relationship with his or her context.

Development of Empathy and Prosocial Behavior in Social Interactions

Before we discuss empathy in cultural contexts, we will address the question concerning how empathy and prosocial behavior are related. Most studies on prosocial behavior have concentrated on adults and have focused on situational determinants (cf. Berkowitz, 1972) and cognitive factors like attribution, self-concept, and social norms (cf. Rushton & Sorrentino, 1981). These approaches are largely a-developmental in nature.

With regard to the developmental literature, there has been a similar emphasis on cognitive abilities as primary sources of prosocial behavior. Traditionally, the development of role taking—which in early studies was treated as synonymous with empathy—and of moral judgments were primary targets of study (for review, see Eisenberg, 1986). Only recently has the role of emotions become recognized. Examples include the extent to which feelings of anger, guilt, justice, and positive and negative mood (cf. Montada, Schneider, & Reichle, 1988), but also feelings of empathy (Eisenberg & Strayer, 1987), can lead to prosocial behavior. A major contribution to this change can be seen in the work of Hoffman (1982, 1983, 1984). In his work, emotions, and empathic feelings in particular, have been accorded a key role for the development of prosocial behavior in childhood.

Emotional Reactions Until Age Two. The emotional basis of prosocial behavior may be most important early in development. Radke-Yarrow and Zahn-Waxler (1984) observed that, in the first year of life, infants react with distress and "prosocial" behavior to the distress of other children. These early and spontaneous emotional reactions have been referred to as "emotional contagion" or "distress." According to Hoffman (1982), the development of empathy (Eisenberg's, 1986, term is *sympathy*) is dependent on the emergence of certain cognitive abilities. At the end of the second year of life, the child has acquired a concept of the self as distinguished from other persons. This distinction allows the child to disentangle his or her own self from the perception of other people, and to now only partly identify with another person's emotions. In this view, the experience of empathy is primarily based on self–other distinctions. Experimental studies support Hoffman's (1982) assumption (e.g., Bischof-Köhler, 1989).

Emotional Reactions After the Second Year. It is still unclear how the development after the second year continues. Several studies on the relation between empathy and prosocial behavior in children yielded inconsistent results (for a review, see Eisenberg & Miller, 1987). It may be assumed that during further development new cognitive abilities emerge, such as an understanding of prosocial norms and of one's own problem-solving abilities, and that these contribute increasingly to the occurrence of prosocial behavior. At the same time, emotional reactions, such as empathy, may play an increasingly minor role.

The reason for the inconsistent results on empathy and prosocial behavior in children may be that the developmental changes in emotional reactions and their specific relation to prosocial behavior during development have been neglected. According to Hoffman (1982), it should be assumed that "personal distress" decreases during development because of the decreasing egoistic concern and increasing ability to take the perspective of the other person. However, it is unclear whether a decrease in distress is related to an increase in empathy and an increase in altruistic motivation.

Accordingly, the inconsistent results on the relation between empathy and prosocial behavior during childhood may be a result of insufficient attention to children's developmental ages and related emotional and cognitive developments. There is reason to expect that studies on how emotional responses and their relations to prosocial behavior develop across childhood could be helpful for our understanding of the causes of prosocial behavior.

Development of Individual Differences in Person-Context Relations

Effects of Parental Socialization. Traditionally, the study of empathy and prosocial behavior has proceeded along quasi-normative questions. Individual differences, and their change across childhood, have largely been ignored. A focus on maturational arguments and normative explanations may be a further reason for the inconsistent results on the relation between emotional reactions and prosocial behavior. Because individual differences in prosocial action exist, besides possible universal developmental processes (e.g., maturation), specific individual socialization conditions affecting this development (e.g., cultural environment; quality of mother–child interaction) should be studied.

Presently, no systematic model of the development of individual differences in prosocial motivation is available that takes into account the multiple child-context interactions. Hoffman (1982, 1984) presented an integrative complex model on the development of prosocial motivation and moral judgment that has not yet been empirically studied with respect to development after the second year of age. According to Hoffman (1982) and Staub (1986), one may assume that warm and responsive parental behavior are related to empathy and a prosocial motivation of the child. This view is supported by the empirical findings of Barnett (1987), Fabes, Eisenberg, and Miller (1990), Radke-Yarrow and Zahn-Waxler (1984), and Trommsdorff (1991). However, despite the fact that these studies followed a more learning-theoretical approach, which would call for attention to details in interactions, the different kinds of emotional reactions that can occur in children's social interactions (e.g., empathy, distress) were not differentiated from one another, and maternal behavior was almost always measured in the form of aggregated self-reports using global behavior categories.

It is interesting to note that alternative approaches are possible and would lead to similar patterns of predictions. An attachment theoretical approach (Bowlby, 1988, 1991) would lead one to expect that prosocial behavior is influenced by experiences of security during early childhood. A warm mother–child relationship and responsive behavior on the part of the adult attachment figure (mostly mother) allows the child to use the caregiver as a secure base. This is crucial for the child's socioemotional development. For example, secure patterns of attachment are related to later social competence in interactions with peers, curiosity, persistence in problem solving, or coping with failure (Turner, 1991).

Perhaps most promising would be a combination of both approaches. Complementing an attachment approach with learning theoretical assumptions leads one to expect that a prosocial and responsive attachment figure should influence the kind of emotional reactions in the child and stimulate the modeling of prosocial behavior. Some empirical findings are encouraging in this regard. Studies on infants show that emotional warmth and the responsiveness of mothers are related to fewer experiences of distress in infants (Ungerer et al., 1990). For preschool children, Kestenbaum, Farber, and Sroufe (1989) demonstrated that secure attachment in early childhood is related to prosocial motivation.

In essence, this would be a framework of the influence of person-context relationships on socialization. A child's relationship with his or her caretaker or attachment figure is assumed to determine the nature of socializing interactions between the child and the attachment figure. With regard to prosocial motivations, mothers' *emotional behavior* in interactions may be most important (Maccoby, 1992). In fact, one of the rare longitudinal studies in this area suggests long-lasting effects of maternal emotional tone. Kochanska (1991) showed that between the ages of 8 and 10 years, children's reactions to another person's distress signals were indeed related to the quality of emotional interactions they had experienced with their parents during infancy. This study underlines that the appropriate emotional reaction of parents does not consist in simply matching the child's emotion but in reacting calmly to his or her negative emotions, thus providing emotional security and reducing distress. This requires high emotional control on the part of the parents. In contrast, if mothers react with distress to their child's distress, they increase their child's negative emotions (Bryant, 1987).

In addition, a focus of person-context relations also includes the notion that the caregivers' relationships with their children must not necessarily remain stable during the children's further development. At different times in development, the same kind of emotional behavior toward the child at different developmental ages may have different effects on the child. For example, it was shown that German mothers' empathic reaction to their children in a stressful situation was related to low distress for 3-year-olds but to high distress in 5-year-olds (Trommsdorff, 1993d). Presumably, it is the adequateness and responsiveness of emotional behavior that is the decisive factor for children's emotional and prosocial development.

To summarize, the child's tendency to react with empathy and altruistic behavior to the perceived distress of another person should be influenced by a specific kind of child-context relation: the child's early experience of security in interaction with the caretaker.

Finally, it should be noted that during further development, certainly other factors beside children's interaction with parents need also to be considered; relationships with peers and teachers, for example, are prime candidates for socializing factors outside the family.

Effects of Cultural Contexts. To examine the extent to which parental behaviors have an influence on children's development of prosocial motivation, a cross-cultural framework is suggested here. In contrasting different cultures that represent differences in socializing conditions for empathy and prosocial development, variations in the outcomes of these socialization practices can be observed. This is especially useful when the differences across the cultures that are selected for comparison are larger than the differences normally encountered within a given culture. This also has methodological advantages when two or more cultures can be selected that are similar in some and different in other aspects of theoretical relevance.

Individualistic Versus Group-Oriented Cultures. A characteristic of cultures that is of high theoretical relevance for our purposes is the value that specific cultures place on different modes of person-context relations. Such a general differentiation was suggested by Triandis (1989), who referred to Hofstede's (1980) value dimension of *individualism* and *collectivism.* "Individualistic" values give priority to the individual's interests and the person's independence and autonomy, whereas "collectivistic" values give priority to the group's interests and demand conformity to group norms. These concepts have met much enthusiasm, but also much criticism in the literature. It is yet unclear whether these concepts form independent dimensions or extreme ends of the same dimension, and whether it is possible to describe cultures in these broad terms, and to not account for intracultural individual differences. (A differentiation of cultures is based on different constructs as compared to a differentiation of individuals). Also, it is unclear whether individualistic and collectivistic (group-oriented) values belong to parts of the same dimension.

For our question about the development of specific person-context relations—empathy and prosocial motivation—it seems promising to compare samples from cultural environments differing in individualistic and group-oriented values. These values define and prescribe to some extent specific relations that people are supposed to form with their social partners. For individuals, they represent specific guidelines for their understanding of how the social system works, and what their role is within the social system.

A central target of inquiry could be the extent to which individuals' beliefs of control (in terms of basic beliefs serving individuals' needs for security and predictability) are affected by these values. Obviously, individualistic versus collectivistic cultures would provide different blueprints for beliefs about how people can be in control of their lives. Theoretical distinctions between "primary" versus "secondary" control or "assimilative" versus "accommodative" control seem to capture these differences (Brandtstädter & Renner, 1990; Rothbaum, Weisz, & Snyder, 1982; Weisz, Rothbaum, & Blackburn, 1984). In essence, one may assume that preferences for a primary control orientation is emphasized in individualistic cultures that value independence and autonomy. Secondary control orientations should be more prevalent in group-oriented cultures that value cooperation, obedience, social cohesiveness, and group harmony (Essau, 1992; Seginer, Trommsdorff, & Essau, 1993; Trommsdorff, 1989). Accordingly, socialization in individualistic cultures should stress autonomy and independence, whereas in group-oriented cultures conformity should be emphasized.

These different socialization conditions should affect the development of empathy and prosocial motivation. Children growing up in an individualistic cultural environment learn to differentiate between self and other and see themselves as independent, separate entities. In a group-oriented culture, the development of self is embedded in the social context; here, the self is part of this context. This differentiation between an "independent" and an "interdependent" self (see recent discussions by Markus & Kitayama, 1991, or Johnson, 1985) allows us to study culture-specific child-context relations and to clarify the role of emotions in prosocial action.

Among children who are socialized in cultures that emphasize "independence," as compared to cultures that stress "interdependence," one should expect fewer emotional reactions when experiencing the distress of another person, and especially less fusion of their own feelings with those of others. Also, one may assume that in group-oriented cultures that value harmonious positive social relations, the expression of negative emotions is more inhibited than in individualistic cultures. If children rarely experience the negative emotions or distress of another person, they should be more upset and distressed than children from an individualistic culture in which the expression of negative emotions is less negatively sanctioned.

Furthermore, one may assume that in a group-oriented cultural environment in which harmonious social relations are valued, more altruistic and prosocial behavior should occur than in an individualistic cultural value system. Accordingly, children from a group-oriented culture should more actively attempt to re-establish the well-being of another person in distress.

Cultural Differences in Prosocial Motivation

With the exception of the famous Six Cultures Study by Whiting and Whiting (1975), only very few cross-cultural studies on prosocial behavior exist. Research on adolescents' attitudes in Japan (a group-oriented society) as compared to Germany (an individualistic society) showed that German adolescents, upon being asked for help, were less willing to spontaneously help a stranger (e.g., give directions), and that Japanese adolescents' overall readiness to help is higher (Youth Affairs Administration, Japan, 1989). This may be an indication that it is the relationship between a person and his or her context that determines prosocial behavior. However, again, these data are based on self-reports only; an intention to help does not necessarily correlate with helping in real situations. In addition, as mentioned earlier, these studies focus on adults, and emotional determinants were not included. So far, cross-cultural studies do not exist that would allow us to determine the influences between person-context relations, including their emotional feature, and individuals' prosocial behavior. However, the intention to help does not necessarily correlate with real helping in real interaction situations.

So far, no cross-cultural studies on the relation between emotional reactions (e.g., empathy) and prosocial behavior exist. Some indirect information may be gained from the recent cross-cultural studies on the development of aggression in different group-oriented (Japan, Bali, Batak) and individualistic (Germany, Switzerland) cultures by Kornadt, Hayashi, Tachibana, Trommsdorff, and Yamauchi (1992) and by Kornadt (1991). Significant differences in the occurrence and kinds of aggression motive (for adolescents) and in developmental conditions are demonstrated in these cultures. One of the most striking differences is that the aggression motive is lower for adolescents in group-oriented (East Asia) than for those in individualistic (Western) cultures. This is interesting in view of the fact that the aggression motive is often understood to counteract prosocial motivation.

Cultural Differences in Socialization

These motivational differences in aggression were related to different patterns of socialization. Mothers from Eastern cultures showed more understanding for their child and preferred prosocial values more than did mothers from Western cultures. Similar differences in socialization goals and values have been demonstrated in studies comparing Japan with other Western societies (Azuma, 1986; Hendry, 1986; Lebra, 1976; Trommsdorff, 1983, 1986, 1993c). These differences in childrearing goals are reflected in different modes of mother-child interaction; this relation is closer in Japan as compared to individualistic societies (e.g., Caudill & Weinstein, 1969; Morikawa, Shand, & Kosawa, 1988; Otaki, Durrett, Richards, Nyquist, & Pennebaker, 1986).

One may conceive of these different socialization practices as indicators of different cultural values that organize people's thinking, feeling, and behavior with respect to their relation to the environment. These may reflect different modes of control orientation. As a matter of fact, there is evidence for more primary and less secondary control in socialization goals and practices of German mothers in interaction with their children than in those of Japanese mothers. German mothers reported more conflicts and Japanese mothers reported more cooperation and giving in by the child (using scenario techniques; cf. Kornadt & Trommsdorff, 1990; Trommsdorff, 1989).

Accommodating behavior requires the evaluation of the needs and wishes of the social environment to adjust one's own actions accordingly. Therefore, responsiveness and empathy should be more pronounced in people who have secondary control beliefs. This is in line with the results of Trommsdorff and John (1992) on the relations between secondary control, empathic concern, and the accurate decoding of emotions in interaction with an intimate partner.

This view is supported by systematic observations of real mother-child interactions in Japan and Germany. Japanese mothers were more responsive to the needs of their 5-year-old daughters than were German mothers (Trommsdorff & Friedlmeier, 1993). Furthermore, mothers' responsiveness was related to their daughters' secondary control in both cultures. A more accommodating interaction was observed for Japanese and a more assimilative interaction for German mother-child interactions. Japanese, as compared to German mothers, induced more cooperation and task involvement in their children. Also, Japanese children were better able to cope with stressful situations.

These findings are consistent with the literature on Japanese socialization and mother-child relations, reporting a strong emotional bonding and feeling of "oneness" ("ittaikan") (Azuma, 1984) for Japanese mother-child relations, whereas German mothers and children act as separate individual entities. Such a culture-specific mode of mother-child relationship characterizes the early experiences of the child with respect to his or her environment; this should affect other aspects of child-context relations, especially the development of empathy and prosocial behavior.

In line with the aforementioned hypothesis, one may expect, on the one hand, more empathic concern and prosocial behavior in a group-oriented versus an individualistic culture. On the other hand, one may expect more distress in a group-oriented culture, in which the child is rarely exposed to the negative emotions of others and thus may be upset. In contrast to the previous hypothesis, one may also assume that prosocial behavior may be blocked if children in group-oriented cultures are more oriented to secondary than to primary control. However, we do not assume that each individual in the one culture is different from each individual in the other. In contrast, there should be within-culture differences across individuals.

A STUDY OF EMPATHY AND PROSOCIAL BEHAVIOR IN INDIVIDUALISTIC AND GROUP-ORIENTED CULTURAL ENVIRONMENTS

Starting from the assumption that group-oriented and individualistic cultural environments transmit certain conditions for the development of specific person-context relations, including empathy and the development of prosocial motivation, children from Japan and Germany were compared. These cultural environments represent theoretically relevant socialization conditions that may help to better understand the development of prosocial motivation.

The goals of our cross-cultural studies were to clarify:

- Whether and what kind of emotional reactions (empathy, distress) occur when children observe another person in distress.
- Which role such emotional reactions—especially empathy—have for prosocial behavior (and its different qualities).
- Whether certain cultural contexts (e.g., culture-specific values; parental socialization) affect those emotional reactions and related prosocial behavior.

The developmental conditions for prosocial motivation and the specific elements in the development of a prosocial action system should thereby be clarified.

Method

The method chosen for our study is designed to overcome the theoretical and methodological deficits of previous studies described earlier. First, we have established a *real* interaction situation in which the child's reactions can be *observed* directly. These reactions are *differentiated* according to observable phenomena of different qualities of emotions (empathy and different kinds of distress) and prosocial behavior. To understand the development of the prosocial action system after the second year of age, children of different developmental ages are studied. To take into account individual differences in this prosocial action system, we also investigate specific socialization conditions of the child, especially the mothers' attitudes and behavior toward the child (observations and self-reports of mother–child interactions). Furthermore, because the cultural environment presumably affects the development of such a prosocial action system, the development of empathy and prosocial behavior is studied here in different cultural contexts—in a more group-oriented versus a more individualistic culture.

Samples. It was possible to carry out this study in Japan and compare a Japanese sample from Yokohama with a German sample from Konstanz. Japan is a culture representing group orientation and Germany is an individualistic culture. Both cultures represent highly modern, industrialized societies, and they differ with respect to their value orientations. In each culture, a nonrandom sample of 24 Japanese and 25 German mother–child pairs was selected. The children (all girls) were 5 years old and were recruited from middle-class kindergartens (in Yokohama and in Konstanz).

Procedures. The general procedure for induction of emotional reactions was designed as a naturalistic, quasi-experimental approach. Before the real experiment took place in a laboratory (children's playroom), the children had several encounters with a female university student in the kindergarten. This student later played the role of the playmate (victim). The playmate played with the child for two sessions so that the child could become sufficiently acquainted with her. After the second session and a certain amount of relaxed play, the playmate met with misfortune: her toy broke. The playmate reacted with sadness.

Child and playmate (kindergarten apprentice) played together for half an hour with different toys. Then they started playing a new game in which the child and the playmate each blew up a balloon, painted and dressed this balloon up like a doll, gave each balloon-doll a name, and let the balloon-dolls play with each other. The child was asked whether she would like to build a tower for the dolls. After a while—when the players were relaxed and happy—the child observed the playmate's balloon pop; it was popped (by the playmate) in such a way that the child was not able to see that it had not been an accident. The playmate told the child in a sad voice that her balloon had popped, that she could not continue to play with her balloon, and that she was very sad about this. She covered her face in her hands and sobbed a little. She continued demonstrating her sadness for about 3 minutes. Then she raised her head with a deep sigh. She started to change her mood, telling the child that she would try to get a new balloon later. She showed the child that this idea made her happy and that she was not suffering anymore; she suggested another game. In the end, the players were relaxed and in a positive affective mood. The child's reactions during the period of the playmate's sadness were videotaped with a hidden camera (3 minutes).

To examine aspects of the *mother–child* socialization process, each dyad was observed in three situations differing with respect to situational demands: (a) no specific demand (free interaction), (b) difficult task for the child (mild stress), and (c) unsolvable task for the child (high stress). The experiments took place in the playroom of a kindergarten. Altogether, the interactions lasted about 20 minutes. The subject's behavior was videotaped with a hidden camera (for a detailed description of this procedure see Trommsdorff & Friedlmeier, 1993). Mothers also answered open-ended questions related to 12 everyday conflict situations (e.g., mother wants to leave the playground, child wants to stay; these were administered using a scenario technique).

The appropriateness of the methods (situations, tasks, and materials used) with regard to cultural differences was established through pilot studies done in both cultures. In these studies, the appropriateness was ensured. Cross-cultural equivalence of the instructions was established via back-translation.

Assessment of Emotional and Other Reactions. Emotional and other reactions in children were assessed in the time span from directly after the playmate's misfortune until the end of the playmate's distress. Ratings were conducted by two independent raters simultaneously. All ratings were done on 6-point scales (1 = none, . . . , 6 = very strong).

Specific qualities of emotional reactions were rated separately. The following categories were rated on an event basis for their frequencies of occurrence. Ratings of intensity were also done on 6-point scales (1 = none, . . . , 6 = very strong).

The following categories were first coded as global characteristics and then as events. For the analyses of events, the rater marked each event in the videotaped sequence. The criterion for a new event was a change in the direction in which the eyes were focused, or in behavioral orientation.

Empathy was defined as an emotional reaction that is congruent with the emotion of the playmate. Here, the focus of the child's attention was on the victim. Empathy was coded when, in facial expression and gestures, the child expressed sadness and felt with the other person. The operationalization of empathy follows the measurement of *sympathy* by Eisenberg et al. (1988).

Distress was defined as expressions of negative emotions. Distress was coded when the child behaved as if upset by the situation and as feeling anxious and uneasy. Indicators for distress were the child's facial expression and gestures showing tension as well as dysfunctional characteristics. So far, the operationalization is in line with Eisenberg et al. (1988). Furthermore, distress was differentiated as *Self-Focused* versus *Other-Focused Distress.* In the first case, the child tries to disregard the distress situation of the victim; in the second case, the child concentrates on the victim. In the first case, a tendency to leave the field can be observed, whereas in the second case, a feeling of helplessness and an orientation toward the other person can be observed.

Active Versus Passive Distress. In case of Active Distress, the child shows facial or gestural movements; in case of Passive Distress, the child is nearly motionless.

A global category of *General Emotional Reaction* was used as a general measure of emotional reactions and did not differentiate between the emotional qualities of empathy and distress. Here, the intensity was again rated on a 6-point scale (1 = none, . . . , 6 = very strong).

Inner Conflict. Strong emotional tensions are indicated by frequent eye movements, and by frequent and quick changes in facial expressions.

Problem Solving. Here, no emotional reactions occur; however, gestures and facial expressions indicate that the child is dealing with the situation cognitively and trying to find solutions.

Dominant Emotional Reaction. This variable was measured to differentiate between nonemotional and emotional responses. When the child had only a scale value of 1 or 2 for empathy or distress (and when "problem solving" was not a dominant reaction), the child was rated as "not affected." If an emotional reaction was given a rating higher than 2, the child's Dominant Reaction was rated accordingly (Empathy, Distress Other-Focused, or Distress Self-Focused).

Assessment of Prosocial Behaviors. Occurrences of prosocial acts on the part of the target child were coded independently of the aforementioned ratings by two independent observers.

The ratings of these behaviors were done on the basis of event analyses. First, the rater measured whether prosocial behavior was shown at all, and, if it was, what kind (category) of prosocial behavior was shown (giving advice, verbal comforting, helping or sharing). Second, a global rating of the intensity of Prosocial Behavior was measured on a 6-point scale (1 = none, . . . , 6 = very strong).

Assessment of Socialization Conditions. To analyze the mother-child interactions, a category system was developed that was to measure the theoretically relevant characteristics of the mothers observed. In addition, maternal self-reports were obtained on several variables of interest.

Mothers' *Child Orientation* was rated from (a) the observations and (b) the mothers' self-reports on the extent to which mothers were oriented toward the child or the task (1 = problem-solving behavior and giving directions about how to solve the task, 2 = task and child orientation, and 3 = focusing on the needs and emotions of the child). Mothers' *Empathy* was rated according to the extent to which mothers focused on the child's emotions by verbalizing or matching these emotions (1 = very low, . . . , 6 = very high empathic reaction). *Emotional Quality* of maternal behavior was rated according to mothers' facial expressions and gestures in interaction with the child (1 = very negative, . . . , 6 = very positive emotions).

Finally, mothers gave self-reports of their typical *Interpretations* and explanations of their child's misbehavior (1 = very negative, . . . , 5 = very positive attribution of intentions), and of the overall *Interaction Quality* with their children (1 = very negative, conflicting, . . . , 5 = very positive, harmonious relation).

Results

First, interobserver correlations were examined to determine the reliability of the ratings of global emotional reactions, the observations of prosocial behaviors, and the ratings of socialization conditions. Correlations ranged from .72 to .95 and were highly significant.

Next, differences in children's emotional reactions and their prosocial behavior and then relations between these variables were examined.

A first set of analyses examined the kind of emotional reactions. German and Japanese girls showed no differences in Empathy but significant differences in the intensity of total Distress ($t = 3.23$, $df = 43$, $p < .05$) and Inner Conflict ($t = 2.37$, $df = 43$, $p < .05$). No differences in overall Prosocial Behavior occurred (see Table 6.1). (Results on differences in the qualities of Prosocial Behavior that cannot be reported here are summarized in Trommsdorff, 1993d.) The distribution of scale values for all categories is shown in Tables 6.1 and 6.2.

With regard to the Dominant Emotional Reaction, Japanese girls showed more frequent Distress reactions than did German girls (70% vs. 28%). When differentiating Distress reactions with respect to Self- and Other-focused Distress, more Self-focused Distress occurred in Japanese girls, whereas in German girls no Self-focused Distress occurred at all (see Fig. 6.1).

A *second* set of analyses focused on the emotional characteristics of those girls who showed prosocial behavior toward the playmate during the experimental procedure. The correlations between Empathy and overall Prosocial Behavior were significantly positive for children from both cultures ($r = .79$, $df = 24$ and $r = .73$, $df = 19$ for German and Japanese girls, respectively). Pearson correlations between total Distress and overall Prosocial Behavior were negative for the German girls ($r = -.49$, $df = 24$) and nonsignificant for

TABLE 6.1
Emotional Reactions and Prosocial Behavior of German and Japanese Children

	German			Japanese			
	M	SD	N	M	SD	N	t-value
General Emotional Reaction	2.46	.85	25	2.78	.96	20	−1.17
Empathy	2.80	1.35	25	2.30	1.38	20	1.22
Distress							
- Total	2.12	1.75	25	3.25	1.15	20	−3.23***
- Self-focused	1.76	.93	25	3.15	1.46	20	−3.70***
- Other-focused	2.48	1.66	25	3.35	1.60	20	−1.77†
- Active	1.96	.98	25	2.90	1.41	20	−2.64*
- Passive	2.20	1.73	25	3.10	1.92	20	−1.65
Inner Conflict	1.40	.91	25	2.10	1.07	20	−2.37**
Prosocial Behavior	2.56	1.39	25	2.10	1.59	20	1.04

Note: Scales from 1 = very low to 6 = very high.
†$p < .10$; *$p < .05$; **$p < .01$; ***$p < .001$.

TABLE 6.2
Distributions of Scale Values in German and Japanese Children

		N	M	SD	MIN	MAX
General Emotional Reaction	Germany	25	2.46	.85	1.00	4.00
	Japan	20	2.78	.96	1.00	4.25
Empathy	Germany	25	2.80	1.35	1.00	6.00
	Japan	20	2.30	1.38	1.00	5.00
Distress						
- Total	Germany	25	2.12	1.18	1.00	5.00
	Japan	20	3.25	1.15	1.00	5.00
- Self-focused	Germany	25	1.76	.93	1.00	5.00
	Japan	20	3.15	1.46	1.00	6.00
- Other-focused	Germany	25	2.48	1.66	1.00	6.00
	Japan	20	3.35	1.60	1.00	6.00
- Active	Germany	25	1.96	.98	1.00	5.00
	Japan	20	2.90	1.41	1.00	5.00
- Passive	Germany	25	2.20	1.73	1.00	6.00
	Japan	20	3.10	1.92	1.00	6.00
Inner Conflict	Germany	25	1.40	.91	1.00	5.00
	Japan	20	2.10	1.07	1.00	5.00
Prosocial Behavior	Germany	25	2.56	1.39	1.00	6.00
	Japan	20	2.10	1.59	1.00	6.00

Note: Scales from 1 = very low to 6 = very high.

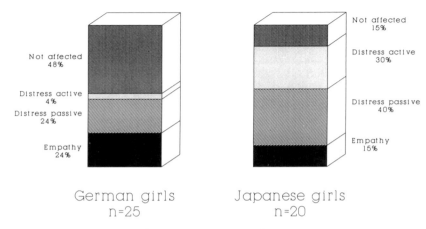

FIG. 6.1. Dominant emotional reactions.

the Japanese girls ($r = -.07$, $df = 19$). A more differentiated look at the specific correlations showed that "Other-focused Distress" and "Passive Distress" both correlated negatively with Prosocial Behavior in German girls ($r = -.38$, $df = 7$; $r = -.53$, $df = 6$, respectively) and nonsignificantly in Japanese girls ($r = -.05$, $df = 6$; $r = -.23$, $df = 7$, respectively). Also, differences between the Pearson r correlations of Japanese and German children were nearly significant ($z = 1.49$, $p < .07$). The frequencies for the different kinds of Distress for German children were too small; therefore no correlations could be computed.

In Japan, girls who showed Prosocial Behavior also showed higher General Emotional Reaction than those in Germany ($m = 3.28$ vs. 2.39, $df = 28$, $t = 2.72$, $p < .01$); this is because they showed more Distress ($m = 3.44$ vs. 1.83, $df = 28$, $t = 4.47$, $p < .01$; see Table 6.3).

German children expressing (vs. not expressing) Prosocial Behavior showed less Distress (total; Other-Focused; Passive Distress; see Table 6.4), whereas Japanese children expressing Prosocial Behavior showed more General Emotional Reaction, more Empathy, and more Active Distress (see Table 6.5).

A closer look at the relation between Distress and total Prosocial Behavior showed that a linear relation existed for German girls, whereas for Japanese girls the relation was an inverted u-curve: Low and high total Distress were related to low, whereas mild Distress was related to high overall Prosocial Behavior (see Fig. 6.2).

A *third* set of analyses focused on the relations between *socialization conditions* based on observations and self-reports of mothers, as well as children's empathy and prosocial behavior. Significant cultural differences were found with respect to empathy and child-oriented behavior. Japanese, compared to German mothers, showed significantly more Empathy, more

TABLE 6.3

General Emotional Reaction, Distress, and Prosocial Behavior

| | German | | | Japanese | | | |
	M	SD	N	M	SD	N	t-value
General Emotional Reaction	2.39	.85	21	3.28	.72	9	−2.72*
Distress Total	1.83	.93	21	3.44	.85	9	−4.47****

Note: Scales from 1 = very low to 6 = very high. Only values for demonstrating prosocial behavior are reported.

$^{\dagger}p < .10$; $^{*}p < .05$; $^{**}p < .01$; $^{***}p < .001$; $^{****}p < .0001$.

TABLE 6.4

Emotional Reactions and Prosocial Behavior: German Children

| | Expression of Prosocial Behavior | | | | | | |
| | No | | | Yes | | | |
	M	SD	N	M	SD	N	t-value
General Emotional Reaction	2.81	.88	4	2.39	.85	21	.90
Empathy	2.00	.82	4	2.95	1.40	21	−1.31
Distress							
- Total	3.63	1.31	4	1.83	.93	21	3.33**
- Self-focused	2.75	1.50	4	1.57	.68	21	1.54
- Other-focused	4.50	1.29	4	2.10	1.45	21	3.09**
- Active	2.75	1.50	4	1.81	.81	21	1.85†
- Passive	4.50	1.29	4	1.76	1.45	21	3.52**
Inner Conflict	1.25	.50	4	1.43	.98	21	−.35

Note: Scales from 1 = very low to 6 = very high.

$^{\dagger}p < .10$; $^{*}p < .05$; $^{**}p < .01$; $^{***}p < .001$; $^{****}p < .0001$.

TABLE 6.5

Emotional Reactions and Prosocial Behavior: Japanese Children

| | Expression of Prosocial Behavior | | | | | | |
| | No | | | Yes | | | |
	M	SD	N	M	SD	N	t-value
General Emotional Reaction	2.36	.95	11	3.28	.72	9	−2.37*
Empathy	1.64	.67	11	3.11	1.62	9	−2.56*
Distress							
- Total	3.09	1.38	11	3.44	.85	9	−.67
- Self-focused	3.18	1.72	11	3.11	1.17	9	.10
- Other-focused	3.00	1.55	11	3.78	1.64	9	−1.09
- Active	2.27	1.49	11	3.67	.87	9	−2.48*
- Passive	3.09	1.97	11	3.11	1.96	9	−.02
Inner Conflict	2.09	1.22	11	2.11	.93	9	−.04

Note: Scales from 1 = very low to 6 = very high.

$^{\dagger}p < .10$; $^{*}p < .05$; $^{**}p < .01$; $^{***}p < .001$; $^{****}p < .0001$.

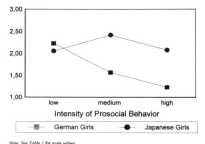

FIG. 6.2. Distress and total proso-cial behavior.

Note: See Table 1 for scale values

positive Emotional Quality, and more Child Orientation (observations). In their self-reports, their Interpretation of their children's misbehavior was more positive; their Interaction Quality with their children was more positive, and they generally showed more Child Orientation (see Table 6.6).

Finally, in both cultures, mothers high in Empathy had children who showed more total Distress (in Japan $r = .42$, $df = 19$, $p < .05$; in Germany $r = .52$, $df = 24$, $p < .05$).

THE ROLE OF EMOTIONS FOR PROSOCIAL ACTS: THE DEVELOPMENT OF ACTION PROCESSES IN CULTURAL CONTEXTS

The purpose of this study was to investigate specific aspects of child-context relations—the role of emotions for children's prosocial behavior. The underlying assumption was that one's own emotional reactions, when perceiv-

TABLE 6.6
German and Japanese Mothers' Behavior in Interactions with their Children

	German			Japanese			
	M	SD	N	M	SD	N	t-value
Observation							
Empathy[1]	3.22	1.59	18	5.15	.93	20	−4.61****
Emotional Quality[2]	4.47	1.26	19	5.10	.91	20	−1.78†
Child Orientation[1]	1.57	.94	14	2.15	.59	20	−2.21*
Self Report							
Interpretation[3]	2.63	.56	21	3.85	.35	24	−8.95****
Interaction Quality[3]	2.84	.77	21	3.65	.49	24	−4.28****
Child Orientation[4]	2.55	.54	21	3.17	.62	24	−3.57***

[1]Scales from 1 = very low to 6 = very high; [2]Scales from 1 = very negative to 6 = very positive; [3]Scales from 1 = negative to 5 = positive; [4]Scales from 1 = very low to 5 = very high.
†$p < .10$; *$p < .05$; **$p < .01$; ***$p < .001$; ****$p < .0001$.

ing another person in distress, should influence the occurrence of prosocial behavior, and that this is especially true for children. Thus, the current study is in contrast to most existing investigations. Traditionally, most studies on the relation between empathy and prosocial behavior has focused on adults (cf. Batson & Coke, 1991; Cialdini et al., 1987); the small number of existing empirical studies on children has yielded inconsistent results.

In this study, a method of cross-cultural contrasts was used, guided by the expectation that differing overarching cultural values should highlight interindividual differences in the relation between emotional antecedents and prosocial behaviors. Positive relations were found in two different environments. At the same time, cross-cultural differences were observed with respect to the role of distress for prosocial behavior.

Based on these results, we suggest a general model describing how prosocial actions are influenced by cultural environments in general, and by the structure of person-context relationships that activate affective and social-cognitive processes in particular. This model is presented in Fig. 6.3. We assume that witnessing the distress of another person induces unspecific arousal that may give rise to different kinds of emotional reactions: empathy, (empathy- or egoistic-based) distress, or no emotional reaction. Depending on the kind of cognitive processes (general control orientation; individualistic or social values; independent or interdependent self-concept; culturally and individually defined relationship with victim), altruistic or egoistic motives should be activated that (again depending on cognitive processes) may give rise to prosocial behavior (occurrence and quality; see Fig. 6.3).

Related action models focusing on prosocial moral reasoning (Eisenberg, 1986) and the aggression motive (Kornadt, 1982) specify some of the factors included here in more detail.

In summary, our model depicts a cultural frame for activation of prosocial behavior in the child. The action process is thus influenced by the action context of the child—the present situation-specific interaction, and past experiences in the social context, including the developmental conditions (e.g., individualistic or social orientation) in a given cultural environment.

On the other hand, it is assumed that the person actively constructs his or her own development, while these activities are effective in the context of and in interaction with cultural factors (e.g., Trommsdorff, 1993a; Valsiner, 1989). In such a model of interrelations between the person and the cultural context, it becomes difficult to clearly differentiate between the organism and the environment; both are interconnected in such a way that they can hardly be defined independently (Rogoff, 1990).

CULTURAL ENVIROMENT

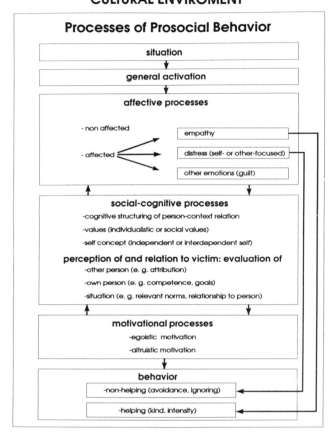

FIG. 6.3. General model of the influences of cultural environments on prosocial actions.

Limitations of the Study and Implications for Further Research

The results from this study must be discussed with respect to methodological shortcomings affecting the generalization of the findings. First, *inter- and intracultural differences* exist with respect to individualistic and group-oriented contexts. However, our small samples of children are not representative. Furthermore, the two cultures—Japan and Germany—represent only certain selected aspects of individualistic and group-oriented societies. To account for other aspects of these variables relevant for our theoretical questions, the same study is presently being carried out in Russia and Israel; these cultures share some elements of group orientation, but also differ with respect to individualistic values. It is assumed that certain collectivistic values have been officially implanted by the political system, whereas individualistic values may operate on the individual level as well. In these cultures, collectivistic values (some based on a shared fate and history) and individualistic values of the Occident or of modern industrialized societies exist simultaneously. Therefore, a simple contrast of "individualistic" versus "collectivistic" cultures is too stereotypical to be adequate.

Also, the study of only one gender (girls) and one age group (5-year-olds) does not allow us to generalize our results with respect to developmental questions. Especially in some group-oriented cultural environments, one should expect *gender differences*. For Russian children, Kienbaum (1993) indeed found gender differences with respect to prosocial action (see also Trommsdorff & Kienbaum, 1992). Children of different developmental ages should react differently; for example, distress may decrease with increasing cognitive and social development as has been assumed in the developmental model of Hoffman (1982). Therefore, we are presently observing children of *different age groups* in cross-sectional and longitudinal studies (2-, 3-, 5-, and 8-year-old girls). This should allow us to analyze the developmental pathways of child-context relations with respect to empathy and prosocial behavior.

Furthermore, it is obvious that individual differences occur even within each of these cultures. These will be studied more closely by analyzing the specific socialization conditions of children in more detail. The cultural environment is too global a variable; thus it should be studied with respect to the "cultural niches" (e.g., parental socialization goals and behavior, etc.) that are relevant to the child's development (Super & Harkness, 1986). Starting from an attachment theoretical framework, we are presently studying areas relevant for the development of individual differences in prosocial action: the quality of the mother-child relationship (in real interaction situations and as perceived by the mother) and especially the quality of emotional reactions of the mother in the event of of the child's distress (Trommsdorff, 1993d; Trommsdorff & Friedlmeier, 1993).

The experimental situations that allow behavioral observations have some disadvantages. Emotional reactions and prosocial behavior can be observed only in specific situations. Still we assume that this is an indicator of a personality variable that has consistency across situations. In the same vein, the interaction took place between the child and a student. We plan to replace the student by a peer to test whether the age (and related status) of the victim affects the child's behavior. For 8- and 11-year-old German boys, Friedlmeier (1993) has already successfully carried out such studies. Especially in a culture in which age is an important aspect for social behavior (e.g., Japan), we should expect cultural differences with respect to prosocial behavior in *interaction with a peer* versus an *adult* victim (Kobayashi & Trommsdorff, 1993).

Finally, so far we have reported on the children's emotional reactions and prosocial behavior for the whole situation without going into the details of the action process. The study of *action sequences* as a process of emotional reactions would allow us to specify which emotion is related to the occurrence of prosocial behavior. Such detailed sequential analyses are now being carried out.

Emotional Reactions and Prosocial Behavior in Different Cultural Environments

The results on emotional reactions and prosocial behavior clearly show some cultural similarities, especially with respect to the intensity of empathic reactions, the degree of prosocial behavior, and the relation between the two—empathy and prosocial behavior. However, the global measurement of a general intensity of emotional reactions would be misleading if this were simply interpreted as an indicator of empathy. Although this is often the case in the literature, a more refined study of the quality of emotional reaction shows that one must differentiate between *empathy* and *distress*. Whereas no cultural differences were found for empathy and for the relation between empathy and prosocial behavior, significant differences nevertheless occurred with respect to distress: Compared to the German girls, the Japanese girls showed more distress (other-focused, as well as self-focused). Also, prosocial behavior was less for German girls who were distressed, whereas for Japanese girls showing prosocial behavior, either empathy or distress occurred.

Empathy can thus be understood as an important precondition of prosocial behavior for children of this developmental age in both cultures. Contrary to most studies in the literature that have produced inconsistent results, these findings are based on observations of children's behavior in *real* situations. In this age group, a spontaneous empathic reaction may activate prosocial/altruistic motivation, which in turn induces prosocial behavior. This is in line with our theorizing on the development of prosocial action. For 3-year-old German girls, we also found a close relationship between empathy and prosocial behavior (Trommsdorff, 1993d). However, it remains to be clarified whether this relation changes during further cognitive, emotional, and social development. Cognitive factors, such as self-concept, social norms, and evaluation of costs and benefits may later also influence prosocial behavior. Although an increasingly close relationship is assumed in the literature, Friedlmeier (1993) found that for 11-year-old German boys the relation between empathy and prosocial behavior is less pronounced than for 8-year-old boys.

It was shown here that preschool children from very different cultural environments—such as Germany and Japan—do not differ with respect to prosocial *child-context relations* as indicated by their empathy and subsequent prosocial behavior. However, children from these different cultural environments do differ with respect to the intensity of distress and the relation between distress and prosocial behavior. Japanese as compared to German girls express more distress. Although for German children distress prevents prosocial behavior, for Japanese children mild distress induces prosocial behavior. Such distress in Japanese children is focused on the other person and is also characterized by activity. These cultural differences not only demonstrate a different type of emotional reaction to another person's sadness and misfortune, but they also show that distress has a different role for prosocial behavior in Japan than it has in Germany. Therefore, not only a differentiation between empathy and distress, but also a differentiation between different kinds of distress is useful to predict prosocial behavior.

When a cultural environment tends to not expose children to the *distress* of another person—as, for example in Japan, where the expression of negative emotions is considered immature and disturbing and is thus somewhat suppressed—children should be upset when faced with another person's distress. Then, children may ask themselves whether they are the source of the other person's distress and feel guilty or helpless, not knowing how to deal with this situation, especially because it is unclear what kind of behavior may really comfort the victim. This can be seen in the finding that internal conflicts were higher in Japanese girls than in German girls. Still, Japanese girls help when mildly distressed. This emotional state may enable sufficient emotional arousal and at the same time a self-other differentiation that is necessary to engage in active prosocial behavior.

Being distressed, Japanese girls react with self- as well as with other-focused distress, whereas German girls tend to only react with other-focused distress. This may indicate a more advanced development of self-other differentiation for German than for Japanese girls. According to Hoffman (1982, 1984), children develop a sense of self-other differentiation in the second year of life. During their further development, the distress they experience when faced with the distress of another person should decrease because they can disentangle the others' emotions from their own. The occurrence of distress may simply not be an indicator of less developmental advancement but rather of a different quality of developmental processes as induced by certain socialization experience.

The experience of certain socialization conditions may hinder this self-other differentiation for 5-year-olds. In both cultural contexts, children showed more distress witnessing the sadness of the playmate when their mothers reacted with high empathy toward their child in a stressful situation. Children who experience too strong a degree of empathy on the part of their caretaker may experience more distress because of a less developed self-other differentiation. Especially for Japanese children, the differentiation between self and other seems to be organized differently, possibly because of different socialization processes. In this group-oriented cultural environment, self and other are generally more fused than in individualistic cultures. This is similar to Markus and Kitayama's (1991) assumption that processes of self-development (independent vs. interdependent self) in individualistic cultures differ from those in group-oriented cultures.

This is also similar to the assumption that a secondary control orientation is more pronounced in Japan, a group-oriented culture, as compared to Germany, an individualistic culture (Trommsdorff, 1989). A person with high secondary control tries to accommodate to the needs of another person (in this case, a victim); the other person and oneself are seen as being mutually dependent. However, because it is not clear how one could fulfill the other person's needs, inner conflicts and distress arise. In case of only mild distress, helping is still possible as was observed for the Japanese children.

In contrast, a person with high primary control may expect another person to assimilate and help him or herself. Both people constitute two independent, separate entities. The responsibility for the other person's (inner) state lies more with the other person than with oneself. Accordingly, less distress and inner conflicts arise as we have seen for the German girls. This is in line with the finding that more German than Japanese children showed no significant emotional reaction even though one may assume higher control over the expression of emotions for Japanese than for German children.

Accordingly, the emotional reaction and prosocial behavior of children in different cultural environments demonstrate aspects of child-context relations that have been developed as elements of child-context interactions during the socialization processes. Children's behavior, in turn, affects their relations to their environments. The emotional relations between the child and his or her context differ in different cultural environments; however, in both group-oriented as well as individualistic cultural environments, universal processes are operating at the same time and induce the development of empathy—feeling with the other person's emotional state. When empathy has been induced, there is a high probability that children will help, independent of their primary or secondary control orientation, and independent of the cultural environment in which they are growing up.

ACKNOWLEDGMENTS

This research was supported by grants from the German National Science Foundation (Deutsche Forschungsgemeinschaft) and by the Japan Foundation. The study was also supported by the Keio University and funds from the University of Konstanz. I would like to express my great appreciation to Professor Hiroshi Namiki, Keio University, who cooperated in the Japanese part of the study. Special thanks go to Ryozo Kobayashi, presently at Konstanz

University, who carried out the Japanese part of this study and who helped in the qualitative analyses of the Japanese sample. I am grateful to Doctor Wolfgang Friedlmeier for his cooperation and help in this study, especially for the organization of data collections and data analysis. Bertrand Lisbach carried out most of the quantitative data analysis. I also wish to thank the mothers and children who participated in the research. Correspondence concerning this chapter should be addressed to Gisela Trommsdorff, Lehrstuhl für Entwicklungspsychologie, Postfach 5560 D 14, D-78434 Konstanz, Germany.

REFERENCES

Azuma, H. (1984). Secondary control as a heterogeneous category. *American Psychologist, 39,* 970–971.

Azuma, H. (1986). *Child development and education in Japan.* New York: Freeman.

Barnett, M. A. (1987). Empathy and related responses in children. In N. Eisenberg & J. Strayer (Eds.), *Empathy and its development* (pp. 146–162). Cambridge, England: Cambridge University Press.

Batson, C. D., Batson, J. G., Griffitt, C. A., Barrientos, S., Brandt, J. R., Sprengelmeyer, P., & Bayly, M. J. (1989). Negative-state relief and the empathy-altruism hypothesis. *Journal of Personality and Social Psychology, 56,* 922–933.

Batson, C. D., & Coke, J. S. (1981). Empathy: A source of altruistic motivation for helping? In J. P. Rushton & R. M. Sorrentino (Eds.), *Altruistic and helping behavior* (pp. 167–188). Hillsdale, NJ: Lawrence Erlbaum Associates.

Batson, C. D., Fultz, J., & Schoenrade, P. A. (1987). Distress and empathy: Two qualitatively distinct vicarious emotions with different motivational consequences. *Journal of Personality, 55,* 19–39.

Batson, C. D., & Oleson, K. C. (1991). Current status of empathy-altruism hypothesis. In M. S. Clark (Ed.), *Prosocial behavior* (pp. 62–85). London: Sage.

Berkowitz, L. (1972). Social norms, feelings, and other factors affecting helping and altruism. In L. Berkowitz (Ed.), *Advances in experimental social psychology* (Vol. 6, pp. 63–106). New York: Academic Press.

Bischof-Köhler, D. (1989). *Spiegelbild und Empathie. Die Anfänge der sozialen Kognition.* [Selfobjects and empathy. The beginning of social cognition]. Stuttgart: Huber.

Bowlby, J. (1988). *A secure base: Clinical applications of attachment theory.* London: Routledge.

Bowlby, J. (1991). Ethological light on psychoanalytical problems. In P. Bateson (Ed.), *Development and integration of behavior* (pp. 301–313). Cambridge, England: Cambridge University Press.

Brandtstädter, J., & Renner, G. (1990). Tenacious goal pursuit and flexible goal adjustment: Explication and age-related analysis of assimilative and accommodative strategies of coping. *Psychology and Aging, 1,* 58–67.

Bryant, B. K. (1987). Mental health, temperament, family, and friends' perspectives on children's empathy and social perspective taking. In N. Eisenberg & J. Strayer (Eds.), *Empathy and its development* (pp. 245–270). Cambridge, England: Cambridge University Press.

Caudill, W. A., & Weinstein, H. (1969). Maternal care and infant behavior in Japan and America. *Psychiatry, 32,* 12–43.

Cialdini, R. B., Schaller, M., Houlihan, D., Arps, K., Fultz, J., & Beaman, A. L. (1987). Empathy-based helping: Is it selflessly or selfishly motivated? *Journal of Personality and Social Psychology, 52,* 749–758.

Eisenberg, N. (1982). Introduction. In N. Eisenberg (Ed.), *Development of prosocial behavior* (pp. 1–24). New York: Academic Press.

Eisenberg, N. (1986). *Altruistic emotion, cognition, and behavior.* Hillsdale, NJ: Lawrence Erlbaum Associates.

Eisenberg, N., McCreath, H., & Ahn, R. (1988). Vicarious emotional responsiveness and prosocial behavior. Their interrelations in young children. *Personality and Social Psychology Bulletin, 14,* 298–311.

Eisenberg, N., & Miller, P. A. (1987). Empathy, sympathy, and altruism: Empirical and conceptual links. In N. Eisenberg & J. Strayer (Eds.), *Empathy and its development* (pp. 292–316). Cambridge, England: Cambridge University Press.

Eisenberg, N., Reykowski, J., & Staub, E. (Eds.). (1989). *Social and moral values: Individual and societal perspectives.* Hillsdale, NJ: Lawrence Erlbaum Associates.

Eisenberg, N., & Strayer, J. (Eds.). (1987). *Empathy and its development.* Cambridge, England: Cambridge University Press.

Essau, C. (1992). *Primary and secondary control and coping.* Regensburg: Roderer.

Fabes, R. A., Eisenberg, N., & Miller, P. A. (1990). Maternal correlates of children's vicarious emotional responses. *Developmental Psychology, 26,* 639–648.

Friedlmeier, W. (1993). *Entwicklung von Empathie, Selbstkonzept und prosozialem Handeln in der Kindheit* [Development of empathy, self-concept, and prosocial behavior in childhood]. Konstanz: Hartung-Gorre.

Hendry, J. (1986). *Becoming Japanese. The world of the preschool child.* Honolulu: University of Hawaii Press.

Hoffman, M. L. (1981). Is altruism part of human nature? *Journal of Personality and Social Psychology, 40,* 121–137.

Hoffman, M. L. (1982). Development of prosocial motivation: Empathy and guilt. In N. Eisenberg (Ed.), *The development of prosocial behavior* (pp. 281–313). New York: Academic Press.

Hoffman, M. L. (1983). Empathy, guilt, and social cognition. In W. F. Overton (Ed.), *The relationship between social and cognitive development* (pp. 1–51). Hillsdale, NJ: Lawrence Erlbaum Associates.

Hoffman, M. L. (1984). Interaction of affect and cognition. In C. E. Izard, J. Kagan, & R. B. Zajonc (Eds.), *Emotions, cognition, and behavior* (pp. 103–131). Cambridge, England: Cambridge University Press.

Hofstede, G. (1980). *Culture's consequences. International differences in work-related values.* London: Sage.

Johnson, F. (1985). The Western concept of self. In A. J. Marsella, G. DeVos, & F. L. K. Hsu (Eds.), *Culture and self: Asian and Western perspectives* (pp. 91–138). New York: Tavistock.

Karylowski, J. (1987). Focus of attention and altruism: Endocentric and exocentric sources of altruistic behavior. In N. Eisenberg & J. Strayer (Eds.), *Empathy and its development* (pp. 139–154). Cambridge, England: Cambridge University Press.

Kestenbaum, R., Farber, E. A., & Sroufe, L. A. (1989). Individual differences in empathy among preschoolers: Relation to attachment history. In N. Eisenberg (Ed.), *New directions for child development* (Vol. 44, pp. 51–64). San Francisco: Jossey-Bass.

Kienbaum, J. (1993). *Empathisches Mitgefühl und prosoziales Verhalten deutscher und sowjetischer Vorschulkinder* [Empathy and prosocial behavior of German and Soviet preschoolers]. Regensburg, Germany: Roderer.

Kobayashi, R., & Trommsdorff, G. (1993, August). *Emotional responses and prosocial behavior of German and Japanese children.* Paper presented at the 6th European Conference on Developmental Psychology, Bonn, Germany.

Kochanska, G. (1991). Socialization and temperament in the development of guilt and conscience. *Child Development, 62,* 1379–1392.

Kornadt, H.-J. (1982). *Aggressionsmotiv und Aggressionshemmung* [Aggression and aggression inhibition] (Vol. 1). Bern: Huber.

Kornadt, H.-J. (1989). Frühe Mutter-Kind-Beziehungen im Kulturvergleich [Early mother-child relationships in cross-cultural perspective]. In G. Trommsdorff (Ed.), *Sozialisation im Kulturvergleich* [Socialization in cross-cultural perspective] (pp. 65–96). Stuttgart: Enke.

Kornadt, H.-J. (1991). Aggression motive and its developmental conditions in Eastern and Western cultures. In N. Bleichrodt & P. J. D. Drenth (Eds.), *Contemporary issues in cross-cultural psychology* (pp. 155–167). Amsterdam: Swets & Zeitlinger.

Kornadt, H.-J., Hayashi, T., Tachibana, Y., Trommsdorff, G., & Yamauchi, H. (1992). Aggressiveness and its developmental conditions in five cultures. In S. Iwawaki, Y. Kashima, & K. Leung (Eds.), *Innovations in cross-cultural psychology*. Selected papers from the Tenth International Conference of the International Association for Cross-Cultural Psychology held at Nara, Japan (pp. 250–268). Amsterdam: Swets & Zeitlinger.

Kornadt, H.-J., & Trommsdorff, G. (1990). Naive Erziehungstheorien japanischer Mütter— deutsch-japanischer Kulturvergleich [Naïve parenting theories of Japanese mothers: German-Japanese comparison]. *Zeitschrift für Sozialisationsforschung und Erziehungssoziologie, 2,* 357–376.

Lebra, T. S. (1976). *Japanese patterns of behavior.* Honolulu: University of Hawaii Press.

Lipps, T. (1903). Einfühlung, innere Nachahmung und Organempfindungen [Empathy, inner imitation, and organic sensations]. *Archiv für die Gesamte Psychologie, 2,* 185–204.

Lipps, T. (1907). *Vom Fühlen Wollen und Denken* [On feeling, wanting, and thinking]. Leipzig: Barth Verlag.

Maccoby, E. E. (1992). Trends in the study of socialization: Is there a Lewinian heritage? *Journal of Social Issues, 2,* 171–185.

Markus, H. R., & Kitayama, S. (1991). Culture and the self: Implications for cognition, emotion, and motivation. *Psychological Review, 98,* 224–253.

Montada, L., Schneider, A., & Reichle, B. (1988). Emotionen und Hilfsbereitschaft [Emotions and helping]. In H. W. Bierhoff & L. Montada (Eds.), *Altruismus. Bedingungen der Hilfsbereitschaft* [Altruism: Conditions of helping] (pp. 130–153). Göttingen: Hogrefe.

Morikawa, H., Shand, M., & Kosawa, Y. (1988). Maternal speech to prelingual infants in Japan and the United States: Relationships among functions, forms and referents. *Journal of Child Language, 15,* 237–256.

Otaki, M., Durrett, M. E., Richards, P., Nyquist, L., & Pennebaker, J. W. (1986). Maternal and infant behavior in Japan and America. *Journal of Cross-Cultural Psychology, 17,* 251–268.

Radke-Yarrow, M., & Zahn-Waxler, C. (1984). Roots, motives, and patterns in children's prosocial behavior. In E. Staub, D. Bar-Tal, J. Karlowski, & J. Reykowski (Eds.), *Development and maintenance of prosocial behavior* (pp. 81–99). New York, London: Plenum.

Rogers, C. (1959). A theory of therapy, personality, and interpersonal relationships as developed in the client-centered framework. In J. S. Koch (Ed.), *Psychology: A study of a science (Vol. 3). Formulation of the person in the social context* (pp. 184–256). New York: McGraw-Hill.

Rogoff, B. (1990). *Apprenticeship in thinking: Cognitive development in social context.* New York: Oxford University Press.

Rothbaum, F., Weisz, J. R., & Snyder, S. S. (1982). Changing the world and changing the self: A two-process model of perceived control. *Journal of Personality and Social Psychology, 42,* 5–37.

Rushton, J. P., & Sorrentino, R. M. (Eds.). (1981). *Altruism and helping behavior: Social, personality and developmental perspectives.* Hillsdale, NJ: Lawrence Erlbaum Associates.

Seginer, R., Trommsdorff, G., & Essau, C. (1993). Adolescent control beliefs: Cross-cultural variations of primary and secondary orientations. *International Journal of Behavioral Development, 16*(2), 243–260.

Staub, E. (1986). A conception of the determinants and development of altruism and aggression: Motives, the self, and the environment. In C. Zahn-Waxler, E. M. Cummings, & R. Iannotti (Eds.), *Altruism and aggression* (pp. 135–164). Cambridge, England: Cambridge University Press.

Super, C. M., & Harkness, S. (1986). The developmental niche: A conceptualization at the interface of child and culture. *International Journal of Behavioral Development, 9,* 545–569.

Titchener, E. B. (1908). *The psychology of feeling and attention.* Norwood, MA: Norwood Press.

Triandis, H. C. (1989). The self and social behavior in differing cultural contexts. *Psychological Review, 96,* 506–520.

Trommsdorff, G. (1983). Value change in Japan. *International Journal of Intercultural Relations, 7,* 337–360.

Trommsdorff, G. (1986). Some comparative aspects of socialization in Japan and Germany. In I. Lagunes & Y. H. Poortinga (Eds.), *From a different perspective: Studies of behavior across cultures* (pp. 231–240). Lisse/Amsterdam, Holland: Swets & Zeitlinger.

Trommsdorff, G. (1989). Sozialisation und Werthaltungen im Kulturvergleich [Socialization and values in cross-cultural perspectives]. In G. Trommsdorff (Ed.), *Sozialisation im Kulturvergleich* [Socialization in cross-cultural perspective] (pp. 97–121). Stuttgart: Enke.

Trommsdorff, G. (1991). Child-rearing and children's empathy. *Perceptual and Motor Skills, 72,* 387–461.

Trommsdorff, G. (1993a). Entwicklung im Kulturvergleich [Development in cross-cultural perspective]. In A. Thomas (Ed.), *Einführung in die kulturvergleichende Psychologie* [Introduction into cross-cultural psychology] (pp. 103–135). Göttingen: Hogrefe.

Trommsdorff, G. (1993b). Kulturvergleich von Emotionen beim prosozialen Handeln [Cultural comparison of emotions during prosocial behavior]. In H. Mandl, M. Dreher, & H.-J. Kornadt (Eds.), *Entwicklung und Denken im kulturellen Kontext* [Development and thinking in cultural context] (pp. 3–25). Göttingen: Hogrefe.

Trommsdorff, G. (1993c). Besonderheiten sozialen Handelns in Japan: Fragen an die sozialwissenschaftliche Forschung [Characteristics of social action in Japan: Questions for social science research]. In H.-J. Kornadt & G. Trommsdorff (Eds.), *Deutsch-Japanische Begegnungen in den Sozialwissenschaften* [German-Japanese exchange in the social sciences] (pp. 227–251). Konstanz: Universitätsverlag Konstanz.

Trommsdorff, G. (1993d). *Rolle von Emotionen beim prosozialen Handeln. Bericht für die DFG* [The role of emotions during prosocial behavior: Report for the German Society for the Advancement of Scientific Research]. Unpublished manuscript, University of Konstanz.

Trommsdorff, G., & Friedlmeier, W. (1993). Control behavior and responsiveness in Japanese and German mothers. *Early Development and Parenting: An International Journal of Research and Practice, 2,* 65–78.

Trommsdorff, G., & John, H. (1992). Decoding affective communication in intimate relationships. *European Journal of Social Psychology, 22,* 41–45.

Trommsdorff, G., & Kienbaum, J. (1992, July). *Cross-cultural studies on the function of emotions in prosocial behavior.* Paper at the IACCP XIth International Congress, Liège, Belgium.

Turner, P. J. (1991). Relations between attachment, gender, and behavior with peers in preschool. *Child Development, 62,* 1475–1488.

Ungerer, J. A., Dolby, R., Waters, B., Barnett, B., Kelk, N., & Lewin, V. (1990). The early development of empathy: Self-regulation and individual differences in the first year. *Motivation and Emotion, 14,* 93–106.

Valsiner, J. (1989). *Child development in cultural context.* Göttingen: Hogrefe.

Weisz, J. R., Rothbaum, F. M., & Blackburn, T. C. (1984). Standing out and standing in: The psychology of control in America and Japan. *American Psychologist, 34,* 955–969.

Whiting, B. B., & Whiting, J. W. M. (1975). *Children of six cultures: A psychocultural analysis.* Cambridge, MA: Harvard University Press.

Youth Affairs Administration. Prime Minister's Office. (Ed.). (1989). *A summary report of the world youth survey.* Tokyo: Youth Affairs Agency.

CHAPTER SEVEN

Life Events' Spacing and Order in Individual Development

Alexander von Eye
Michigan State University

Kurt Kreppner
Max Planck Institute for Human Development and Education

Christiane Spiel
Universität Wien

Holger Weßels
Freie Universität Berlin

Life events are those events that have an effect on an individual's life course. In General Psychology and in Developmental Psychology, researchers have investigated events covering the whole spectrum from the ubiquitous, behavior-shaping reinforcements to critical events that change individuals' life courses. Examples of the former include the experimenters' "hm-hm" or the token given to children for behaving well. Examples of the latter include accidental pregnancies or retirements.

In the area that is labeled life event research, the focus is on events of critical importance to individuals. In this chapter, we cite a definition of *critical life events* (Brim & Ryff, 1980; Dohrenwend & Dohrenwend, 1974; Filipp, 1982; Filipp & Gräser, 1982), specify domains of critical life events, present a typology (Brim & Ryff, 1980), and discuss approaches to statistical analysis of such events. We place special emphasis on the analysis of critical life event patterns that differ in order and spacing. First, we use elementary combinatorics to specify and enumerate patterns of life events. The number of permutations, variations, or other patterns of life events is important to know for design and planning of investigations. For example, the number of patterns is one important determinant of required sample sizes. Subsequently, we illustrate how complete lists of life events can be statistically analyzed.

DEFINITION AND CLASSIFICATION OF LIFE EVENTS

Before presenting definitions of critical life events, we note that a plethora of events has been investigated under the label of life events (Hultsch & Plemons, 1979). Thus, the term *life event* seems to be an umbrella term involving all events that can possibly be important to humans. To be able to discriminate critical events from just any event that happens to individuals, we stress the highly subjective nature of life events. The same event, for instance, a political change, can be perceived as a catastrophe by some and as a routine transition by others.

Definition of Life Events

Filipp (1982) proposed the following definition of critical life events (hence-forth brief: life event):

1. Individuals perceive life events as massive changes of their current situation. These changes are not necessarily abrupt. Some life events have an obvious and predictable history as, for instance, the death of a spouse after a severe illness such as cancer. In each case, life events can be localized in time and space.

2. Individuals perceive life events as distinct and profound. As such, life events are different from more enduring developmental circumstances such as being raised in one-parent families.

3. Life events often disturb an existing equilibrium or, person-environ-ment fit. As a result, reorganization of the person-environment system is necessary. Mechanisms that help reorganize this system are termed coping mechanisms.

4. Life event research focuses on events that are of critical importance to the individual. Here, the term *critical* has a very broad meaning. It involves such catastrophical events as the loss of a spouse and such highly desired events as a marriage. Each of these events dramatically changes the course of the life of individuals.

5. Life events are critical only if they are affectively-emotionally important. This proposition includes both positive emotions as experienced when one falls in love and negative emotions as experienced when a great loss occurs.

6. The source of life events is located either inside or outside the indi-vidual. Examples of the former type of life events include illnesses. Examples of the latter type include earthquakes.

Classification and Systems of Life Events

Many classifications and systems of life events have been proposed (cf. Elliott & Eisdorfer, 1982). Well-known examples include the system proposed by

Brim and Ryff (1980) and the Holmes and Rahe (1967) social readjustment rating scale in which life events are rank ordered according to stressfulness. On this scale, death of a spouse ranks as the most stressful life event, and vacations and minor violations of the law are considered least stressful life events.

Brim and Ryff (1980) introduced the distinction into biological, social, and physical life events. *Biological life events* involve all morphological and physiological changes, changes in body size and shape, illnesses, and changes in functionality. Biological life events are rooted within the individual. Whereas some of these changes may go unnoticed, others may be critical in Filipp's (1982) sense.

Social life events, typically rooted outside the individual, change the individual's role and status in the social world. Normative[1] social life events include starting a new job, marriage, and becoming a parent. Non-normative social life events include becoming imprisoned, being involved in social binge drinking, and having children out of wedlock.

Physical life events are rooted in the physical world. Examples include earthquakes, car accidents, and fires. Many of these events are unpredictable and catastrophical in nature. In addition, most of them cause negative emotional responses.

Brim and Ryff (1980) proposed a *typology of life events* from crossing the following three variables: the probability of events (high, *h*, vs. low, *l*), the correlation of the event with chronological age (strong, *s*, vs. weak, *w*), and the number of individuals that can be expected to experience a particular life event (many, *m*, vs. few, *f*). Cross-tabulating these three variables yields a table with eight cells. Table 7.1 contains this cross-tabulation as well as a brief characterization of each cell and examples of each configuration of life events (see Brim & Ryff, 1980, p. 375).

For the present purposes we classify critical life events in the two groups of expected and unexpected ones. Whereas many social life events such as falling in love may be unpredictable, others, such as school entry, are predictable. Expected life events have characteristics that are known a priori. Most notably, they are either avoidable or occur by necessity. Avoidable are life events that occur by choice. Examples include marriages. Normative life events such as military service and the beginning of school, and biological life events such as the onset of menarche occur with high degrees of necessity. Individuals typically have good knowledge of the time of occurrence of expected life events.

---

[1]The multiple meanings of the terms normative and non-normative cannot be discussed in the present context. Specifically, there is no space to distinguish between the term normative in a descriptive sense and in a prescriptive sense. The former implies that most people experience a particular event, for instance, entering school. The latter implies that there are strong social expectations that a particular event takes place (or may not take place).

TABLE 7.1
Brim and Ryff's Typology of Life Events

Configuration	Description and Examples
hsm	highly likely, strong correlation with age, experienced by many
	(e.g., entering school, heart attack, birth of sibling, accidental pregnancy)
hsf	highly likely, strong correlation with age, experienced by few
	(e.g., inheriting a billion, dying of AIDS contracted via heterosexual
	contacts, outbreak of schizophrenia)
hwm	highly likely, weak correlation with age, experienced by many
	(e.g., death of sibling, getting mugged)
hwf	highly likely, weak correlation with age, experienced by few
	(e.g., tornadoes)
lsm	unlikely, strong correlation with age, experienced by many
	(e.g., whooping cough epidemic, military draft)
lsf	unlikely, strong correlation with age, experienced by few
	(e.g., participation in 1,300 mile run; *New York Times*, 10/3/1991)
lwm	unlikely, weak correlation with age, experienced by many
	(e.g., war, political changes, severe economic depression)
lwf	unlikely, weak correlation with age, experienced by few
	(e.g., cured of drug dependency, dismembered in car accident)

By definition, individuals do not anticipate unexpected life events. Examples of such events include accidents and falling in love. Also by definition, unexpected life events cannot be avoided nor prevented, and neither can they be induced. Time of occurrence is unknown a priori. It should be noted that whereas some characteristics of life events may be unexpected, other aspects may be expected nevertheless. For instance, the existence of car insurances is based on the assumption that car accidents will happen. However, time and place of car accidents typically is unknown. On a similar note, one may try to prevent car accidents, burglaries, and wars, and one can attempt a minimization of their consequences. However, it seems impossible to prevent them 100% from happening.

Many social life events cause negative emotional responses, others are responded to more positively. In more general terms, degree of predictability and *emotional response* can be considered characteristics of any life event.

LIFE EVENTS: A COMBINATORIAL PERSPECTIVE

In the following paragraphs we discuss constellations of life events from a combinatorial perspective. Specifically, we show how to calculate the number of possible constellations using elementary combinatorics. In subsequent sections we present approaches to statistical analysis of constellations of life events. (In the present context we use the term *constellation* in a very broad sense. We introduce more precise terms in the following paragraphs.)

Permutations of Life Events

Consider the following three life events: Being involved in a Car Accident (A); Accidental Pregnancy (P); and Death of Parent (D). The last of these three life events is unavoidable; the first two come unexpected, the last one is expected. Time of occurrence, however, often is not predictable.

The three life events can be placed in the six sequences APD, . . . , PDA. These sequences, or orders, are termed the six *permutations* of A, P, and D. In more general terms, for k life events there is a total of

$$P_k = k! = k(k-1)(k-2) \ldots (k-(k-1)) \tag{1}$$

permutations. Calculation of permutations of life events implies the following assumptions:

1. The researcher is interested only in the sequencing of events; spacing in time or other events are not of interest.

2. Each life event can occur at any point in time. There are obvious contradictions to this assumption that constrain the range of applicability of permutations in life event research. For example, consider the two life events Entering School and Military Service Draft. For these events, there is an obvious sequence and they only occur during a priori specified periods of the life span.

3. Each life event occurs only once. Obviously, each of the life events A, P, and D, can occur more than once.

4. All k life events occur to each individual in a sample. This assumption, again, constrains the range of applications for Formula (1).

Variations of Life Events

In the last section the researcher used all the k life events under study. In this section we assume that the researcher selects k out of n life events. For instance, a researcher may be interested in the effects of the k negative out of n life events.

The number of sequences of k out of n life events, with $k \leq n$, is called number of *variations*. It is given by

$$_nV_k = \frac{n!}{(n-k)!}, \tag{2}$$

with $0!_{\text{def}} = 1$. Again, the calculation of variations of events implies the following assumptions:

1. The researcher is interested only in the sequencing of a subset of events; spacing in time or other events are not of interest.
2. Each of the k life events can occur at any point in time; the same constraints apply as for permutations.
3. Each of the k life events can occur only once; the same constraints apply as preceding.
4. All of the k events occur to each individual in a sample.

Spacing and Repetitions of Life Events

In the following paragraphs we deal first with the problem of spacing and, then, with the problem of repeated occurrences of life events.

Spacing in Time in Permutations or Variations of Life Events.

In the preceding paragraphs the focus was on sequences of life events. In this paragraph we consider *spacing in time* in addition to order of life events. Rather than measuring length of time between life events we emphasize the subjective characteristics of time. We propose that, regardless of the actual amount of time spent before, between, or after life events individuals will view these periods as short, long, or just about right. In many instances time periods are experienced as too short or too long. For instance, the time between two imprisonments is, from the perspective of the individual involved, most likely too short. The time before marriage often is too long.

It seems hard to find a period that, relative to life events, is just about right. Because of the typically strong emotional responses to life events, most time periods can be expected to be viewed as either short (s), in the case of undesired events, or long (l), in case of desired events. For the present purposes, we, therefore, confine the discussion to these two types of periods.

We consider two cases next. For Case 1 the time spent before the first life event under study is either not considered at all or not known. In this characteristic Case 1 is comparable to left-censoring in event history analysis. For Case 2, we do consider the time spent before a life event.

To be able to include the two types of periods, we consider each period a separate event. Thus, rather than studying k life events, we now consider $k + 2$ events. The two additional events, however, do not have the same status as the k life events. For both permutations and variations we noted that each life event occurs only once. If $k > 2$, the same type of interval can occur more than once and, if $k > 3$, at least one interval type must occur more than once.

Consider the same example as preceding. We have six permutations of the three life events A, P, and D. For each of these permutations we have two intervals. Each of these intervals can be either short (s) or long (l).

Thus, we obtain for each triad of life events the following event interval-alternatives: E1-s-E2-s-E3, E1-s-E2-l-E3, E1-l-E2-s-E3, E1-l-E2-l-E3. In more general terms, we have $k-1$ intervals between k life events. If the number of time intervals considered is c, the number of different period constellations of k life events is

$$I = c^{k-1}, \tag{3}$$

and the number of life event-period constellations is

$$C_P = k!\, c^{k-1}. \tag{4}$$

Formula (4) applies if one investigates permutations of life events and their spacing. If one studies variations of life events and their spacing, one obtains

$$C_V = \frac{n!}{(n-k)!}\, c^{k-1}, \tag{5}$$

instead. For the present example with $k = 3$, one obtains $C_P = 3!\,2^2 = 24$. If any three events are examined from a total list of $n = 5$ events, one obtains $C_V = 240$ variations. If one also considers the time spent before the first life event (Case 2), one substitutes k for $k-1$ in the exponent for c in (4) or (5).

Repeated Occurrence of Life Events. The range of applicability of Formulas (1) and (2) is dramatically constrained because it was posited that each life event may occur only once. However, whereas some life events can occur only once, other life events can occur repeatedly.

Consider the three life events involved in Car Accident (A), Accidental Pregnancy (P), and Death of Friend (D). Each of these events happens unexpectedly and can occur more than once. Suppose a researcher is interested in effects that three life events from this group may have. Then, the researcher must consider the 27 constellations from AAA, AAD, through PPD, and PPP. In general, for n events the researcher must consider

$$_nP_k^R = n^k \tag{6}$$

permutations with repetitions where $k = n$. If $k > n$ or $k < n$ and $\{k, n\} > 0$, Formula (6) gives the number of *variations with repetitions*. Considering time intervals as before, one obtains

$$_nV_k^R = n^k c^{k-1}. \tag{7}$$

Somewhat more complicated is the case in which the number of times an event can be repeated is constrained. Examples of life events that cannot be repeated many times include Falling in Love for the First Time (which cannot be repeated at all), Death of a Parent (two possible occurrences), Entering Elementary School (cannot be repeated), and Suffering a Heart Attack (can be repeated a few times). In fact, no life event can be repeated ad libitum. Therefore, the following considerations apply to life events that, within a given observation period, can occur only $k' < k$ times.

Consider, again, the example with the life events A, D, and P. For these life events we have the six permutations ADP through PDA. To derive the next formula, we add event E to our list of life events. We place the constraint that E can occur only once. There is no constraint concerning timing or position of E. This set of rules yields, for permutation ADP, the following four constellations: $EADP$, $AEDP$, $ADEP$, and $ADPE$. Accordingly, one obtains constellations $EAPD$ through $APDE$ for permutation APD, and so forth.

In more general terms, for each of the P_k permutations of k life events, the addition of a new event E that can occur r times leads to the following factor:

$$m = \binom{k+r}{r} = \frac{(k+r)(k+r-1)\ldots(k+r-(k+r)+1)}{r(r-1)\ldots(r-r+1)}. \tag{8}$$

This factor is defined by the well-known binomial coefficients (see Goldberg, Newman, & Haynsworth, 1972). Using (8) we obtain for the number of permutations after inclusion of one life event that can be repeated r times $(r > 1)$

$$P_k^R = k!\binom{k+r}{r}. \tag{9}$$

Accordingly, we obtain for the number of variations

$$V_k^R = \frac{n!}{(n-k)!}\binom{k+r}{r}, \tag{10}$$

and for the number of permutations where each of the n life events can be repeated up to k times

$$P_k^R = n^k\binom{k+r}{r}. \tag{11}$$

Formulas (5) and (7) which consider spacing in time can be adapted accordingly. For instance, Formula (7) becomes

$$V_k^R = n^k c^{k-1}\binom{k+r}{r} \tag{12}$$

when one adds one life event that can be repeated r times.

We now consider the case in which J life events are added to the k events under study. The jth life event $(0 < j \le J)$ of the added events can be repeated r_j times. The number of permutations for the jth life event can be calculated using the following recursive formula:

$$P_{k,j}^R = V_{k,j-1}^R \binom{k+r_j}{r_j}, \qquad j>1, \tag{13}$$

where the number of permutations for $j = 1$ is given in (9).

Accordingly, we obtain for the number of variations

$$V_{k,j}^R = V_{k,j-1}^R \binom{k+r_j}{r_j}, \qquad j>1, \tag{14}$$

where the number of variations for $j = 1$ is given in (12). Spacing can be considered as before.

Cross-Classifying Life Events

In the preceding sections we presented formulas for calculation of numbers of life event constellations. As is obvious, these numbers can be quite large. As an alternative to considering k events, their spacing in time, and their repetitions, life events have been cross-classified (Müller, 1980, 1981; Thober, 1981; von Eye & Brandtstädter, 1981). This approach usually leads to smaller numbers of constellations. It requires variables that have two or more categories. Suppose k life events are listed as did occur versus did not occur. Then, the cross-classification of these k events has

$$t = 2^k \tag{15}$$

cells or configurations. These configurations describe patterns of events. Consider, again, the three life events A, P, and D of the first example, aforementioned, each scored as 1 = did occur or 0 = did not occur. Then, Pattern 111 describes individuals that experienced all three life events. Pattern 010 describes individuals that experienced only life event P.

One of the advantages of cross-tabulating life events is that alternative events can elegantly be taken into account. In addition, one can consider individuals that do not report life events or phases in which no life event occurs. In many instances, there is a number of alternatives to a life event. For example, after passing their high school diploma, many individuals face the decision whether to go to college, to take a job, or to do nothing. Only some of these alternatives can be considered life events. In more general terms, suppose we study k life events. The kth event has j_k alternatives, only some of which are life events. Then, the number of cells of the cross-classification of these k events is

$$t = \prod_{i=1}^{k} j_i \tag{16}$$

One of the main drawbacks of cross-classifications of this type is that there is no obvious order in the patterns of life events and alternatives. In contrast to permutations and variations, the order of life events is not taken into consideration. In the following paragraphs we present two approaches to dealing with this problem.

The first approach exploits the fact that many life events occur in an a priori specified sequence. For instance, Birth of a Sibling typically occurs before Death of Mother. In these instances, one can disregard the "confound" between age and life event. For instance, Pattern 10 describes individuals that do have a sibling and whose mother is alive. Pattern 11 describes individuals that have siblings and whose mother died. Pattern 00 describes individuals that have no siblings and whose mother is alive. Pattern 01 describes individuals that have no siblings but whose mother died. For each of these patterns the sequence of events is part of the definition of the life events under study because there is a strong correlation with age (see Table 7.1).

The second approach involves combining combinatorics and cross-classifying variables. Suppose we study k life events, with $k > 1$. These life events can be subdivided into the two sets, N and R. Set N contains those life events that either are confounded with age or for which the sequence of occurrence is of no importance. Set R contains those life events for which the sequence is of importance. The second approach generates all permutations or variations of the elements in R and, then, cross-classifies these permutations with the elements in N. Each of the resulting constellations describes a different group of individuals. More specifically, it describes individuals that experienced the life events in R in a particular sequence.

In more general terms, we have the set, N, of life events. This set contains I life events, with $I \geq 0$. The number of configurations that can be formed with these I life events is, according to (16)

$$t_I = \prod_{i \in I} j_i , \tag{17}$$

where j_i denotes the number of alternatives for the ith life event in I, for $i = 1, \ldots, I$.

Set R contains K life events, with $K \geq 0$. The number of permutations of these K life events is, according to (1)

$$t_K = K! . \tag{18}$$

The cross-classification of the t_I cells with the t_K permutations has

$$t_{INK} = (\prod_{i \in I} j_i) K! \tag{19}$$

cells.

It is important to note that, so far, the second approach treats life events from set N and life events from set R in different ways. For life events from N the events themselves, their alternatives, and their nonoccurrence are considered. For life events from R only the events themselves are considered. This implies the assumption that every individual in the sample experienced every life event in R. This may be an overly strong assumption as was illustrated using the example with the variables Presence of a Sibling (S) and Death of Mother (D), aforementioned. Therefore, we now consider for each life event in R the possibility that it may not have occurred in an individual's life. (The following considerations apply accordingly to the topics discussed in the sections about permutations, variations, and spacing in time.)

To include this option we consider the nonoccurrence of an event in R a separate event. For each permutation or variation we then calculate the number of constellations that results from combining life events that did occur with those that did not occur. Consider the life events, S and D. Both are scored as 1 when they did occur and 0 when they did not occur. For permutation SD we then obtain the event Patterns 11, 10, 01, and 00. This applies accordingly to permutation DS. In more general terms, when there are k life events, each scored as did versus did not occur, there are 2^k event patterns that describe which life event did occur and which did not occur. When one considers c_k alternatives for the kth life event of set R, with $c_k > 1$ and $k = 1, \ldots, K$, one obtains

$$t_c = \prod_{k \in K} c_k \tag{20}$$

configurations. If all events are scaled dichotomously, Formula 20 simplifies to $t_c = 2^k$. The cross-classification of the t_l cells with the t_C configurations that are based on the t_K permutations has

$$t_{I\wedge C} = \left(\prod_{i \in I} j_i \right) K! \left(\prod_{k \in K} c_k \right) \tag{21}$$

cells. From the discussion in the last section it is obvious how spacing and repetitions can also be considered, and how the present concepts can be applied to variations of life events.

Summary

One of the results of the discussions presented in this chapter is that we are able to completely enumerate constellations of life events. This is important for two reasons. First, we can select and interpret constellations of special importance. For instance, we can select constellations with predominantly negative life events and constellations with predominantly positive life events. We then can compare individuals that experienced these life event patterns on such variables as coping skills, self-definition, locus of control, and cognitive complexity.

Second, we can calculate from a priori probabilities how likely certain event constellations are. These calculations can be an important precondition for subsequent statistical analysis. The following sections are concerned with calculation of probabilities of life event constellations. In addition, they give a glimpse of statistical methods for analysis of life event frequencies. Specifically, we discuss how to apply methods of Configural Frequency Analysis (CFA; Krauth & Lienert, 1973; Lienert, 1978; von Eye, 1990) to life event analysis (cf. Spiel & von Eye, 1993; von Eye & Brandtstädter, 1981).

STATISTICAL ANALYSIS OF LIFE EVENT FREQUENCIES

In this section we present methods for analysis of frequencies of life events. Rather than asking how life events affect outcome variables, we ask whether life events occur more often or less often than expected under some model. We use prior probabilities for calculating expected cell frequencies.

We use methods of CFA for statistical analysis of life event frequencies. Specifically, we use variants of parametric CFA as proposed by Spiel and von Eye (1993). This approach is parametric in the sense that it estimates expected cell frequencies from such a priori information as theoretical assumptions or population parameters rather than from sample characteristics.

Nonparametric Configural Frequency Analysis (CFA)

CFA analyzes multivariate frequency distributions focusing on single cells of contingency tables rather than on the variables that make up a cross-classification (Krauth & Lienert, 1973; von Eye, 1990). In its basic form, CFA asks whether observed cell frequencies, o, statistically differ from expected cell frequencies, e, or, whether

$$o < e \text{ or } o > e \tag{22}$$

for each cell. Statistical tests used for comparison of observed and expected cell frequencies include the binomial test and X^2 tests. Tests typically are performed under protection of the local experimentwise error alpha (for details, see von Eye, 1990).

Classical, nonparametric CFA (Krauth & Lienert, 1973) estimates expected cell frequencies from the data using the log-linear main effect model

$$\log e = \lambda_0 + \lambda_{(i)}^A + \lambda_{(j)}^B + , \ldots , \tag{23}$$

where lambda denotes the effect parameters and A, B, . . . denote variables. This approach is nonparametric in the sense that it draws information from only the sample. A priori information, population parameters, or parameters specifying sampling distributions typically are not taken into account.

The log-linear main effect model proposes that a frequency distribution can be statistically explained from the main effects of the variables under study. In other words, it assumes total independence of all variables. If, for one or more cells, the null hypothesis that negates the propositions made in (22) must be rejected, one can assume that variables are, at least locally, associated (cf. Havránek & Lienert, 1984). If such a local association is described by $o > e$, the pattern of cell indexes describes a *type*. If $o < e$, the pattern of cell indexes describes an *antitype*. Types and antitypes are considered concepts of special importance and meaning in a sample. In the present context, patterns of cell indexes describe patterns of life events, as discussed earlier in this chapter.

Estimation of expected cell frequencies from (23) can be done using

$$e_{ijk...} = \frac{o^A_{i...}\, o^B_{.j..}\, o^C_{..k...} \cdots}{N^{d-1}} \qquad (24)$$

where $o^A_{i...}$ denotes the ith marginal frequency of variable A, $o^B_{.j...}$ is the marginal frequency of variable B, $o^C_{..k...}$ is the marginal frequency of variable C, and so on; N denotes the sample size, and d is the number of variables under study. Obviously, (24) exclusively uses sample information for estimation of expected cell frequencies.

Although the nonparametric main effect model may be appropriate in many contexts (see Lienert, 1978), we propose that, in life event research, population parameters can fruitfully be used. Population parameters describe the probabilities of life events. More specifically suppose a variable has I categories with $I > 1$, and $i = 1, . . . , I$. With probabilities for all variable categories known we estimate expected cell frequencies in a fashion analogous to (24) as follows:

$$e_{ijk...} = N \pi_{i...}\, \pi_{.j...}\, \pi_{..k...} \cdots \qquad (25)$$

In contrast to (24), Equation (25) uses no sample information concerning marginal distributions at all. Rather, only information describing the population is used. Parametric CFA estimates expected cell frequencies using (25) rather than (24).

As was pointed out by Spiel and von Eye (1993), interpretation of types and antitypes may not be straightforward. There may be two reasons why types and antitypes can be detected. Sole application of CFA does not provide one with explanations for discrepancies between observed and expected cell frequencies. The first reason is, as in standard, nonparametric CFA, the presence of local variable associations. The second reason is that the sample may not belong to the population described by the parameters used in (25). These two reasons for identification of types and antitypes can be present simultaneously.

To enable clear-cut interpretation of types and antitypes, one has to test whether the sample under study was drawn from the population that is described with the parameters used in (25). If one has reason to assume the sample stems from some other population, application of (24) for estimation of expected cell frequencies and interpretation of results with no reference to the population is recommended. If, however, the null hypothesis of no differences between the sample and the population cannot be rejected, types and antitypes may indeed reflect local associations that are present in the population. For the following example we assume no discrepancy between population and sample characteristics.

The example uses the two variables, married (M; yes = 1, no = 0) and birth of a child (C; yes = 1, no = 0). These variables had been observed in a sample of N = 601 couples that, at an earlier point in time, had expressed their wish for a child. The two life events, M and C, are crossed with the variable waiting time for a child. This time can, subjectively, be either long or short (W; l, s). Table 7.2 contains the cross-classification of these variables. According to (16) or (20), the cross-classification of the variables, M, C, and W has 2^3 = 8 cells. The left-hand block in Table 7.2 gives all cell indexes or configurations.

It is important to recognize the character of the variable W in Table 7.2 as subjective. The categories "long" and "short" do not necessarily reflect duration as measured in standard units of time. Rather, they reflect individuals' evaluations of the length of time spent before the child arrived. If there is no child, these categories describe individuals' perceptions concerning the length of the waiting time during which no child has arrived.

Keeping this in mind, one can interpret configurations as illustrated using the following sample cases: Configuration 1/1 signifies that, in the eyes of a married individual, it took long before a child arrived; configuration 1/0 indicates that, in the eyes of a married individual, there is already a long waiting period but still, no child; configuration 0/1 indicates that, in the eyes of an unmarried individual, it took long before a child arrived.

The next column in Table 7.2 contains the population probabilities for each configuration. Population probabilities typically are taken from census reports (see, e.g., Spiel & von Eye, in preparation). These joint probabilities were calculated using (25). The prior probabilities were $\pi(M{=}1)$ = 0.6, $\pi(M{=}0)$ = 0.4, $\pi(C{=}1)$ = 0.6, $\pi(C{=}0)$ = 0.4, $\pi(W{=}l)$ = 0.8, $\pi(W{=}s)$ = 0.2. The joint probabilities reflect the assumptions of the main effect model. Specifically, they reflect the assumption that the variables, M, C, and W are totally independent of each other. The estimated expected cell frequencies

TABLE 7.2
Parametric CFA of the Cross-Classification of the Variables,
Marital Status (M), Waiting Time (I), and Parenthood (C)

Configurations CWM	π_{ijk}	o	e	X^2	p	T/A
1/1	.29	207	174.29	6.14	< a*	T
1/0	.07	49	42.07	1.14	0.29	
1s1	.19	109	114.19	0.24	0.62	
1s0	.05	35	30.05	0.82	0.37	
0/1	.19	105	114.19	0.17	0.68	
0/0	.02	25	12.02	14.02	< α*	T
0s1	.13	60	78.13	4.21	0.04	
0s0	.03	11	18.03	2.74	0.10	

Note: $N = 601$.

in the next column result from multiplying the joint probabilities with N. The next column contains Pearson X^2-components for the comparisons of observed with expected cell frequencies. The last column contains either the tail probabilities for the X^2-components or a label indicating that this tail probability is less than α^*. To control the local experiment-wise α we used the Bonferroni method that resulted in the adjusted threshold $\alpha^* = 0.05/8 = 0.00625$.

CFA revealed two types. The first is described by configuration 1/1. As was pointed out before, these are individuals that are married and had to wait a subjectively long period of time before they had a child. From the independence assumption, we expected about 174 individuals to display this pattern; however, 207 were observed. The second type is described by configuration 0/0. These are also individuals for which the waiting time is too long. However, they are not married and have no child. More than twice as many individuals as expected showed this pattern.

DISCUSSION

This chapter presents a methodological discussion of life events' spacing and sequencing. The discussion covers two basic issues. The first issue concerns constellations of life events. We discussed the patterning of life events that are experienced once, of life events that are experienced repeatedly, and of the time elapsed before, between, or after life events. We used elementary combinatorics and specified functions using elementary combinatorics to calculate numbers of combinations, variations, and of other constellations. In addition, we are able to completely enumerate all possible constellations.

This chapter covered only sample cases. In the combinatorial domain more elaborated approaches to combinatorics have been discussed. Substantively, additional characteristics of life events can be of interest. For example, thus far, life events were treated as having no temporal extension. However, many events can be thought of as spanning periods of time. For example, car accidents typically take only a few seconds to happen; in contrast, the birth of a child often takes many hours. If one considers puberty a life event, it lasts a number of years. Thus, one characteristic of life events to be considered when enumerating patterns is their temporal extension.

If duration is a characteristic of life events, they can overlap. For example, during a wedding celebration, accidents can happen or, during puberty, one can fall in love. Thus, patterns of life events may have to consider overlapping or partly overlapping events.

As was pointed out earlier, individuals respond emotionally to life events. These responses may vary depending on individuals' temperamental and personality characteristics. For instance, whereas some individuals may respond coolly to a big win in the lottery and not change their style of living at all, others may quit their jobs and retire on the Mediterranean coast.

Because of these highly subjective characteristics of life events, it may be problematic to use life events as main effects in an analysis of variance or log-linear design. Because of individuals' different responses, they cannot be considered exposed to the same "treatment." Life events can only be used as factor levels if individuals respond in similar ways to these events. As an alternative one can generate patterns of life events in which the same event is subclassified according to the emotional responses shown by individuals experiencing them.

From a life-span perspective of interest, emotional responses to life events may vary with age. For instance, death of a parent can be expected to arouse different responses when a child is 15 versus 50 years of age. Thus, whenever researchers form patterns of life events, the age of individuals that experience these events needs to be taken into account.

The second issue concerns statistical analysis of patterns of life events. We used the Parametric Configural Frequency Analysis (CFA; Spiel & von Eye, 1993) as an example of a statistical method suited for analysis of complete sets of life event patterns. CFA allows us to answer questions concerning the observed frequency of life event patterns relative to some model that determines expected frequencies (Krauth & Lienert, 1973; von Eye, 1990). Additional questions concerning life events, responses to life events, and characteristics of individuals that experience life events are easily derived. Sample questions concern the patterns of environmental and personality characteristics that predict successful coping with adverse life events. Questions of this type can be answered using logistic regression or prediction CFA. In addition, one can ask questions concerning covariation patterns of life events, personality, temperament, and environmental variables. Questions of this type can be answered using methods of cluster analysis, structural equations modeling, log-linear modeling, or, again, CFA.

One important result that can be derived from this chapter is that, in completely enumerating constellations of life events, their sequences and spacing can lead to large numbers of patterns. To be able to analyze these patterns one needs large sample sizes. Thus, to be able to analyze more than one or two life events, one may have to consider strategies to reduce the size of cross-classifications. Sample strategies include collapsing across categories, consideration of selected categories, and confining analyses to effects of low order.

Whatever method for statistical analysis is applied, an important step, to be performed before data analysis, involves the specification of the patterns of life events under study. This specification can be accomplished using combinatorics. This is why this chapter placed strong emphasis on elementary combinatorics.

ACKNOWLEDGMENTS

The authors are indebted to Tom Feagans for helpful philosophical discussions and to Scott Hershberger, Peter C. M. Molenaar, Mike Rovine, Mark Stemmler, and Pat Wamboldt for critical discussions of earlier versions of this chapter.

REFERENCES

Brim, O. G., Jr., & Ryff, C. D. (1980). On the properties of life events. In P. B. Baltes & O. G. Brim, Jr. (Eds.), *Life-span development and behavior* (Vol. 3, pp. 367–388). New York: Academic Press.

Dohrenwend, B. S., & Dohrenwend, B. P. (Eds.). (1974). *Stressful life events: Their nature and effects*. New York: Wiley.

Elliott, G. R., & Eisdorfer, C. (Eds.). (1982). *Stress and human health. Analysis and implications of research*. New York: Springer.

Filipp, S.-H. (1982). Kritische Lebensereignisse als Brennpunkte einer angewandten Entwicklungspsychologie des mittleren und höheren Erwachsenenalters [Critical life events as focal points of an applied developmental psychology of middle and late adulthood]. In R. Oerter & L. Montada (Eds.), *Entwicklungspsychologie* [Developmental psychology] (pp. 769–788). München: Urban & Schwarzenberg.

Filipp, S.-H., & Gräser, H. (1982). Psychologische Prävention im Umfeld kritischer Lebensereignisse [Psychological prevention when individuals face critical life events]. In J. Brandtstädter & A. von Eye (Eds.), *Psychologische Prävention: Grundlagen, Programme, Methoden* [Psychological prevention: Bases, programs, methodology] (pp. 155–195). Bern: Huber.

Goldberg, K., Newman, M., & Haynsworth, E. (1972). Combinatorial analysis. In M. Abramowitz & I. A. Stegun (Eds.), *Handbook of mathematical functions with formulas, graphs, and mathematical tables* (pp. 821–873). New York: Dover.

Havránek, T., & Lienert, G. A. (1984). Local and regional vs. global contingency testing. *Biometrical Journal, 26,* 483–494.

Holmes, T. H., & Rahe, R. H. (1967). The social readjustment rating scale. *Journal of Psychosomatic Research, 11,* 213–218.

Hultsch, D. F., & Plemons, J. K. (1979). Life events and life-span development. In P. B. Baltes & O. G. Brim, Jr. (Eds.), *Life-span development and behavior* (Vol. 2, pp. 1–37). New York: Academic Press.

Krauth, J., & Lienert, G. A. (1973). *KFA. Die Konfigurationsfrequenzanalyse und ihre Anwendung in Psychologie und Medizin* [CFA. Configural frequency analysis and its application in psychology and medicine]. Freiburg: Alber.

Lienert, G. A. (Ed.). (1978). *Angewandte Konfigurationsfrequenzanalyse* [Applied configural frequency analysis]. Frankfurt am Main: Athenäum.

Müller, N. (1980). Functions on life-trees for explaining social phenomena, with special reference to political socialization. *International Journal of Policy Analysis and Information Systems, 4,* 317–330.

Müller, N. (1981). *Die Life Tree-Konzeption: Einige Gedanken und Thesen* [The life-tree concept: Some thoughts and propositions]. Unpublished manuscript, University of Osnabrück.

Spiel, C., & von Eye, A. (1993). Configural frequency analysis as a parametric method for the search of types and antitypes. *Biometrical Journal, 35,* 151–164.

Spiel, C., & von Eye, A. (in preparation). *Wen bilden wir aus—oder stammen Österreichs Psychologie- und Publizistikstudenten aus dieser Welt? Eine Anwendung der parametrischen KFA* [Who do we train—or do Austria's students of psychology and communications sciences belong to the general population? An application of parametric CFA].

Thober, B. (1981). *Methodische Überlegungen zum Life Tree-Ansatz* [Methodological considerations concerning the life tree-concept]. Unpublished manuscript, University of Osnabrück.

von Eye, A. (1990). *Introduction to configural frequency analysis the search for types and antitypes in cross-classifications.* Cambridge, England: Cambridge University Press.

von Eye, A., & Brandtstädter, J. (1981). Lebensbäume als entwicklungspsychologische Modelle: Ansätze zur Analyse von Lebensereignissequenzen [Life trees as models for developmental psychology: Approaches for analysis of life event sequences]. *Trierer Psychologische Berichte, 8*(2).

CHAPTER EIGHT

Adolescents' Adaptation to Structural Changes in Family Relationships With Parental Divorce: A Combinatorial Model

Michelle L. Batchelder
University of Texas at Austin

Divorce is an event that changes the lives of many parents' children around the world. The prevalence of divorce in Western industrialized societies has accompanied social concern for the future well-being of these children. Divorce is certainly an event that requires active psychological adaptation on behalf of all family members involved, adults and children alike. Yet, common expectations that divorce has negative impact on the development of children may prevent us from considering how parental divorce may indeed benefit some children. Whether the impact of divorce on psychological well-being is detrimental or beneficial, all participants in divorce must adjust to losses and novelties in family relationships as those relationships undergo radical changes.

This chapter focuses on young women's psychological transformations as they adapt to parental divorce and family reconstitution in adolescence. The goal is to investigate the role of family members as social contexts in the coping processes of individuals. The analysis focuses on how the structure of family relationships changes as family members disperse in the process of divorce, and how the dispersed family structure becomes reintegrated in new ways as the former spouses separately construct new families.

On the basis of interviews with a small sample of young women from divorced families, the chapter highlights the *variability* in the reorganization of individual-context relations as well as in the organization of individual adaptation to relational changes following divorce. The empirical evidence illustrates that, whereas the divorce-related experiences of individuals may

165

be nominally similar (e.g., parental divorce, remarriage of custodial parent, conflict between parents), the structure of the relationship transformations and life events, the meaning of those changes for individuals and families, and the subsequent outcomes of individuals and family relationships vary greatly. The discussion centers around the extent to which many of these forms of individual adaptation may provide the basis for sufficient coping with parental divorce, whereas others may leave young women with persistent sensitivity in several domains of family relationships long after the event.

Parental Divorce and the Restructuring of Interpersonal Relationships: A Metaphor Borrowed From Chemistry

Social scientists often import metaphors from other sciences to help capture the complexities of social phenomena. Changes in family relationships brought on by divorce can be compared to the structural transformation of molecules during chemical changes. A common molecule, such as water (H_2O), is comprised of atoms of different chemical elements, two atoms of hydrogen and one of oxygen. A water molecule has bonds and exchanges of energy between its atoms, which *in tandem* maintain the molecule in a steady state. When heat or electricity disrupts the stability of the molecule, its structure changes. The arrangement of the atoms and the previous amount of energy in the molecule transform as the bonds between atoms of hydrogen and oxygen break. Forces of attraction and repulsion between atoms of the original molecule and other atoms in the environment determine what form the reorganization takes. Whereas some of the original atoms of the water molecule remain and rebuild some of the old bonds, other atoms of the original structure form new bonds with different atoms and reorganize as new molecules. When water boils, for example, the two hydrogen atoms of the molecule sometimes recombine to form a hydrogen molecule (H_2), while the oxygen atom may bond with a nearby oxygen atom to form a new oxygen molecule (O_2). The newly formed molecules arrive at a state of restructured stability, that is, at least until the molecules enter another phase of structural reorganization. This metaphor offers a conceptualization of how divorce influences changes in family relationships.

Divorce as a Transformation of Family Relationships

Divorce brings about dissociation in the relationship between parents but inevitably also has some effect on the parents' relationships with their children: Parent-child relationships cannot be isolated from changes in the relationships between parents. Perhaps the closest comparable change in parent-child relationships to that found in divorce may be the case where a child loses a parent through death. Yet, even loss through death may be less complex: Although the young child whose parent dies must adjust to living with a single parent whose marriage has ended, the experience of transformed family relationships is different from the divorce experience (cf. Hetherington, 1972). A family in which death has permanently removed the parent from the child's family environment contains fewer members and, therefore, fewer active relationships.

In contrast, a child of divorced parents must develop new ways of relating with her two living-but-separated parents, that is, the parent with whom she continues to live and the parent who lives in a separate residence (Ahrons, 1979). The breakup in the parents' relationship necessitates the formation of new relationships between the child and each parent. When faced with parental divorce, the child who is forced to alter her relationships necessarily develops coping mechanisms for dealing with these changes. Because human beings are actively relating to their environments, they start to cope with traumatic events the very moment they begin.

Traditionally, psychological approaches to traumatic events have de-emphasized the active coping process that begins simultaneously with the inception of trauma. Classical approaches to coping processes, moreover, have highlighted intrapersonal cognitions about life stressors and personal resources for adjustment (Lazarus & Folkman, 1984). My focus is on active coping processes that consist of the reorganization of relationships between individuals and their environments.

Divorce creates a situation of disorganization in relationships between (previously) closely related persons. In psychologically coping with the trauma of divorce, the child seeks ways of relating to her altered environment that afford sufficient psychological adaptation (Valsiner, 1989). In some cases, this coping effort succeeds and the person overcomes much of the effects of the divorce. For others, the coping effort does not completely resolve the divorce trauma and leaves vestiges of interpersonal difficulties lingering later in development.

Research on Children and Divorce

A number of psychological studies have been conducted in the past three decades to examine how different aspects of parental divorce influence the lives of children. Typically, this research focuses on gender and age-specific processes of adaptation, comparing children from divorced families and intact families.

Comparisons of children by gender reveal gender-specific styles of response to parental divorce. A longitudinal investigation of school-age middle-class children revealed that boys "externalize" their psychological problems by manifesting behavioral problems, whereas girls "internalize" their psychological problems in ways such as depression (Hetherington, Cox, & Cox, 1978, 1979, 1985). While much research confirms the work of Hetherington and her colleagues (Guidubaldi, Cleminshaw, Perry, Nastasi, & Lightel, 1986), other findings suggest that marital dissolution has a greater impact on girls than on boys with girls presenting more problem behavior, dissatisfaction, and distress (Allison & Furstenberg, 1989).

Studies have also evaluated whether responses to parental divorce depend on the gender of children's custodial parent. These studies show that children benefit more from living with their same-sex parents after divorce (Allison & Furstenberg, 1989; Hetherington et al., 1985; Peterson & Zill, 1986; Santrok & Warshak, 1979). Still another set of studies has evaluated gender differences in child adjustment to the remarriage of custodial parents: Psychological adaptation appeared to be optimal for boys whose mothers remarry and add stepfathers to the family residence (Allison & Furstenberg, 1989; Clingempeel, Brand, & Ievoli, 1984; Ganong & Coleman, 1987; Hetherington et al., 1985; Peterson & Zill, 1986; Santrok, Warshak, Lindbergh, & Meadows, 1982; Vuchinich, Hetherington, Vuchinich, & Clingempeel, 1991).

In addition, age at separation was shown to influence psychological adaptation to parental divorce. Wallerstein's (1984, 1985, 1987; Wallerstein & Kelly, 1980) longitudinal study revealed that 10 years after parental divorce children who were in middle childhood when the separation occurred experienced more psychological difficulty than children younger or older at the time of breakup (Wallerstein, 1984, 1985, 1987; Wallerstein & Kelly, 1980). Gender differences were found at various periods of development. In contrast, other work has found that younger children have more psychological maladaptation in the long run (Allison & Furstenberg, 1989; Hetherington, 1972).

This research may be beneficial for therapeutic endeavors with large populations grouped by global variables, such as gender or age at separation. Government pamphlets might provide general advice to divorcing parents for guiding the adjustment to divorce of daughters versus that of sons. However, the data may be of little help to therapists or parents who want to optimize children's adaptation. These limitations are inherent to population-based statistical methodology for making inferences about systematic functioning within individuals (Valsiner, 1986). Investigators have often contrasted groups of subjects, for example, boys and girls from divorced families or mother-custody and father-custody children, to find generalities of the effects of gender or custody arrangements on the behavior of children and adults. However, this strategy for studying complex psychological issues involves at least two inappropriate assumptions. The first assumption is that the complex, structurally organized psychological phenomenon of divorce is reducible to its supposed constituent parts, such as the gender of children and of custodial parents. The second assumption is a consequence of searching for modal or prototypical ways that children cope with parental divorce; that is, the most frequent or average way of coping is assumed to be normative (i.e., "the" only way children adapt).

In contrast, focusing on tranformations in the relationships between person and environment addresses individual differences in children's adaptation. Children do not all respond to the stressors of divorce in one definitive manner (a point also made by other investigators; e.g., Hetherington, 1979, and Wallerstein, 1984). Instead of normative development, the amount of variability within the population created by the idiosyncratic psychological patterns of its members is of interest to psychological research (Valsiner, 1984). As each family and its members cope with divorce individually, variability of responses is normal and expected.

CONCEPTUAL BACKGROUND OF THE MODEL

To analyze the multiplicity of possible forms that intrafamily relationships may assume through divorce and family reconstitution, a theoretical model, which represents all possible versions of these relationships and their transformations for a specified set of conditions, is necessary. This combinatorial model of intrafamily relationships applies to the case of nuclear and neolocal families in contemporary Western industrialized cultures that practice strict but sometimes serial monogamy. It should be noted that the very fact that otherwise strict monogamy sometimes becomes serially organized sets the stage for divorce and psychological problems related to it.

To consider what family relationships after divorce are like, I outline a basic structure of relationships that families may adopt when their composition changes (cf. Kreppner, 1983, 1985; Kreppner, Paulsen, & Schuetze, 1982). The basic unit of the model is the dyadic relationship. A family of three, for example, that consists of mother, father, and child has three dyadic relationships: The relationship between the parents, between the mother and child, and between the father and child.

Each individual in a dyad also has a relation to the other. The dyadic relationship between mother and child, for example, contains two relations; the mother has a relation to the child, $M \rightarrow C$, and the child has one to the mother, $C \rightarrow M$. To describe the quality of dyadic relationships, each relation is assigned a valence, positive (+), neutral (0), and negative (−). A relation with a valence attached is called an *orientation*, to denote a directional attitude toward another person, which constitutes the quality of the respective relation (see Newcomb, 1961). Thus, the relation between mother and child has two orientations (e.g., $M \rightarrow C = 0$ and $C \rightarrow M = +$). Because I arbitrarily limit the quality of these orientations to three valences, I clearly oversimplify the reality of family relationships: Some orientations may be ambivalent, that is, simultaneously positive and negative; in addition, the valence of orientations may change over time.

Each dyadic relationship and its relational structure can be represented in a 3-by-3 matrix. Figure 8.1 presents a general matrix for mother-father relationships that contains all possible orientations and possible outcomes in marital relationships. Two clear-cut marital outcomes are assumed to exist: In cases when mother and father have mutually positive orientations the marriage persists, and in cases when mother and father have mutually negative orientations the marriage ends in divorce (Levinger, 1979). When at least one partner has a negative orientation toward the other (outcome = D?), the marital relationship may end in divorce. In the case where at least one partner has a neutral orientation toward the other (outcome = M?), the marriage is considered "at risk" for divorce, because it may continue if the other is willing to tolerate the partner's indifferent attitude. Figure 8.2 depicts the nine possible pathways of transformation in a highly conflictual relationship between mother and father (mother has a positive orientation toward father and father has a negative orientation toward mother). A relationship between spouses organized in this way may not last long. It may transform in five different ways, that end in divorce, or in three different ways that put the marriage "at risk" for divorce. Only in the last transformation is the marriage expected to persist.

When the organization of the relationship between spouses leads to divorce, children then have to cope with it. This may involve many forms of family reorganization, and in fact, these family reorganizations are probably as diverse as the divorced families themselves. Consider first the dyadic relationships of an intact family of three, consisting of mother, father, and child. Since each dyad contains two relations (as illustrated in Fig. 8.1; e.g., M → F, F → M) and a family of three members has three dyadic relationships, the total number of relations that exists in a family of three is six.

The potential for diversity in the conditions of dyadic family relationships is augmented by matching each relation in a dyad with an element from the set of valences that each may adopt (e.g., positive, neutral, and negative). All possible combinations of the resulting orientations in a family of three

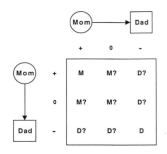

FIG. 8.1. General matrix description of mother-father relationships with orientations that may lead to divorce (D, D?), to being "at risk" for divorce (M?), or to continuation of marriage (M).

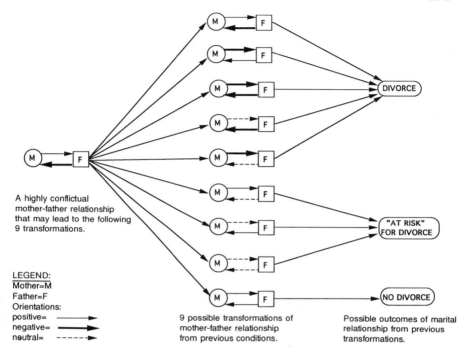

FIG. 8.2. Possible pathways of transformation in mother-father relationships that may lead to divorce, or "at risk" for divorce, or to continuation of marriage (i.e., no divorce).

sum up to 27 (that is, 3 dyadic relationships multiplied by the 9 possible combinations of orientations within each dyad as shown in the matrix of Fig. 8.1; see the Appendix for computations of the number of possible relationship combinations in families of different sizes).

The presence of more than one child in a family further increases the potential variability in family relationships and relationship transformations in the case of divorce and family reconstitution. Figure 8.3 presents sets of possible dyadic intrafamily relationships as a function of the number of children per family.

The combinatorial model of possible family relationships after parental divorce includes three graphs. As the general case, the first graph shows the number of dyadic orientations among members of any family in its present state according to the number of children in the family. Here, the number of orientations equals the number of dyadic relations in a family because each relation is assigned a specific valence (i.e., M → C +).

The second graph represents all possible combinations of orientations in dyadic family relationships, given the possibilities that are pertinent to divorce by the number of children in the family (i.e., nine possible combina-

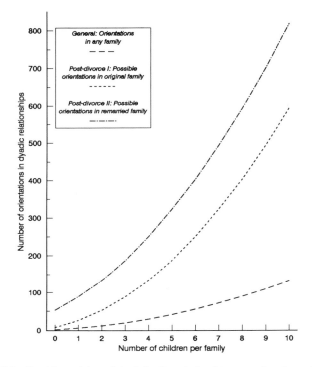

FIG. 8.3. Combinatorial model of dyadic relationships as a function of the number of children per family for a general case and postdivorce original and remarried families.

tions of orientations for each dyad minus the mutually positive orientation between original parents). The third graph adds two stepparents to the set of dyadic family relationships. In the case when both original parents eventually remarry, the number of possible combinations increases with the total number of children. For this graph, the number of children in a family includes those from the predivorce family and any stepsiblings or half siblings added through family reconstitution.

The graphs illustrate how the complexity of family relationships increases with the number of children and adults in a family (see also Visher & Visher, 1979). Any family with 1 child contains only 6 dyadic orientations. However, all possible combinations of dyadic orientations among members of an original family with only 1 child postdivorce total 26, and a reconstituted family with only 1 child has 89 possible combinations. At the other extreme, whereas any family with 6 children has 56 dyadic orientations, a postdivorce family with 6 children has 251 possible dyadic orientations, and a reconstituted family has 404 possible orientations. If after divorce a family with 2 children from the original family reconstitutes by adding 2 stepparents and

4 stepsiblings to the family (2 stepsiblings per stepparent), the number of adults in the family increases from 2 to 4 and the number of children increases from 2 to 6. Thus, after divorce, the number of possible combinations of orientations in dyadic family relationships rises from 53 in the original family to 404 in the reconstituted family.

How does our formal combinatorial model relate to the actual composition of U.S. families, some of which end in parental divorce and others that reconstitute? Table 8.1 compares statistical data regarding the percentages of families in the United States in 1989 with up to four children, and the corresponding possible combinations of dyadic orientations from the combinatorial model. (Note that after parental divorce children are counted as members of their custodial parent's family only.)

The very fact that outcomes of family relationships following divorce can be so complex sets the stage for wide variability in family environments. The model illustrates that any family has only a subset of all possible orientations. Across a sample of many families, the whole pool of possible orientations may be present. This picture is still oversimplified because accurate descriptions of any one dyadic relation may require more than one valence (as for ambivalent orientations). Moreover, the model does not account for transformations in relationships over time. Whereas this combinatorial model demonstrates the potential for variability in family relationships after divorce, the life experiences of individuals and families are necessarily more complex.

REORGANIZATION OF FAMILY RELATIONSHIPS
THROUGH DIVORCE WITHIN CULTURAL CONTEXTS

Children's coping with parental divorce takes place in the context of cultural meanings about marriage, divorce, remarriage, as well as child development. More often than not, in the cultural environments of Western industrialized societies, the effects of divorce on children have overall negative connotations. Folk models that focus on the deleterious effects of divorce on children are widespread. These stories can serve as preventive measures that keep some parents from divorcing "in the best interests of the child." In some cases, a child may be exposed continuously to conflict and dissatisfaction in the relationship between parents. As a consequence, the child may suffer detrimental psychological effects. Even though this is not the intention of a culture, it is the outcome of the culture's primary motivation to keep families together.

To consider the context-dependent adaptation of children to divorce, the following section presents a discussion of transformations in the psychological and social environments that are specific to contemporary Western cultures.

TABLE 8.1

Comparison of Numbers of Children in U.S. Families in 1989
and Postdivorce Possible Relationship Combinations

	Families[a]		Postdivorce Possible Relationship Combinations	
Number of Children[b]	Percentage in Population		Original Family	Reconstituted Family
0	50.9		8	53
1	20.7		26	89
2	18.7		53	134
3	7.1		89	188
4+[c]	2.7		134	251

[a]From U.S. Bureau of Census, *Statistical Abstract of the United States*, 1991.
[b]Children are counted only as members of custodial parent's family.
[c]4+ = four or more children.

Domains of Adjustment in Family Relationships

Family living arrangements after divorce change when one parent moves out of the family residence. This situation introduces a new psychological environment to which all family members must adapt. The following discussion presents some specific domains of adjustment in family relationships after divorce (see also Ahrons & Rodgers, 1987).

Child as Replacement for Absent Parent. For most children of divorce, when one parent moves out of the family residence, a household previously headed by two parents becomes a single-parent household. The child must now cultivate a new relationship with the single parent as the role of the other parent in the home diminishes. Depending on the custodial parent's ability to cope as a single parent, he or she may turn to one or more of the children at home to help maintain family life for those members who remain after divorce. The custodial parent may expect the child to perform the emotional or behavioral roles of the former spouse and residential parent. The child may become the custodial parent's confidante as the parent shares information that had previously been discussed among adult family members only (i.e., financial or sexual matters). This sharing may emerge as a new form of intimacy in the parent–child relationship (Wallerstein & Kelly, 1980). On the other hand, exposure to adult sexuality may be difficult to adjust to for a child whose socialization has excluded such "horrors" of the "adult world."

The absent parent also leaves behind the responsibility of daily household chores for the remaining family members. A child who performs household chores that had been carried out by the now absent parent may require psychological adjustment to these new responsibilities. The child may respond in different ways, such as enjoyment in new adult roles, neutral feelings, or resentment for having to take on the chore. Whereas the child's helping with the task may alleviate the emotional burden of her parent, the child herself may experience an emotional burden requiring psychological adjustment and social support.

Visitation Arrangements. In American White, middle-class subculture and other cultures, parents end their marriage contracts with divorce decrees that often regulate the postdivorce relationship between children and non-custodial parents. In the decree, a "visitation" schedule may lay out when and for how long a noncustodial parent and child spend time together, which serves as the framework for the maintenance and transformation of this relationship. For the child, these arrangements may involve cherished, rare times spent with the parent who is now free of the everyday management of the child's life. Or perhaps, the child may experience this contractual relationship as forced and unpleasant. We see later some complications in the relationship between noncustodial parent and child that may occur during visitation in noncustodial reconstituted households that include stepparents and stepsiblings.

Child as a Mediator Between Parents. Former spouses with children from their terminated marriage may have a more complicated relationship after divorce than those without children. Although spouses have ended their marital relationship, both still continue the role as parents of the children from their former marriage. If parents wish to continue relationships with their children, they most likely will have to interact with each other long after the divorce decree is signed. As the needs of the children change with development and their own needs change with their respective life situations, parents will have to confer about child care and financial matters.

Although this type of communication may have been customary before the divorce, afterward interactions may be difficult or even impossible. Parents in this situation may enlist their children, who maintain relationships with the former spouse, as "go-betweens." If one parent, for example, wants to alter the predetermined visitation schedule for some reason, arranging changes may be easier with a child than with the ex-spouse (especially when the ex-spousal relationship is conflictual). When the child serves as an intermediary, she may have any of a variety of responses, such as feeling embroiled in parental conflict, mature in the adult role, or loyalty conflicts between parents.

Adaptation to Remarriage of Parents. After parents end their marriage, one or both may restructure their families by remarrying a new partner who is not the parent of their children. Accompanying these increases in family size are qualitative changes in the family environment. Formerly unfamiliar people join together in family activities that range from special occasions, like holiday celebrations, to routine activities, such as mealtime gatherings. Children may live in or visit the stepfamily. As illustrated in the combinatorial model of Fig. 8.3, parental remarriage is likely to augment the complexity of family relationships after divorce. Children must adapt not only to the transformation in old relationships with members of the original family but also to expectations of family members to form intimate relationships with stepparents and stepsiblings. Mixing relationships with different levels of intimacy can foster confusion and doubts about where relationships stand. The roles of stepparents and stepchildren are often not clearly defined in the American culture and may be subject to experimentation. Consequently, adding the task of negotiating new relationships in reconstituted families after divorce may overburden a child. On the other hand, the addition of stepfamily members to a child's family network may provide supplementary social support for children's processes of adaptation.

Adaptation in Sibling Relationships. Divorce often creates a situation in which parents become less prominent in family life than in the predivorce family. The increased financial burdens of maintaining two households and a new social life outside the family are only two changes that may reduce the amount of time that the custodial parent is able to spend at home with the children. In divorced families with more than one child, this situation can give way for siblings to depend more on one another than on parents and develop support networks between children at home. At times, previously rivalrous siblings may put aside their former conflicts to develop coping strategies for the divorcing process. Sibling rivalries, of course, may also intensify in the context of divorce.

Child's Psychological Support Systems. Adaptation of children and adolescents to parental divorce can take many forms. They may focus on activities outside the family or delve into religion, books, or drugs. They may also explain divorce-related events to themselves, a therapeutic method for adjusting that provides knowledge of one's own experience. Talking to others about parental divorce is another way. Communication may come easily when friends share their own experiences of the divorce or with difficulty if an individual perceives the topic as taboo to "social others."

Whereas coping with parental divorce by oneself may be a solution, it may not be a sufficient solution. As demonstrated in the combinatorial model, the number of potential partners who may be interested in forming a supportive relationship with a child increases with the number of family members, especially in the case of family reorganization through parental remarriage. Social support networks that include extended family members, parents and siblings from the original and reconstituted family, and friends who share divorced family situations can provide much needed support for coping processes. Structured peer groups (e.g., religious youth groups) can offer friendship or even support geared toward divorce-specific coping. Each child's adaptation may include some combination of these social support systems.

METHOD OF THE STUDY

The respondents in this study were 11 female university students who were enrolled in introductory psychology courses (mostly freshmen and sophomores). The selection of only females was based on the folk model that women share intimate thoughts and feelings more readily with other women; the author was the female interviewer.

Respondents were interviewed in library cubicles for two 1-hour sessions held approximately 1 week apart. All but one of the 11 subjects agreed to have the interview audiotape-recorded. Interviews followed a semi-structured outline of possible divorce-related events gathered from pilot interviews, but respondents were also welcome to discuss other events. Completed interviews were transcribed roughly verbatim and the texts analyzed.

The structure of the interviews varied in form for each respondent. Although some spoke fluidly from the start, others were more guarded in their responses. The respondents had diverse areas of sensitivity and differed in their willingness to share them with a stranger. The recency of divorce may have also influenced the nature of responses; age at time of separation in the sample ranged from 3 to 18 years. Furthermore, the importance of divorce and its aftermath for each respondent varied at the time of interview regardless of the amount of time passed since parental separation.

Note that these data, in the form of retrospective interviews, may lack some accuracy compared with interviews held concurrently with family transformation. Respondents' memory may be altered by reinterpretation and reconstruction of past events. Salient and interpersonal events, however, often involved in the transformation of family relationships, are more likely to be remembered than other events (Fitzgerald & Surra, 1981). Replications of this study based on interviews concurrent with events of parental divorce may further substantiate these findings.

Description of the Cases

The divorce-related events and family life environments of the 11 respondents are presented in Table 8.2. The table first presents basic facts about each individual in the sample (Respondents A through K), their original families, and some divorce-related life events. The second part describes events related to parental remarriage (at least one parent of 7 respondents remarried). For example, Column J presents a history of life events for

TABLE 8.2

General Description of Cases in Sample

	Respondents										
Basic Facts	A	B	C	D	E	F	G	H	I	J	K
Original Family											
Number of Children	3	5	2	2	3	3	3	1	2	1	4
Respondent's Birth Order	1	3	1	1	3	1	1	1	1	1	4
R's Age at Separation	14	13	10	14	10	13	18	3	15	3	14
Parental Problems[a]	L	AQ	AQ	LIQ	AQ	Q	AQ	H	AQ	na	na
Initial Benefits of Divorce	+	–	–	+	–	–	–	na	–	na	–
R's Anticipation of Divorce	+	–	+/–	+	–	–	+	na+[b]	–	na	–
Custodial Parent	M	M	M	M	M	F	M	M	M	M	M
Parental Dating	MF	F	MF	MF	F	MF	MF	MF	MF	MF	MF
Visitation Frequency[c]	C > A	A	A > B	B	A >[d] C	A	A	C	A	C	C
Split-Sibling Residence	–	+	–	–	–	+	+	na	–	na	na
Changed Residential Parent	–	+	+	–	–	+	+	–	–	–	–
Mental Health Support	F	–	MF	FR	–	all	–	–	R	R	–
Religious Support	+	+	–	–	–	–	+	–	+	–	+

Reconstituted Family

Custodial Parent	–	–	+	–	+	+	–	–	–
Noncustodial Parent	+	+	+	+	+	–	–	+	+
Stepsiblings	0	na	0	2	6[e]	0	na	0	2
Half Siblings	2	na	0	0	0	1	na	1	0
Second Divorce	–	na	–	–	–[f]	+	na	+	–

'+' = presence; '–' = absence; '+/–' = ambivalence; na = not applicable for respondent and/or family; M = mother; F = father; R = respondent; all = entire family.

[a]*Parental Problems*: A = affair(s); L = alcoholism; I = mental illness; H = homosexual interests; Q = quarrels.

[b]Respondent H anticipated the second divorce that ended the reconstituted family of her custodial parent but did not expect the divorce that broke up her original family.

[c]*Visitation Frequency*: A = more than once a month. B = more than holidays only but at most once a month. C = holidays and vacations only. '>' = change in frequency over time from period soon after divorce to recent.

[d]Respondent E's older brother, who was having emotional problems, went to a boarding school for his junior year in high school.

[e]Respondent F has stepsiblings from the remarriage of both her parents, three from each reconstituted family.

[f]Only Respondent F has stepsiblings from the remarriage of both remarried parents in the home of Respondent F's single-parent family, the respondent's step-mother and children moved to a new residence. A new home for the reconstituted family was under construction: The remarried partners had not initiated a second divorce at the time of interview.

Respondent J: She has no siblings and her parents divorced when she was 3 years old. Her mother had child custody. Respondent J always lived with her mother and visited her father on holidays and vacations only. Although both her parents dated, only her father remarried. He had another child, the respondent's half sister, and terminated his second marriage. She also reported receiving some support from mental health professionals but not from religion or religious social groups.

Structural Comparison of Three Prototypical Cases. An analysis of the various structural transformations that family relationships undergo through divorce and the adaptation of individuals to such changes demonstrates high variability in families' and individuals' psychological adaptation to divorce-related events. In the following section, similarities and differences of life events in the divorcing process are discussed for three selected respondents in the sample. These three case studies were chosen because they represent a variety of transformations in family relationship structure after divorce and variations in the degree of sufficient coping with those transformations (e.g., beneficial effects of parental divorce vs. severe lingering effects). The discussion focuses on the positive and negative experiences of respondents in relation to relationships transformations. Figure 8.4 provides a comparative representation of the reorganized structure of family relationships postdivorce for Respondent A, Respondent B, and Respondent C. (To specify segments of the family transformations, I represent the column of Respondent A, for example, with "Fig. 8.4A" and the third box in column A with "Fig. 8.4.A.3.")

How the relationships in the families of these three respondents changed with parental separation, family reconstitution, and relationship closeness illustrates some key similarities and differences in individual and family psychological functioning after divorce. Although all three respondents have childhood experiences of parental separation and divorce in common, these events took place at different times in their lives, involved different interpersonal processes, for different reasons, and took on different psychological meaning for family participants.

The *parental separation* in Respondent A's case occurred when she was in high school; the separation was related to her father's alcoholism (see Fig. 8.4.A). The family's living arrangements changed when the father moved into an apartment. This family ultimately coped positively with these changes as the members supported one another emotionally and benefitted from the support of outside sources. In comparison, the divorcing process was much more complex for Respondent B (see Fig. 8.4.B). When she was in junior high school, her father moved out of the original family residence some time after her mother found out that he was having an affair. He moved in with the other woman and had a child with her out-of-wedlock. Respondent

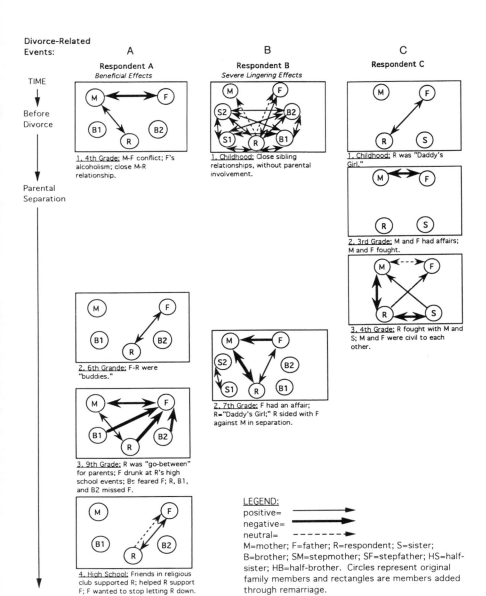

Divorce-Related
Events:

A

B

C

TIME

Before
Divorce

Parental
Separation

Respondent A
Beneficial Effects

1. 4th Grade: M-F conflict; F's
alcoholism; close M-R
relationship.

2. 6th Grade: F-R were
"buddies."

3. 9th Grade: R was "go-between"
for parents; F drunk at R's high
school events; Bs feared F; R, B1,
and B2 missed F.

4. High School: Friends in religious
club supported R; helped R support
F; F wanted to stop letting R down.

Respondent B
Severe Lingering Effects

1. Childhood: Close sibling
relationships, without parental
involvement.

2. 7th Grade: F had an affair;
R="Daddy's Girl;" R sided with F
against M in separation.

Respondent C

1. Childhood: R was "Daddy's
Girl."

2. 3rd Grade: M and F had affairs;
M and F fought.

3. 4th Grade: R fought with M and
S; M and F were civil to each
other.

LEGEND:
positive=
negative=
neutral=   - - - - - - - ▶
M=mother; F=father; R=respondent; S=sister;
B=brother; SM=stepmother; SF=stepfather; HS=half-
sister; HB=half-brother. Circles represent original
family members and rectangles are members added
through remarriage.

181

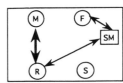

4. 5th Grade: F's remarriage; R wanted to live with F and SM; R argued with M.

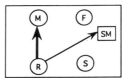

5. 7th-8th Grade: R cried often, did poorly in school, and told M that she hated M.

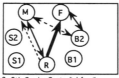

3. 9th Grade: Custodial family moved to smaller house; B2 moved in with father and future SM; B1 away at college; R talked to M with menstruation.

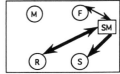

6. 9th Grade: SM had hysterectomy; SM resented R and S; R felt caught between parents.

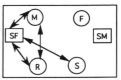

7. 11th Grade: M's remarriage; close custodial family.

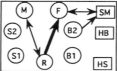

4. 12th Grade: R rejected F for "mistreating" M, i.e., not paying child support & having a child "out of wedlock."

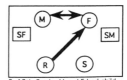

8. 12th Grade: M and F had child support court battle; F secretly ended R's romantic relationship.

Present

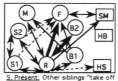

5. Present: R=best friends with M & F; B1, B2, F have close relations; M has financial problems with F.

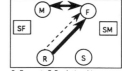

5. Present: Other siblings "take off the rose-colored glasses" about F's behavior toward family.

9. Present: R-F relationship neutralizes.

FIG. 8.4. Transformations of family relationships across time of Respondent A, Respondent B, and Respondent C.

182

B's parents did not consummate their divorce until 5 years after the father had left the original family residence. The drawn out nature of parental separation and the postponed divorce as well as the complexity of adding new relationships to the family system in ways stigmatized by U.S. middle and upper class subcultures (i.e., cohabitation between unmarried adults and bearing children out-of-wedlock) contributed to the respondent's difficulty adapting to divorce-related events. In the third case, although both parents of Respondent C were reportedly unhappy with their marriage a year before separation (i.e., she witnessed her parents fighting and knew that both had affairs), they terminated their marriage cordially when she was in elementary school (see Fig. 8.4.C). Thus, although all three respondents experienced the same nominal event, parental divorce, the structural changes and conditions of the event varied widely.

The three cases illustrate differences in patterns of *family reconstitution*. At the time of the interviews, neither parent of Respondent A had remarried, whereas Respondent B had experienced her father's remarriage and Respondent C had experienced the remarriage of both her original parents. In the two cases of remarriage, the fathers moved in with their lovers soon after the parents had separated. Whereas the remarriage of Respondent B's father brought half siblings into her network of family relationships, no stepsiblings were added to the reconstituted family networks of either respondent.

The changes in *stepfamily relationships* also followed different courses for these two respondents. Respondent B described no orientation to her stepmother until a period just before the interview when the respondent felt positively toward her; Respondent B felt sorry for her stepmother because of what the stepparent had endured living with the respondent's father. In contrast, Respondent C's previously positive relationship with her noncustodial stepmother turned sour soon after her father's remarriage, when the stepmother had a medically necessary hysterectomy. Several years later, the same respondent formed a positive relationship with her live-in stepfather. Therefore, parental remarriage (if it occurs) adopts different structures as part of the reorganization of family relationships, and the outcomes of stepfamily relationships differ greatly across individuals and families.

Finally, transformations in *closeness of family relationships* further illustrate differences and commonalities in adaptation to parental divorce. Each respondent followed different pathways of closeness (or lack thereof) in the history of family relationships. Respondent A, whose father was an alcoholic, maintained a positive relationship with her mother but alternated between negative and positive-neutral relations with her father as she coped with the separation and his alcoholism. At the time of the interview, she shared close relationships in both her custodial and noncustodial family networks.

In contrast, before parental separation, Respondent B participated in a tight network of close relationships with her four siblings. When her father moved out of the original family household and in with his female lover, Respondent B first sided with her father against her mother. Before the breakup in the parents' marriage, the respondent had been a "daddy's girl" and close to her father. Respondent B later switched alliances and maintained closeness with her mother while developing acrimonious feelings for her father. At the interview, she had close relationships with all custodial family members but not with her father nor her older brother, who had formed a close bond with her father early in the course of family transformation. Similarly, Respondent C reported being a "daddy's girl" and having close ties to her father before and soon after parental separation. She, too, held negative feelings for her mother in early adolescence that became positive in late adolescence.

Both Respondents B and C had negative feelings for their fathers late in the divorcing process. Differences in their father–child relationships after divorce emerged nonetheless. At the time of interview, Respondent B was enduring intensely negative feelings for her father that seemed to consume her emotionally (see Lingering Negative Effects later), whereas Respondent C's negative feelings for her father were negative but neutralized. Although Respondent C still was angry at him for ending one of her romantic relationships the previous summer and disagreed with her father about politics, her anger had become less intense and her feelings more neutral.

In sum, even though aspects of an individual's divorce-related experiences consist of nominally similar life events, the form that relationship transformations take, their meaning for individuals and family members, and the subsequent outcomes vary greatly.

Thematic Case Descriptions

This section presents themes that emerged from qualitative analysis of the transcripts. These themes demonstrate specific transformations in family relationships and individual adaptation in divorced family contexts. Emphasis is placed on the three cases discussed previously, but information from other cases in the sample is also included.

Parental divorce may entail a combination of positive *and* negative functions for individual family members and families that undergo this relationship transformation. Differences across individuals and families may occur in the degree, timing, and form of positive and negative functions. When, for instance, the behavior of a parent has a negative impact on the network of family relationships, removing that parent from the family through divorce may relieve the network of stressors. Although adaptation to losing a parent who contributed primarily negatively to the lives of other family members may come more easily than losing a parent who contributed positively, family members still may have to make emotional and behavioral adjustments to relationship loss and transformation. The following five themes demonstrate how individuals and their families adapted to the changing family context of divorce in a wide variety of ways, and how the divorce itself had positive, negative, and often both positive and negative functions for family members.

Positive Functions of Parental Divorce. The potential variability in the role of divorce for psychological functioning was underscored by the different attitudes the respondents held toward their parents' divorce. Two respondents of the sample, A and D, thought that they and other family members benefitted immediately from parental divorce. Both respondents described the divorce as a "relief" in homes where the atmosphere was "tense." Both respondents were anticipating the separation when it occurred; conflict between parents was evident to them. The salient feature of family life that these respondents had in common was an "alcoholic" father. These two respondents described a double-sided home life, one with the father present and one with him absent. When he was away, the home was pleasant and relaxed. But when he was home, the environment was shadowed by a "moody" and "bad-tempered" or "sick" father. One respondent described the transition from one state to the other with, "I knew that as soon as my dad walked in the door my mom's mood would change." Having friends visit was difficult when the father was home; either he forbade friends from coming over or the children did not want to bring home friends when he was there.

The transformation of family relationships in these two cases was also similar in other ways. After parental separation, both custodial families could not count on financial support from a father whose alcohol-related problems included not being able to hold a job. Important life events, such as graduating from high school or cheerleading at sports events, were upset by the attendance of an inebriated father. Another commonality was that because the father did not participate much in the everyday life of the predivorce family, his postdivorce absence was not felt so strongly (although her younger brother(s) mentioned missing the father).

Respondent A and her family adjusted in the most positive ways of all cases in the sample to divorce and the life circumstance of parental alcoholism. At the time of interview, her father, with the help of psychotherapy, the respondent's emotional support, and his own will, had not been drinking for 4 years. His life had stabilized considerably and he had begun participating constructively in the lives of his children. Respondent A reported, "He's growing up finally." For more than a year, he and his sons shared close relationships. He also visited the respondent at college every 2 weeks. Contributing to her positive feelings for her father was their helping one another with life problems. She said, "I feel real lucky to have him now."

Figure 8.4.A.5 illustrates the tight bonds between the father and his children at the time of interview.

The successful adaptation after parental divorce of this respondent and her family is associated with very strong social support from both within and outside the family network. The three children supported their mother when she needed help emotionally as well as financially. The respondent and her older brother, for instance, sometimes gave the mother money that they had earned in outside jobs without expecting repayment. The children's school-related behavior also prevented their mother from having to deal with problems at school, as they were all successful in academics and in extracurricular activities.

The most influential support for the custodial family network came from participation in religious organizations. All members were active in the family church. The respondent also formed strong, mutually supportive relationships with members of a national religious club for high school athletes. Male friends from church and the club helped her brothers cope with their father's absence by serving as father figures. Respondent A benefitted further from the guidance of religious doctrine and encouragement from these friends in forgiving her father for "letting her down." This social support at the point when she felt most angry and frustrated with her father enabled her to change her attitude toward him and to begin supporting him in his struggle to stop drinking (Fig. 8.4.A.4).

Thus, at the time of the interview, the adjustment of this family to parental divorce and to alcoholism in particular had improved. All family members had to cope with the father's alcoholism at some point in the family's development (Fig. 8.4.A.1 and 8.4.A.3). With the exception of the relationship between the parents, this family had developed a close-knit network of relationships. As Respondent A explained:

> I don't feel like I'm a victim of divorce like everybody else feels . . . because I don't think it affected my life tragically . . . because I have a really good relationship with both my parents now. And both my brothers have very good relationships with both of them. And my dad's fine, you know, good, doing well now. So he gives money to the family, gives me money. And he's taking care of himself . . . But I don't feel like there's like lost love in our family. I feel like we grew closer together.

A comparable picture emerged from the description provided by *Respondent D*, the other case in the sample in which parental divorce was precipitated by the father's alcoholism. The respondent was relieved when her father left the household. Yet, Respondent D's adjustment to transforming family relationships differed from that of Respondent A as the changes were complicated by the father's mental illness. Although her father had been diagnosed as manic-depressive 2 years before the interview, problems had occurred long before. She stated several times that, more than the divorce, the family had to adjust to the father's "problems that he couldn't straighten out." Rather than providing financial or emotional support for the family over the course of relationship transformation, his behavior brought about a long list of traumatic events, including his losing a job, getting evicted from an apartment, having a car accident while intoxicated, and giving up his car, property, and family heirlooms. Although at the time of interview, her father's condition and lifestyle had been stabilized somewhat with medication, he had not completely repaired his family relationships. In sharp contrast, the respondent's custodial family relationships nevertheless showed strong positive bonds.

Summary. For both respondents and their families, adapting to parental divorce was overshadowed by the father's alcoholism. By removing him from the family residence, divorce eliminated the most eminent conflict. With his departure, each individual in the family could suspend their troubled relationship with him while custodial family members restructured their relationships with one another. Only after the father had changed his problematic behavior could he and his children gradually rekindle the relationships between them. These families, therefore, used divorce as *a means of coping* with problematic fathers.

Whereas these two cases are similar in that divorce was a constructive way to deal with an alcoholic father, the transformations of family relationships took different courses. Whereas the family relationships in Case A received strong social support from friends and involvement in religious organizations, Respondent D did not describe comparable support, even though her mother continued to attend church after the divorce. Moreover, the restructured bonds in Case A were stronger than those for Case D, and included the father. Certainly, the mental illness of Respondent D's father made rebuilding relationships with him more difficult. Finally, noteworthy in these cases is the absence of complications related to parental remarriage. Neither respondent nor family members had to adjust to building new relationships with stepkin.

Lingering Problematic Effects of Parental Divorce. The remaining nine respondents in the study reported different psychotraumatic effects following parental divorce. For some respondents, psychological pain from divorce-related events still lingered at the time of interview. The sources of this pain varied across respondents. Loss in relationships with noncustodial parents through remarriage or emotional distance may make adjustment difficult. New relationships in reconstituted families may be more harmful than helpful to a child in transforming family relationships. For Respondent B, in particular, the divorce crisis was long-lasting, and perhaps even life threatening, as feelings of abandonment and wrongdoing by her father still tormented her.

Of all participants in this study, *Respondent B* (Fig. 8.4.B) was especially affected by the process and aftermath of her parents' divorce. Of great importance were previous events and relationship transformations that involved her father. She described her childhood relationship with her father as "daddy's little girl," and as having a personality and sense of humor like his. She and her four siblings sided with her father against her mother when he moved out. When in junior high school, she would often take refuge from her unhappy and "insecure" mother at her father's nearby home, which he shared with his female lover.

Later, in her mid-teens, the respondent began to break down the bond with her father. As she began to talk with her mother about the divorce and family living and financial arrangements, her perceptions began to change. She also began severing her ties with her father (Fig. 8.4.B.3). She characterized life in the custodial family as "rough times." Family members suffered financially. Her mother, formerly an upper-middle class housewife from a wealthy family, had to support and care for her five children. Because the mother had no marketable job skills, she started to train herself at home by practicing typing. Rather than ask her well-to-do parents for support, the custodial family adjusted their lifestyle: "We cut down the budget, we canceled the paper, we practically ate Campbell's soup." The children took on the housecleaner's work at home but were "slack" about completing their chores. The mother also cried in front of the children and asked how they could "make it." Financial and emotional support in the household, thus, was scarce.

Respondent B was beginning to find out further that her father was not paying child support, despite his comfortable financial standing; he had built his business before the separation with money from her mother's trust fund. At one point after the separation, he even went to court to have the mother send him money. Moreover, without financial support from the father, the custodial family was forced to move out of their large house filled with the respondent's childhood memories to a smaller one that her mother already owned.

Other events contributed to her feeling that the father "was doing her [mother] wrong." For so-called "financial reasons," the time between parental separation and divorce was protracted lasting 5 years. While the marital contract between her parents continued, her father, in the respondent's words, lived "in sin" with a woman and had a child by her "out-of-wedlock." When Respondent B was 16 years old, she became a Christian and developed a "personal bias" against this behavior. She also rejected his efforts to maintain the "daddy's little girl" relationship with her.

At the time of interview, Respondent B was exceedingly dissatisfied with the relationship with her father. She described its present state:

There's tension between us. . . . It really hurts. . . . I really feel let down. I feel so disappointed. I'm so angry inside. . . . This is what kills me: He cannot see that he is wrong. . . . He honestly does not see where he's at fault. That's why it's so frustrating. . . . He can't understand why I feel the way I do.

They also argued about "little things." He called her a snob (as he had called her mother) and asked whether he only meant money to her. She explained their relationship and its impact on her own psychological adjustment by saying: "It's stagnant and it's going to fall out one of these days. And that's just going to be the way it is, I guess. That's probably why I haven't started, you know, healing yet."

An added complication to this respondent's adaptation was her inability to access social support outside her family network. She could not talk with other people about the divorce: From the start she was "unemotional." A year passed before she told anyone about the parental separation. In high school, she told her boyfriend little about it because "he could not understand it . . . he'd never been through it." But, in adolescence she began to talk to her mother about the family and to a friend whose parents had also divorced: "I never really talked it out. Now I do. It seems to get worse every year, you know, every day. It just gets worse and worse. I kept thinking it will get better. . . . It's just been terrible for me."

The account of *Case E* resembles this picture of transformations in the father-daughter relationship in which closeness became mitigated with divorce and the father's remarriage, although the emotional aftermath was less life threatening. Respondent E had a close childhood attachment with her father: "I always used to say that I could ask my dad for anything and he'd give it to me." This closeness was abruptly cut off soon after he moved to another town and remarried the woman with whom he had been having an affair. Although encouraged by both parents to contact her father, the respondent ceased her efforts after one dinnertime call she made to him provoked anger. Problematic relationships between her older brother and stepmother also led to the termination of the children's summer vacations with their father. Although Respondent E, like Respondent B, was reluctant to seek peer support after the divorce because of its social stigma, she broke her silence a few years after the divorce, much earlier than Respondent B. Close relationships in the custodial family network further helped Respondent E adjust. Yet, inasmuch as her father's reconstituted family crowded out her close relationship with him, her longing to be closer to him persisted: "I'm so close with my mom and brothers. I wish I could be close with my dad. But, you know, that's just something that's going to take time. But there's no time. But we're all starting to get closer now."

It should be noted that there were several cases like these in the sample. Another respondent (F) also experienced lingering emotional sensitivity linked with her father's remarriage and the difficulties of living with children from both spouses' previous marriage (see Remarriage of Custodial Parent later).

Summary. Evidently, emotional problems related to parental divorce can linger far beyond the original crisis. Coping processes depend on the dynamics of adaptation to divorce in the family structure. For Respondent B the continuous chain of difficult divorce-related events greatly challenged her ability to adapt to the family environment and left persistent emotional problems. The combined effects of the extremely difficult living situation in her custodial family, her lost closeness with her father that lingered on as unresolved conflict, and her lack of emotional expression about the divorce left her psychological adjustment in critical condition. In comparison, Respondent E, who also continued to suffer from the loss of her previously close father–daughter relationship, benefitted from social supports in custodial family relationships and early communication with peers about the divorce.

These cases illustrate how comparable outcomes can arise from diverse divorce-related family circumstances. The actual circumstances in each family together with how family members approach these determine the outcomes of parental divorce. Although parent–child attachments, for example, can ebb and flow with changing visitation patterns, the outcome ultimately depends on ways that individuals together rebuild their family relationships. Variations in individual and family adaptation to divorce-related circumstances set the stage for variations in outcomes of family relationships.

Dynamics of Living Arrangements in Divorced Families. A child with two parents who live in different residences may have the option of choosing to live with either parent. The amount of time she spends visiting the home of her noncustodial parent and the degree to which she considers this home her own may determine how welcome she feels there. These conditions have an impact on a child's thoughts about living with the noncustodial parent on a more regular basis as well as how she makes use of the alternate residence to retreat from divorce-related crises and conflicts in the custodial parent's home. Four respondents in the sample moved from the home of one parent to the other.

Respondent C thought about moving in with her noncustodial father for a long time after her parents separated. As a child she was a self-proclaimed "daddy's little girl" (Fig. 8.4.C.1). After he moved out, she missed him a lot and, for a while, did not want to visit him because leaving was so difficult. During the same period, she did not get along with her mother: "It was just the whole big thing: I just, I hated my mother. I would tell her I hated her. I said, 'I don't want to live with you. I hate you. I want to live with Dad.' " Whereas Respondent C was close to her father and had conflicts with her mother and sister, her sister was close to her mother (Fig. 8.4.C.3).

During early adolescence, she also experienced other difficulties. She reported feeling sick to her stomach every morning when her school bus approached the schoolyard. She cried often: "Sometimes at night I would just cry all night . . . almost every day probably."

Respondent C began to idealize the possibility of living with her father. She liked how his home looked more than how her mother's home did because he had all new furniture, whereas her mother had the old furniture left from the predivorce family residence. Weekend visits with her father were enjoyable because she got more concentrated attention from him. After he remarried, Respondent C and her stepmother, whom the respondent liked, made preparations for the move by decorating her bedroom at her father and stepmother's home, whereas they left her sister's room there undecorated. The plans for the move never materialized, perhaps related to a change in her stepmother's attitudes toward the respondent and her sister (Fig. 8.4.C.6): After a medically necessitated hysterectomy, her stepmother began to resent the stepdaughters and became hostile to them.

Several years later when Respondent C was in high school, she took a summer job in the city where her father and stepmother lived and spent the summer living with them. At the time she was dating a local boy whom her father disliked. When she found out that the relationship was terminated not by her boyfriend but secretly by her father, she immediately returned to her mother's home, which then contained close reconstituted family relationships (Fig. 8.4.C.7). Her relationship with her father was so affected by this event that she did not return his letters or phone calls for a year. At the time of interview, her feelings for him had become tempered somewhat:

> We're on good terms. It's just that I can only take so much of him. . . . We're really different now because . . . I'm just like my mom. . . . She's real liberal . . . and he's just the total opposite. So if we ever sit down at dinner and talk about politics or anything, it's just 'Ugh!' because I always get real mad at him and he always gets real mad at me for my views.

Other cases also demonstrate how minor conflicts between parent and child may trigger a move from the home of one parent to the other. Respondent G left her mother's home over a trivial argument only to return in 2 days. Similarly, Respondent B once lived with her father for 2 days when she was not getting along with her mother. Respondent F ended a summer vacation with her mother early because the respondent was un-happy living with her.

Summary. Although several cases illustrate moves from one parent's home to the other parent's home, the case of Respondent C, more than the others, speaks to a child's deep emotional and relational involvement in alternative living arrangements when divorced parents keep separate residences. Respondent C's persistent fantasy of living with her father, supported by decorating her room at his home, demonstrates a child's continual desire to maintain a parent–child attachment that may be threatened by conditions inherent to parental separation (i.e., divorced parents often live in separate residences and children with one parent at a time).

This persistent fantasy shows her efforts to live with her father and step-mother, where she perceived relationships to be close and the furniture "nice" and "new," to escape the realities of living conditions (i.e., old furniture from the original family) and conflicts with her mother in the single-parent custodial household. But, several years later when she did finally move in with her father and stepmother, the family relationships in the households of both parents had transformed. The reconstituted family environment at her mother's home included tight-knit relationships, whereas the one at her father's home had deteriorated with tensions in the stepmother-stepdaughter relationship, as well as in her father-daughter relationship. The reality of living with her father and stepmother then differed greatly from her fantasies of early adolescence.

Although the option of changing living arrangements by moving from the residence of one parent to the other exists for children in some divorced families, the conditions of relationships between original and reconstituted family members at the time of the move dictate whether these options are solutions for successful adaptation to divorce-related problems or to other problems. Again, the dynamic nature of the family relationships and circumstances of divorce relegates how individuals adapt to the transformations of family life.

Split-Sibling Residence After Divorce. Although siblings of most divorced families reside primarily together with one original parent, some families arrange child residences so that siblings live apart, with different parents or a third party. The decision for siblings to live with different parents may come about for a variety of reasons. Different conditions in family relationships may influence the decision: Siblings may have different degrees of attachment to their parents, they may have conflicts with parents or among siblings themselves, or a child may be concerned about a parent's living alone. In the sample, four respondents spent some time in split-sibling residences: two respondents from the initial period of parental separation on-ward and two some time after separation.

After living with the custodial mother for 2 years, one of Respondent B's brothers moved into the father's home. His close attachment to the father (but not to the mother) was a motivating factor for the move (Fig. 8.4.B.1): "There really wasn't any problem, it wasn't like [my mother and brother] just couldn't live with each other." Both the respondent and the brother (who was a year older than she) were reaching adolescence, and both were beginning to align with their same-sex parents (Fig. 8.4.B.3). The brother's move to the father's home coincided with the mother's moving her younger children, all female except the younger brother, into a smaller house for financial reasons (meanwhile, the older brother and oldest child was away at college). The younger brother did not want to live with "the girls": "It was just important for him to have a male influence, I guess, in his life. And he was happier that way." He also knew that discipline would be more lenient at the father's home (i.e., curfews could be broken easily). Although the mother did not want her son to leave her household, she was unwilling to fight it in court because she could not afford to and had already been to court over child support.

The respondent reported that split-sibling living was not a major stressor because she saw her brother often at each of the parents' homes and at school every day. Nevertheless, this early change in child living arrangements was related to the later transformation of her family relationships at the time of interview: She reported having recent positive relationships with all cus-todial family members, including the older brother, but negative feelings for her father and the brother who had moved in with her father's reconstituted family during adolescence (Fig. 8.4.B.5).

Other cases illustrate how parent-child alliances that form before and after divorce can influence split-sibling living arrangements and subsequent relational outcomes. In *Case G*, splitting up the respondent's two younger brothers fell clearly along parent–child alliances: Before the divorce, the younger brother had been a "mommy's boy" and the older brother had been close to the father. Relationships in this family transformed according to the split-sib living arrangements. At the time of interview, the relationship be-tween her younger brothers had gone from frequent fights at the time of separation to its present neutral feelings. On the other hand, the relationship between the father and younger brother, who lived with the mother, were beginning to deteriorate.

Many family members were upset by these living arrangements. The respondent was concerned about her father's sharing financial matters and details of his dating relationships with her brother. For her mother: "Mom's thrown tantrums several times. But, it's not been about Dad. It's been about getting custody of [my brother], and wanting him to come live with us . . . because she wants him to live with her. She says she wants her family back together." In light of pressure from the mother to live with her, the older brother himself had offered and had started spending alternate weeks with each parent, an arrangement that made the respondent worried about her brother's psychological well-being. For many in this family, the respondent, her mother, and to some degree, the younger brother who lived with the father, this living arrangement became a greater source of emotional conflict than the divorce itself had been.

In contrast, *Respondent F* had originally lived with the father while her siblings lived with the mother, to prevent her father from having to live alone. But some time after parental separation, all the siblings ended up living with their father. This living arrangement seemed to evolve because of the stability of the father's home environment, close sibling ties, and the wish for a home life with two parents (the father remarried long before the mother did).

Summary. Siblings can perceive the option of living with different parents as a solution to divorce-related family conflicts. But, when split-sibling residences become permanent arrangements, the structure of the arrangements has an enduring impact on relational outcomes.

Despite similarities in conditions of the decision to split-sibling living arrangements, outcomes differ. Like Respondent B, Respondent E had two older brothers, the younger of whom moved out of their custodial mothers' residence during adolescence. Whereas both left because of conflicts in mother-son relationships and close attachments to their fathers in adolescence, the family relationships, their strategies for dealing with the conflict, and relational outcomes differed. Whereas Respondent B's brother had moderate problems getting along with his mother, Respondent E's brother had severe mother-son conflicts in addition to other emotional problems. Respondent B's brother was welcomed in the home of his father and stepmother, but Respondent E's brother went away to preparatory school because his father had moved out of town. At the time of interview, Respondent B reported that she did not get along with her brother (Fig. 8.4.B.5), although Respondent E's brother and his mother had become close.

These cases highlight the variability across families with similar divorce-related living conditions. Each case history has its unique developmental pathway for adjusting not only to divorce and the accompanying changes in living arrangements but also to all other problems of everyday life. Of interest to the examination of individual-context transformations is the individual's adaptation to changing family contexts, that is, processes of coping by constructing temporary solutions for some problems of some family members, although these efforts are undermined by other family members, and new problems emerge for the family across time.

Remarriage of Custodial Parent. Although all reconstituted families include a stepparent, the number and form of stepkin relationships added to a family through remarriage differentiate the structural arrangements of reconstituted families. A child enters a reconstituted family as either a member of one spouse's previous marriage or as a child born or adopted into the reconstituted family. Half siblings most likely live with the remarried couple who are their original parents, but stepsiblings may live primarily in the reconstituted household or primarily in their other original parent's home and visit the reconstituted family.

The three respondents in the sample who lived in reconstituted families represent three very different structural arrangements of family reconstitution. Respondent C's stepfather had never been married and brought no children to the reconstituted household. Although Respondent H's stepfather had three children from a previous marriage, when he married Respondent H's mother the stepsiblings were adults living on their own. This family grew in size when her mother and stepfather bore a child, the respondent's half sibling. Similarly, Respondent F's stepmother had three children from a previous marriage, but only her adolescent son joined the reconstituted family with the respondent's father and siblings. As shown later, the living arrangements in these reconstituted families also varied greatly.

For Respondent C, living with the stepfather was a positive experience. Her mother had dated the man who became the respondent's stepfather for several years before introducing him to the two daughters. The mother remarried 1 year later. Soon after remarriage, the reconstituted custodial family moved from the city where her father lived because her stepfather had a new job. Although the respondent reported feeling "bothered" by her mother's past secrecy about the adult dating relationship, Respondent C had accepted her stepfather at the time of interview and considered him compatible with her mother and with herself: "We get along great." Custodial family relationships were all positive (Fig. 8.4.C.7). Her stepfather also supported the respondent and her younger sister by defending them when her mother disciplined them in ways that he considered unfair: "Like if I had stayed out too late but it wasn't my fault, she'd come down really hard on me. . . . [My stepfather] would go, 'Now wait a minute. You're not being fair.' Stuff like that, he's really good." The stepfather also considered the respondent and her sister as family: "He has Susan [my younger sister] and me, and he enjoys us and we enjoy him." These mutually satisfying family relationships and the simplicity of adding only one person through remarriage influenced the positive reconstituted family relationships.

Respondent H also had a positive relationship with the stepfather, which she described as "perfect." In the early years of the mother's remarriage, her stepfather was close to the respondent's half sister, his daughter. But from the time the sister was 3 years old, the respondent, instead, became his "favorite" because "He can't take close relationships like that [with my half sister]. . . . When something gets close, he has to leave. He started pushing further and further away from [my half sister]." As the stepfather's business trips grew more frequent and his participation in the family diminished, her mother's feelings for him became more negative. Respondent H's adjustment to her mother's second divorce was not difficult as the respondent told herself that her stepfather had just gone on another long business trip. This reconstituted family thus transformed subsequently into a single-parent family structure with positive custodial family relationships.

In contrast, the custodial reconstituted family of Respondent F was the most problematic of these three cases. When her father remarried, the stepmother and stepbrother moved into the home where the respondent and her younger siblings lived with their father. Combining families in this way disrupted the respondent's postdivorce family environment. Whereas her relationship with her stepmother was "not like the mother–daughter thing," the two of them got along well alone but had occasional conflicts. The conflicts between them centered on the relationships between her stepmother and siblings from her original family: When her stepmother clashed with and slighted her siblings, she got "really mad." Whereas Respondent F, nonetheless, conceded that her stepmother's living with three stepchildren must be hard, she still could not understand anyone's not getting along with her younger sister who "is as easy as anybody to get along with, and they clash more than anybody which is wild." She reasoned that her stepmother's problems with her siblings could be similar to the respondent's own mother's difficulties with reconstituted families; her mother experienced stepchildren living in her home as an invasion of privacy. This reconstituted family ultimately solved its difficult living arrangements by moving into two separate households (while waiting for a new home to be built). At the time of interview, Respondent F still felt "uncomfortable" in the reconstituted family and did not like to be at home when everyone was together. Her advice to parents who remarry indicated lingering anxiety about her reconstituted family relationships: "I'd wait until the kids got out of college and then try it . . . kids coming together . . . [is] havoc."

Summary. The three respondents with remarried custodial parents varied in their adjustments to reconstituted family relationships and living arrangements. The first two cases demonstrate how having fewer reconstituted family members can facilitate positive adjustment to remarriage of the custodial parent. In comparison, the remarriage of Respondent F's father, which involved the most people and the most new relationships, posed difficulties for reconstituted family life. Clashes between her stepmother and younger siblings were not only problems in the relationships between them but also for the relationship between the respondent and her stepmother. The decision made by the respondent's father and stepmother to continue their marital relationship in separate households further implicates the negative impact of the conflictual reconstituted family relationships. Whereas Respondent F herself got along with her stepmother, the difficult relationships between others in the reconstituted family network elicited her negative feelings about the reconstituted family.

The complex structure of so many intimate and newly formed relationships sets up a family environment that may be more difficult to adapt to than are simple reconstituted family structures. These cases further illustrate the interrelationship between individual adaptation to divorce-related events and the adaptation of other individuals and relationships in the family network. Adaptation to living in reconstituted family networks can facilitate or inhibit the adjustment of a child.

DISCUSSION: DIVORCE AND ITS CONTEXT

Divorce and its aftermath are dynamic processes. The specific divorce experience of each family and its members depends on the life circumstances of the people involved. In some instances, divorce becomes a "problem" that demands adaptation, oftentimes exhausting all the material and psychological resources that family members can muster. In other cases, parental divorce may be a means for solving some other problems that have infringed upon family life. Such variability in the role that parental divorce plays in the lives of adolescent girls was expected on the basis of the combinatorial model of family relationship structures and their transformations and moreover was found in the empirical interviews.

Every family enters into divorce with a unique structure of life circumstances and family relationships. Families that undergo divorce differ in multitudinous ways, ranging from concrete demographic dimensions (i.e., the number of family members or financial income) to more abstract characteristics (i.e., attitudes about marriage or feelings of self-confidence).

Although this study investigated families who all had in common the same life event, namely divorce, it reveals wide variability across cases. As the sequence and patterning of each family's life events after divorce differ, so does their adaptation to them. The structure of the family's life environment sets up opportunities for different possible ways of coping with these events, including divorce. To fully discover the ways in which family adaptation to difficult life events is organized, research must take into account the culturally structured environments for these coping processes.

Because family and individual adaptation to divorce is a systemic and dynamic process, there are no simple straightforward "remedies" or "cures" that will work for everyone and for every instance of divorce. Outcomes of divorce can vary across different families and for different family members. For some families, the consequences of divorce can be positive, as for Cases D and A. In both of these cases the immediate effects of parental separation provided a solution to a predivorce family problem. For others families, divorce can have no major effects as in Case J. For still others, it can generate severe psychological problems as seen in the cases of Respondent B and of the brother of Respondent E.

The resources that help family members adjust to divorce also vary. They can originate from relationships within families, for example, when the mother and children support one another after the father moves out (Case A and H) or from extrafamily relationships when friends or religious groups provide assistance (Case A).

An individual's adaptation to parental divorce is a complex process that proceeds across time. Individual interpretations of specific divorce-related events affect the individual's adjustment across time. For example, Respondent A interpreted a move to a new home necessitated by strapped family finances as an exciting and delightful event, whereas Respondent B interpreted the same event as a painful reminder of the sacrifices she had made since parental separation. For Respondent A, the family's former home had housed memories of her father's alcoholism and her family's struggle with his illness, while Respondent B described her former home as filled with warm childhood memories of good times spent playing with siblings and neighborhood children.

The different meanings attached to otherwise similar events underline the importance of studying the adaptive actions of family members and the personal values and subjective perspectives that they use to make sense of the events. Meanings that people generate in coping processes are often unto themselves a means of coping with some aspects of life and should not be separated from our study of active coping efforts. However, the meanings that individuals construct are made available to them by their cultural environments. As family relationships are transformed into new states, the meanings used to describe these relationships can be altered by individuals as well. Thus, a respondent may tell us that at a certain time she "hated" her mother or father but that at a later time she "loved" the parent again. Individual's meanings of *hate* and *love*, as well as other terms used to describe one's relationships with others, stem from socialization in particular cultural contexts.

The coping process is by its nature dialectical: It includes forces of psychological improvement and harm. At the same time that an individual makes advances in adapting to parental divorce, she may have relapses. As Respondent B, for example, began to appreciate and understand what changes had occurred in her family relationships and living arrangements and what her mother had experienced during separation, she began to suffer more psychologically. Whereas her relationship with her mother became more supportive, her relationship with her father deteriorated and became a source of psychological suffering. At the time of interview, she and her father were both being taxed by their efforts to renegotiate their relationship. Thus, postdivorce individual transformations are not due solely to the respondent's internal psychological dynamics but are also related to transformations in person-environment relations and, in particular, to transformations in the structure of the family relationships.

Most of what has been analyzed in this chapter is hardly new; it has been well-known to psychotherapists, parish priests, and writers for quite a while. In his most thorough case study of the process of families, Lev Tolstoy (1875–1877/1930) has appropriately summarized the basic issue of family relationships: "All happy families resemble one another, but each unhappy family is unhappy in its own way" (p. 1).

Curiously, psychologists have rarely shared the simple understanding that complex psychological phenomena, like family relationships and divorce events, have their case-specific structure, and that this structure can be analyzed using general principles of structural transformation. If research on family relationships at large, and divorce in particular, is to come closer to the reality of these complex psychological phenomena, then the adoption of a context-related structuralist perspective in conjunction with careful case studies of families' life histories is inevitable. The present exercise in combinatorics applied to interview data is just a small step in that direction.

ACKNOWLEDGMENT

I gratefully acknowledge the seminal guidance and thinking of Jaan Valsiner, whose perspective constantly reaches for the "whole picture."

REFERENCES

Ahrons, C. R. (1979). The binuclear family: Two households, one family. *Alternative Lifestyles*, *2*, 499–515.

Ahrons, C. R., & Rodgers, R. H. (1987). *Divorced families: Meeting the challenge of divorce and remarriage*. New York: Norton.

Allison, P. D., & Furstenberg, F. F. (1989). How marital dissolution affects children: Variations by age and sex. *Developmental Psychology, 25,* 540–549.

Clingempeel, W. G., Brand, E., & Ievoli, R. (1984). Stepparent-stepchild relationships and stepfather families: A multimethod study. *Family Relations, 33,* 465–473.

Fitzgerald, N. M., & Surra, C. A. (1981, October). *Studying the development of dyadic relationships: Explorations into the retrospective interview technique.* Paper presented at the National Council of Family Relations Pre-Conference Workshop on Theory Construction and Research Methodology, Milwaukee.

Ganong, L. H., & Coleman, M. M. (1987). Stepchildren's perceptions of their parents. *Journal of Genetic Psychology, 148,* 5–17.

Guidubaldi, J., Cleminshaw, H. K., Perry, J. D., Nastasi, B. K., & Lightel, J. (1986). The role of selected family environment factors in children's postdivorce adjustment. *Family Relations, 35,* 141–151.

Hetherington, E. M. (1972). Effects of parental absence on personality development of adolescent daughters. *Developmental Psychology, 7,* 313–326.

Hetherington, E. M. (1979). Divorce: A child's perspective. *American Psychologist, 35,* 851–858.

Hetherington, E. M., Cox, M., & Cox, R. (1978). The aftermath of divorce. In J. H. Stevens & M. Matthews (Eds.), *Mother-child father-child relations* (pp. 110–155). Washington, DC: National Association for the Education of Young Children.

Hetherington, E. M., Cox, M., & Cox, R. (1979). Play and social interaction in children following divorce. *Journal of Social Issues, 35,* 26–49.

Hetherington, E. M., Cox, M., & Cox, R. (1985). Long-term effects of divorce and remarriage on the adjustment of children. *Journal of the American Academy of Child Psychiatry, 24,* 518–530.

Kreppner, K. (1983, August). *Family and individual development: Socializing a child within a family.* Paper presented at the 7th Biennial meeting of the International Society of Social and Behavioral Development, Munich.

Kreppner, K. (1985). Individual development within the family: An analysis of the child's growth as a set of potential crises. In T. Garling & J. Valsiner (Eds.), *Children within environments: Toward a psychology of accident prevention* (pp. 145–163). New York: Plenum.

Kreppner, K., Paulsen, S., & Schuetze, Y. (1982). Infant and family development: From triads to tetrads. *Human Development, 25,* 373–391.

Lazarus, R. S., & Folkman, S. (1984). *Stress, appraisal, and coping.* New York: Springer.

Levinger, G. (1979). A social exchange view on the dissolution of pair relationships. In R. L. Burgess & T. L. Huston (Eds.), *Social exchange in developing relationships* (pp. 169–193). New York: Academic Press.

Newcomb, T. M. (1961). *The acquaintance process.* New York: Holt, Rinehart & Winston.

Peterson, J. L., & Zill, N. (1986). Marital disruption, parent-child relationships, and behavior problems in children. *Journal of Marriage and the Family, 48,* 295–307.

Santrok, J. W., & Warshak, R. A. (1979). Father custody and social development in boys and girls. *Journal of Social Issues, 35,* 112–125.

Santrok, J. W., Warshak, R. A., Lindbergh, C., & Meadows, L. (1982). Children's and parents' observed social behavior in stepfather families. *Child Development, 53,* 472–480.

Tolstoy, L. (1930). *Anna Karenina* (L. & A. Maude, Trans.). New York: Random House. (Original work published 1875–1877)

U.S. Bureau of Census (1991). *Statistical Abstract of the United States* (111th ed.). Washington, DC.

Valsiner, J. (1984). Two alternative epistemological frameworks in psychology: The typological and variational modes of thinking. *Journal of Mind and Behavior, 5,* 449–470.

Valsiner, J. (1986). *The individual subject and scientific psychology.* New York: Plenum.

Valsiner, J. (1989). Organization of children's social development in polygamic families. In J. Valsiner (Ed.), *Child development in cultural context* (pp. 67–85). Toronto: Hogofe & Huber.

Visher, E. B., & Visher, J. S. (1979). *Stepfamilies: Myths and realities.* Secaucus, NJ: The Citadel Press.

Vuchinich, S., Hetherington, E. M., Vuchinich, R. A., & Clingempeel, W. G. (1991). Parent-child interaction and gender differences in early adolescents' adaptation to stepfamilies. *Developmental Psychology, 27,* 618–626.

Wallerstein, J. S. (1984). Children of divorce: Preliminary report of a ten-year follow-up of young children. *American Journal of Orthopsychiatry, 54,* 444–458.

Wallerstein, J. S. (1985). Children of divorce: Preliminary report of a ten-year follow up of older children and adolescents. *American Academy of Child Psychiatry, 24,* 545–553.

Wallerstein, J. S. (1987). Children of divorce: Report of a ten-year follow-up of early latency-age children. *American Journal of Orthopsychiatry, 57,* 199–211.

Wallerstein, J. S., & Kelly, J. B. (1980). *Surviving the breakup: How children actually cope with divorce.* New York: Basic Books.

APPENDIX

Combinatorial Calculations of Dyadic Relationships

Relations between Members of Dyads

If we assume that dyadic relationships are bidirectional, each dyad has two relations ($X \rightarrow Y$ and $Y \rightarrow X$). Each relation can adopt one of three valences (+, 0, −). A relation that has a valence ($X \rightarrow Y = +$) is called an orientation; hence, every dyad has 2 orientations (e.g., $X \rightarrow Y = 0$ and $Y \rightarrow X = +$). All possible combinations of orientations for a dyad total 9 (cf. Fig. 8.1).

Number of Dyads by Number of Children

Let n represent the total number of members in a two-parent family and m the number of children per family. Then, $n = m + 2$. Calculate the total number of dyadic relationships in a family of size n with the combinatorics formula for all possible combinations in a group of objects taken 2 at a time. The total number of dyads in a set of size N is:

$$\binom{N}{2} = \frac{N!}{(N-2)!\,(2)!}.$$

Then, the total number of dyadic relationships in a family with m children is:

$$\binom{N}{2} = \binom{n}{2} = \binom{m+2}{2} = \frac{(m+2)!}{[(m+2)-2]!\,(2)!}$$
$$= [(m+2)\,(m+1)]\,/\,2.$$

1. *General: Orientations in any Family.* Because the number of relations in each dyad is 2, the total number of dyadic relations for a family with m children is:

$$2 \left([(m + 2)(m + 1)] / 2 \right) = (m + 2)(m + 1).$$

The total number of dyadic relations for any family also equals the total number of orientations because each dyad has only one valence per orientation (e.g., $M \rightarrow C = +$ and $C \rightarrow M = 0$). The preceding formula, therefore, also represents the total number of orientations in any family.

All Possible Combinations of Orientations in Dyads. To demonstrate the potential for variability in the conditions of dyadic relationships, the total number of dyads in a family with m children is multiplied by the nine possible orientations. Then, all possible combinations of orientations in dyads of an original family equal:

$$9 \left([(m + 2)(m + 1)] / 2 \right).$$

2. *Postdivorce I: Possible Orientations in Original Family.* After divorce, the possibility of both parents having positive orientations toward the other is omitted (i.e., $M \rightarrow F = +$ and $F \rightarrow M = +$). Thus, all possible combinations of dyadic orientations after divorce, before either parent remarries, are calculated by:

$$(9 [(m + 2)(m + 1)] / 2) - 1.$$

3. *Postdivorce II: Possible Orientations in Remarried Family.* If both parents from a child's original family remarry, the maximum number of parental figures the child can have is 4 (i.e., mother, father, stepmother, and stepfather). Therefore, the maximum size of a reconstituted family is $n = m + 4$. (Note that m, the total number of children in a reconstituted family, may include siblings from the predivorce family as well as stepsiblings or half siblings added in the remarriage of either parent from the original family.) Then, the total number of dyadic relationships in a reconstituted family with m children is:

$$\binom{N}{2} = \binom{n}{2} = \binom{m+4}{2} = \frac{(m+4)!}{[(m+4)-2]!\,(2)!}$$
$$= [(m+4)(m+3)] / 2.$$

All possible combinations of dyadic orientations in reconstituted families postdivorce, excluding mutually positive relations between the child's parents from the original family, are calculated by:

$$(9 [(m + 4)(m + 3)] / 2) - 1.$$

Sample Combinatorial Calculations

1. *General: Orientations in any Family.*

   2 *children:* $[(2 + 2) (2 + 1)] = 12.$
2. *Postdivorce I: Possible Orientations in Original Family.*

   2 *children:* $(9 [(2 + 2) (2 + 1)] / 2) - 1 = 53.$

3. *Postdivorce II: Possible Orientations in Remarried Family.*

   2 *children:* $(9 [(2 + 4) (2 + 3)] / 2) - 1 = 134.$

   4 *children:* $(9 [(4 + 4) (4 + 3)] / 2) - 1 = 251.$

Distinguishing "Buddies" From "Bystanders": The Study of Children's Development Within Natural Peer Contexts

Thomas A. Kindermann
Portland State University

Historically, developmental psychologists have always been interested in the influences of children's social contexts. However, in looking at childhood environments, developmental research has largely been dominated by a focus on contexts that are provided by adults, and almost exclusively by adults who fulfill a caretaking or teaching role.

There are many reasons to believe that such an adult-centered perspective may limit our understanding of childhood development. Without doubt, early relationships with adults constitute contexts that are of great developmental importance. However, at least from the time on when children gain competencies to walk independently, they also become capable to have some influence themselves over who and what their contexts should be. Thus, with increasing age, the early predominance of adult caretakers diminishes and gives way to greater self-determination. This is played out in increased instrumental and emotional competencies, as well as in an increased striving to transcend biologically or institutionally assigned contexts, and to form new relationships with others. To a large extent, these new contexts are self-selected and consist of relationships with other children (Hartup, 1978, 1983).

A major reason why the attention of developmentalists has been overall confined to biologically or culturally-institutionally assigned environments may be that these are comparably well defined and stable across time. Stable contexts are frames that can easily be targeted: Context actors are readily identified, and models, empirical designs, and time windows for capturing their influences can be comparably easily specified. For example, teachers are usually assigned to children for clearly specified time periods; primary caretakers usually remain stable across large portions of children's development; relationships with biological relatives often last for a lifetime. In comparison, children's friendships, acquaintanceships, and peer group affiliations lack such clear-cut definitions; they often fluctuate widely and are free to change at almost any time (cf. Cohen, 1961; Matthews, 1986)—even if they extend across longer time periods. Moreover, change in these contexts is expected to proceed with the same pace as change in our target subjects under study. As soon as our interests include developmental contexts that consist of other children, change in these contexts may need to be accorded a role that is as central as change in the individuals themselves.

TRADITIONAL APPROACHES TO THE STUDY
OF PEER RELATIONSHIPS

Folk wisdom has it that if one knew a person's companions, one would know much about the person him or herself. Early attention of social scientists to people's interrelationships can be traced to French sociologists (cf. Le Bon, 1896; Tarde, 1903) who were interested in so-called crowds and "mobs."

Among psychologists, Moreno's 1934 book, *Who Shall Survive*, is regarded by many as a key reference to the current literature on interpersonal relationships. Moreno was interested in what he called *social configurations*. His sociometric method was concerned with identifying patterns in these configurations; it was primarily used with adults, and most often with therapeutic goals. The main assessment strategy was to use individuals' self-reported preferences or "choices" for relationships with specific others. However, it was an explicit goal at the time to also extend the method toward examining people's "actual" interrelations (Moreno & Jennings, 1945, p. 6). Today, much of Moreno's sociometric thinking still prevails. Four approaches are of particular interest for our current discussion.

First, there is the study of *sociometric status* (cf. Asher & Coie, 1990). This approach typically focuses on the classroom as one specific setting in which children are likely to be found outside the family. The central construct is the extent to which a child is nominated by his or her classmates to be liked or disliked (or both, or neither; e.g., Coie, Dodge, & Coppotelli, 1982; Newcomb & Bukowski, 1984). Based on these nominations, children are labeled as popular, average, controversial, negelected, or rejected. Sociometric status is regarded to indicate children's social success or failure in a setting (e.g., Dodge, 1983; Ladd & Asher, 1985; Ladd, Price, & Hart, 1990; Pope, Bierman, & Mumma, 1991; Putallaz & Wasserman, 1990; Rubin, LeMare, & Lollis, 1990), but also to allow predictions for their future development (e.g., Cillessen, 1991; Kupersmidt, Coie, & Dodge, 1990; Morrison & Masten, 1991; for reviews, see Newcomb, Bukowski, & Pattee, 1993; Parker & Asher, 1987).

Attention to individuals' social status within a group is consistent with Moreno's framework. However, contemporary sociometric approaches tend to focus more on individuals, and less on person-context relations. Although a child's social status is assessed within his or her social context, it is then used as a construct of individual differences and as a characteristic that is located within the child. In addition, there seems to be considerable variation in the criteria that are used to determine membership in groups of popular, rejected, and neglected children, as well as considerable heterogeneity within some of the categories, especially in boys (Bierman, Smoot, & Aumiller, 1993; Bukowski & Hoza, 1989; Cillessen, van Ijzendoorn, van Lieshout, & Hartup, 1992; French, 1988). This may indicate that there are interindividual differences in the antecedents, correlates, and consequences of classroom neglect or rejection. However, this may also imply that the categorizations depend not just on factors within the individual but also on specific features of children's interpersonal relationships among each other. Hence, the whole classroom may be a somewhat undifferentiated and artificial unit for analyses (see also Asher & Coie, 1990; Cairns, 1983).

A second approach to children's relationships to age-mates focuses on their *friendships* among each other (cf. Berndt, 1989). This approach *does* include information on the identities of those people that are contextual partners for one another. Children's friendships are seen as indicators of their ability to form and maintain reciprocal relationships among each other, and as key contexts for their social, personality, as well as academic development (Asher, Hymel, & Renshaw, 1984; Berndt, Laychak, & Park, 1990; Hartup, 1978).

Critiques of friendship research point out that the unit of analysis is restricted to dyads of best friends (Furman, 1989), and that the friendship construct is open to individual interpretation, at one point in time as well as across different ages (cf. Adams, 1989). In addition, there are concerns about the reliability of friendship self-reports (see also Cairns, Neckerman, & Cairns, 1989). Many children in a setting may nominate those individuals as their friends who are most popular overall, but these views may not necessarily be reciprocated. Hence, examinations of friendship patterns are often restricted to reciprocal nominations. Although this helps with regard to reliability problems, the unit of analysis is further reduced. Across time, for example, friendships would need to remain reciprocally stable to allow examinations of mutual influences among friends.

A third tradition in the study of social relationships is the study of *social groups* or *networks* in the fields of sociology, social psychology, and social anthropology. These approaches also focus on naturally existing social structures. Proponents argue that the target of analysis, instead of the individual, should be network structures among individuals (e.g., Hallinan & Williams, 1990: Hammer, 1980a; Wasserman & Galaskiewicz, 1994; Wellman & Berkowitz, 1988), as well as the roles and functions that different people play in social networks (e.g., Bryant, 1985; Hammer, 1980b; Heller & Swindle, 1983; Kahn & Antonucci, 1980) or in groups of people that work together on tasks (McGrath, 1984).

Typically, either individuals' self-reports about their friends or peers are used to determine networks and their characteristics, such as size (number of individuals in a given network) and coherence (interconnections within a network), or objective descriptions of these groups are delineated from task characteristics (e.g., expeditions, crews, focus groups). Major objectives of these approaches are to describe the functions that networks have for individuals (e.g., Kahn & Antonucci, 1980) and the effects that task characteristics have on within-group interactions (McGrath, 1984). For sociologists, for example, key questions are about the effects of network properties on larger social systems; for social psychologists, a central interest is in what groups can accomplish over and above individuals; for social support researchers, the focus is on consequences of various characteristics of support systems for individual functioning.

Group research in the area of social psychology is best known for experimentally contrived studies and for studying groups that are formed around certain tasks. The advantage is that the groups are well defined. However, there are questions about the extent to which findings on experimentally formed groups or task-groups can be generalized to natural processes of peer group formation among children. For example, this may depend on the specifics of the experimental designs, or the relevance and generalizability of the tasks for children's everyday life. The Robbers Cave State Park experiment (Sherif, Harvey, White, Hood, & Sherif, 1961) provides an example for what it takes to conduct an experimentally controlled study so that groups are accurately identified and ecological validity of the observed processes exists at the same time.

Conversely, sociological, anthropological, and social support studies focus on groups or networks that are naturally existing in people's everyday life. However, they mostly rely on self-reports about network structures and their characteristics. Often it is assumed that these reports provide good approximations of reality, although efforts are rare to estimate how accurate they actually are (but see Hammer, 1980a). However, it can also be argued that people's perceptions of their networks are something different than their actual characteristics. Hence, methods would be needed that would allow to contrast individuals' perceptions with more objectively defined network structures.

The Current Approach.   Each of the above approaches seems to have specific strengths and shortcomings. One perspective on this is that despite the virtues of these approaches there may be additional avenues for studying children in peer contexts. In the following, an approach is presented that aims to incorporate the strengths of each of these approaches and to overcome some of their problems at the same time.

First, in line with sociometric and sociological traditions, it is assumed that children's development proceeds within peer contexts that have a certain structure, and that this structure has important implications for their development. Second, in line with sociologial and anthropological thinking and the literature of social support, it is assumed that this structure is related to what children do with and for one another. Third, it is assumed that social structure is something that children know about, and that this knowledge is based on children's observations of public social interactions in a setting. Consequently, perceptions on networks structures in a setting are expected to converge among those children who commonly interact with one another. Fourth, in line with friendship research, it is assumed that it is essential to identify exactly who the members of a given child's network are and what characteristics they possess. Hence, the focus in examining contextual influences is not so much on measuring outcomes of context effects within individuals (such as ascriptions of popular or rejected status), but on capturing the relationships between contextual agents and the individual. Fifth, following the example of social psychological group research, it is assumed that methods to examine processes of interpersonal relationships should be open to include different kinds of characteristics of social partners. The traditional focus on people's private perceptions of their social networks will need to be complemented by examinations of more objectively defined characteristics of one's network; for example, self-decriptions of the members of one's network may be included as well as observational accounts.

Methodologically, two major goals have to be met with such an approach. The first goal is to expand efforts to *identify* individuals' networks in such a way that it becomes possible to assess the reliablity of individuals' networks across accounts gathered from many different reporters. The second goal is to determine the *psychological characteristics* of these networks and the *influences* that they may have on a child's development. As contextually oriented developmentalists, we may have interests that go beyond studying the role of general or topographical features of social structures, of groups that are artificially formed by adults, of people's social status within a given setting, or of dyadic reciprocal friendship patterns. We may additionally be interested in the psychological characteristics of those children who comprise an individual child's natural peer contexts, and in the role that these others may play for his or her development.

IDENTIFYING BUDDIES AND BYSTANDERS: COMPOSITE MAPS OF NATURAL PEER NETWORKS

The basic idea of this chapter is that the psychological characteristics of a child's peer context constitute an important determinant for his or her development. In contrast to many of the socialization contexts traditionally studied in developmental psychology, these contexts are self-selected to a large degree. In settings where multiple candidates are available, children will actively choose or be chosen by specific other children as "buddies" or preferred associates. How can we identify, for any individual child, and with some level of reliability, those other children that make up his or her peer group network?

Robert Cairns and his colleagues (Cairns, Perrin, & Cairns, 1985) have proposed a method in which multiple children in a setting are asked to report about "who hangs around together with whom." The method uses children's free recall; groups of any size can be reported (i.e., even dyads are considered to be a group), and children can be reported to belong to one or many more groups at the same time. The practicability of this method in school settings has been demonstrated in several studies (Cairns, et al., 1985; Cairns, Cairns, Neckerman, Gest, & Gariepy, 1988; see also Cairns, Gariepy, & Kindermann, 1990; paper-and-pencil extensions of the procedure have been piloted, Kindermann, McCollam, & Gibson, in press). To illustrate this method, an empirical example is used in the following (Kindermann, 1993).

Multiple Reporters. One advantage of the method is that not just children's reports about themselves but their reports about social configurations in the entire classroom are obtained. Children participate as expert observers and give a list of those individuals that they recall to be members of groups in their classroom. For example, a child may report that the children ANN, BEV, CAM, and DEE are members of one group, and LYN, KIM, and MIA of another.

A second advantage is that many reporters provide information about the same setting, and about publicly and open observable affiliations within that setting. Hence, the amount of consensus about networks that exists among the reporters can be empirically determined. A third advantage is that, if public consensus exists, not each and every student in the classroom needs to be interviewed to achieve a reliable map of its network structure. This may be important in many situations in which time constraints, human subjects' considerations, or parental cooperativeness set limits to the number of children that are available for asessments (for further discussion of the procedure, see Cairns et al., 1985).

Network Identification. Based on the reports of multiple children, the social network structures within the entire classroom are determined. Although for the current discussion only group nominations are of interest, it should be noted that these can be combined with various kinds of additional qualitative information. Labels can be included that children may want to give to these groups (or by which the groups are known), as well as specific descriptions of the agenda or purpose of the groups, or of the functions of specific individuals within the groups.

In the empirical example, 57 students (out of 109 children) from two fourth- and two fifth-grade classrooms were interviewed about group networks in their classrooms. Interviews commenced about 1 month after the beginning of the school year. Based on these reports, composite social maps were formed as summary accounts of network structures. This involved two steps. First, across reporters but separately for each classroom, matrices were formed of the frequencies with which any two individuals were nominated to be together in the same group. Second, these *co-nomination matrices* were examined for network patterns (see Table 9.1 for an example of a classroom of 4th grade girls).

The goal was to find out which classmates could be considered to be members of each individual child's networks. For each student, the question was whether any of his or her classmates were more likely to be nominated together with that student than could be expected by chance. Binomial z-tests were performed on conditional probabilities of co-nominations (or, if nomination frequencies were low, approximations to Fisher's exact test, using Sterling's formula; see von Eye, 1990). For each student, his or her conditional probabilities of being in a group with any other student were compared with the probabilities that these students were nominated for any group at all. (A computer program NETWORKS for conducting these tests is available from the author upon request.) The resulting interconnections among children ($p < .01$) can be represented in the form of Moreno-like network structures, as shown in Fig. 9.1. Lines in the figure connect pairs of children who shared significant connections. Note that in contrast with Moreno's sociograms, individuals' positions are arbitrary and based on drawing convenience only.

These composite network maps can be examined for consistency with the individual reporters' nominations. Normally, errors of commission will only be of concern, because not each and everyone in a classroom can be expected to have the same knowledge about all of the networks. In fourth and fifth grade, for example, boys are likely to know more about boys' networks than about girls', and vice versa. In the sample studied, the composite maps were quite consistent with the individuals' reports. Averaged across all classrooms, *kappa* was .70; no reliability differences were found across classrooms and gender of reporters.

NETWORK DESCRIPTION: FOCUS ON GROUPS VERSUS FOCUS ON INDIVIDUALS' NETWORK MEMBERS

Network descriptions may first focus on overall structural characteristics. In the example, there was high variability across classrooms. Thirteen children were found to belong to no group, but there was also one classroom in which all girls had a group. Also, there were differences in network sizes.

TABLE 9.1

Co-Nomination Matrix for Girls in a Fourth-Grade Classroom

Students	Classmates with Whom Students were Nominated to be in the Same Group													Total Nominations
	ANN	BEV	CAM	DEE	EVE	FAY	GIN	HEA	INA	JAN	KIM	LYN	MIA	
ANN	—	29	12	11	4	19	11	4	4	3	1	1	1	31
BEV	29	—	11	10	4	21	11	4	5	3	1	1	1	33
CAM	12	11	—	19	11	8	13	8	5	4	2	2	4	25
DEE	11	10	19	—	9	6	8	5	5	4	2	2	4	23
EVE	4	4	11	9	—	3	9	4	2	3	5	5	3	17
FAY	19	21	8	6	3	—	14	5	6	4	2	5	3	28
GIN	11	11	13	8	9	14	—	12	7	11	6	4	3	34
HEA	4	4	8	5	4	5	12	—	5	8	3	3	5	16
INA	4	5	5	5	2	6	7	5	—	2	2	1	5	14
JAN	3	3	4	4	3	4	11	8	2	—	1	3	1	14
KIM	1	1	2	2	5	2	6	3	2	1	—	7	4	13
LYN	1	1	2	2	5	5	4	3	1	3	7	—	15	19
MIA	1	1	4	4	3	3	3	5	5	1	4	15	—	19

Note: In total, 159 Groups were reported by 22 respondents in this classroom. Totals of single nominations are necessarily smaller than the sums of multiple co-nominations.

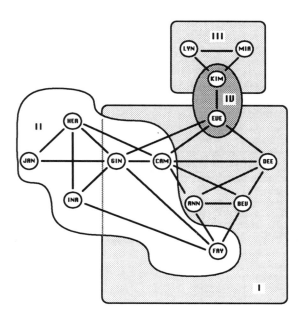

FIG. 9.1. Social networks of girls in a fourth-grade classroom; individuals' connections among each other and group assignments determined via a decision-rule strategy. From Kindermann (1993). Copyright (1993) by the American Psychological Association. Reprinted by permission.

On the average, a child's group consisted of 2.3 classmates; the range was from many dyads up to one group of seven boys in a fifth-grade classroom.

Further description of network characteristics involves a decision that has major theoretical and methodological consequences: Do we want to determine overall group structures as units for analyses, or do we want to obtain descriptors that are composites of a child's individual context? Traditionally, overall group structures are most interesting to network researchers. These can be identified from co-nomination matrices. However, we will also present a more individualized approach, which may be more interesting to developmental researchers.

In many cases, distinct groups of individuals will be readily apparent in the data; but this may not always be the case. In the example of Fig. 9.1, all the girls are more or less interconnected with one another, and at first glance it may be a question whether any further group differentiation exists at all (i.e., beyond the networks of boys and girls, which were entirely separated). However, even in cases in which separate structures emerge more readily (which was the case in many classrooms), there still may be questions about whether subgroups can be distinguished and about interconnections among these subgroups.

Several strategies can be used for this purpose. First, a 50% group inclusion rule was applied to groups with more than two members (see Fig. 9.1). This approach is topographical. Group I was first considered to be formed by students ANN, BEV, CAM, and DEE, and then to also include EVE and FAY, who each had connections with 50% of the first four. In addition, this group included GIN, who again had connections with 50% of the six others. Group II was considered to be formed by children GIN to JAN, and then also included CAM and FAY. Finally, Group III consisted of KIM to MIA, and Group IV of EVE and KIM.

An alternative to topographical strategies can again be based on nomination frequencies. The binomial z-tests can be expanded to include dyads, triads, or higher order clusters of individuals (e.g., to test whether the pair of *ANN and BEV* is connected to further individuals).

In general, this strategy is time consuming when it is used to test all kinds of possible combinations among children, and the number of cases available for the tests is reduced with every higher level of analysis. Nevertheless, analyses of this kind can be very helpful for specific goals. For example, we may have questions about whether there are certain *core* groups within the overall map who have especially strong connections among each other (Gest, Graham-Bermann, & Hartup, 1991). Hence, analyses may focus on dyads or triads of students who share the highest frequencies of co-nominations. In the example classroom (see Fig. 9.2), a first *core group A* can be considered to consist of students ANN, BEV, and FAY; this was a triad of students who were nominated more often to be in the same group than any other pair or triplet. *Core groups B* (CAM and DEE), *C* (LYN and MIA), and *D* (GIN, HEA, and JAN) consisted of students who were less often nominated to be in the same group, but still more often than any other dyad or triad. These core groups can be treated as if they were individuals in higher order analyses, in order to examine their connections to other students. Results are depicted in Fig. 9.2; a comparison with the results of the topological analysis of Fig. 9.1 highlights the level of differentiation that can be achieved with this strategy.

Group I (from Fig. 9.1) broke down into two *core groups, A* and *B*, which were connected by ANN and her joint membership in both clusters. Student GIN was not a core member of either cluster A or B.

The *core group* within Group II was *D*, consisting of GIN, HEA, and JAN; CAM, FAY, and INA were only peripheral members of this group. There was an additional independent connection between HEA and CAM, which provided a link between this group and core group B. Student INA was not found to be a member of any core group; half of her co-nominations were each with core groups A and D, and these were not enough to assign her core membership in either of these. Group III also broke down into two independent groups, which were connected by student LYN. Finally, the dyadic group IV remained unchanged.

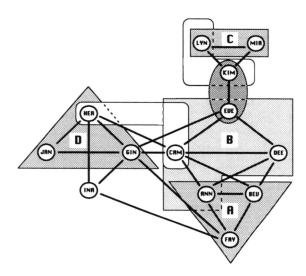

FIG. 9.2. Social networks of girls in a fourth-grade classroom; individuals' connections and core group memberships determined via higher-order conditional probabilities.

There are further alternatives that employ more commonly used statistical methods. In an unpublished paper, Cairns and colleagues (Cairns et al., 1990; see also Gariepy & Kindermann, 1989) discussed hierarchical cluster analyses (in conjunction with Multidimensional Scaling techniques), structural linear equation models (based on covariance patterns in children's co-nomination profiles), and bivariate comparisons of dyadic linkages among children (in combination with methods of Correspondence Analysis).

All of these procedures have specific advantages and disadvantages. Most likely, the results obtained with the different techniques will overall converge, but results can differ for particular children, and especially with regard to multiple group memberships and with regard to subgroups that may exist within larger clusters. Overall, the problems involved in the identification of overall group structures can appear to be thorny (see also Wellman & Berkowitz, 1988), and often it may be wise to employ several methods and to accept only results that converge across methods.

However, this need not be discouraging. As indicated, we may also address the question from an entirely different and more *individual-oriented* angle. We may be less interested in describing overall social structures but more in identifying and describing those contexts (or sets of contextual agents) that are relevant for specific children. The network identification method presented offers an interesting alternative for this purpose.

If we have identified exactly those other individuals who are important contexts for each student in a classroom (first level), we just may be in need of descriptors for their *composite psychological profile*. These composite scores can be based on the individual scores of those others that have been identified as important context agents. Incidentally, it is this composite that seems to be of concern to parents and educators. Often concerns exist about specific children who are "hanging out with the wrong guys," or who seem to be influenced "negatively" by a group of others. Hence, we may be interested in profile scores as descriptors of individuals' contexts, instead of overarching group structures in the classroom.

INDIVIDUALS' NETWORKS OF "BUDDIES": PEER GROUP PROFILES AS CONTEXT DESCRIPTORS

A central assumption for our further discussion is that groups can be described as a joint function of the characteristics of their members, and that it is these characteristics that are likely to influence their members' individual development. This assumption has two consequences. First, it leads to some kind of aggregation across the members of a child's peer group. Second, it opens up a discussion of what kinds of variables, beyond structural network aspects, are promising candidates for investigating peer group effects.

The decision for context aggregation should not be made lightly. Under all circumstances, some level of detail will be lost when aggregates are used. The decision will also depend much on the research question under study. For example, specific hypotheses may hold that an individual's membership in multiple groups constitutes a context that is different from that of another individual who is in only one group. Or, if deviant peer groups were of interest, researchers may focus on these only and probably neglect children's simultaneous memberships in nondeviant groups.

The advantage of an aggregate index is that it allows us to form context accounts that are comparable across children, despite differences in peer group size, overlapping memberships, and even despite changes in peer group members and their characteristics over time. Group change over time is likely to involve membership turnover, and we often may not want to limit ourselves to examining influences of those people only who remain stable interaction partners. Rather, we may want to conduct comparisons, even if, at different points in time, networks are comprised of entirely different individuals. It may be of interest to note that similar problems exist in studies of family transitions (e.g., across divorce or a parent's death); across many transitions, context agents are lost or added, and substitution and aggregation of context accounts will be unavoidable.

In terms of influential aspects of peer groups, target variables can generally include behaviors, competencies, values, or beliefs. One limitation of earlier studies of peer influences has been a reliance on children's perceptions of their peers' characteristics. An advantage of the current method is that any technique can be used to assess peer attributes, including observations, peer self-reports, file data (such as grades), or reports of a child's perceptions of his or her peers as well.

In the empirical example, the impact of peer groups on children's school motivation was of interest; hence, relations between children's own motivation and aggregate profiles of their peer group(s) were investigated. Children's motivation was measured in 109 children from two fourth- and two fifth-grade classrooms. Individuals' motivation was measured independently from that of their peers, namely, via teacher and self-reports of student's *engaged versus disaffected behavior* in the classroom. The measures used were developed by Wellborn (1991); the scales for self- and teacher-reports possess sufficient measurement properties, are moderately intercorrelated among each other, and are highly stable across the school year (cf. Skinner & Belmont, 1993; Skinner, Wellborn, & Connell, 1990). It should be noted that although the concepts include two components of behavioral and emotional engagement, in the current study only the behavioral component was examined. Examples of the items are: "In my class, this student tries as hard as he or she can," or "When I'm in class, I just act like I'm working."

A simple strategy for capturing the composite profile of a target child's peer group(s) is to use the average score of the members of his or her network. This is based on the conservative assumption that we do not know whether any specific members within a child's network are more influential than others. Alternative strategies could use totals of the scores of all the members of one's peer group (if one assumed that the effects of peers are additive and cumulative), standard deviations or variances of the members' scores (if one was interested in the effects of diversity among group members), or individual weights in the averaging procedure (e.g., for core versus fringe members, if there was reason to expect differential contributions).

In the empirical study, we did not differentiate among a child's network members. For each child in the classrooms, their context average scores were formed across all those other children who had been identified as network members of that student. Two averages were used: the average of the teacher reports of their peers' engagement, and the average of their peers' own reports. Thus, in the example of Fig. 9.1, the two peer group profiles of student FAY were the averages of ANN's, BEV's, GIN's, and INA's teacher- and self-reported engagement scores.

GROUP HOMOGENEITY AS AN INDICATOR
OF GROUP SELECTION PROCESSES

If we assume that children and their peers do not just sort themselves at random but form networks according to systematic processes, we would expect significant interrelations between children's individual characteristics and the profiles of their peer networks. Most researchers assume that peer selection processes occur according to similarity criteria (e.g., Cairns et al., 1989; Cohen, 1977; Kandel, 1978a); children are expected to seek out others that are similar to themselves. Thus, children can be expected to be more similar to the members of their own networks than to non-network age-mates, which would lead to significant correlations between individuals' own scores and the composite scores of their peer group members. These correlations can be interpreted as indices of within-group homogeneity (in analogy to item-total correlations in which a child would be an item and his or her network would be the scale).

In the example, expectations about group homogenity with regard to classroom engagement were supported. Significant correlations were found between individuals' engagement and their peer group averages (teacher reports: $r = .55$, $p < .001$; self-reports: $r = .28$, $p < .01$; $n = 96$). Also, analyses of variance were performed on overall group assignments based on the 50% decision rule for group inclusion. These can have methodological problems if multiple group memberships are frequent in a classroom: The tests become overly conservative, because multiple entries of the same people for different groups lead to decreases in between-group variances. (In these cases, analyses can be restricted to core groups, see Fig. 9.2.) Nevertheless, the analyses on overall group assignments (Fig. 9.1) showed that variances between groups were larger than those within groups (teacher reports: $F(34, 77) = 1.74$, $p < .05$; self-report: $F(34, 77) = 2.28$, $p < .01$).

Group homogeneity and between-group differentiation is an indication that peer affiliations can be organized around a variable that is highly valued in school settings: Highly motivated students were affiliated with others who, on the average, were also highly motivated, and vice versa. This is consistent with reports about homogeneity among affiliated peers with regard to students' performance (Tesser, Campbell, & Smith, 1984), school motivation (Berndt et al., 1990), and other personal characteristics (Kandel, 1978a; 1978b). But what happens to individuals and their peer groups across time?

DEVELOPMENT OF PERSON-CONTEXT RELATIONSHIPS

One goal for which the method shows special promise is to examine children's development within *changing* peer contexts. Self-selected peer contexts can be expected to change in many aspects, even across small time frames. In fact, many different kinds of changes can be going on at the same time, and simultaneously with changes in the target children under study.

First, the membership composition of a child's network can change. For a given child, some of his or her peer group members will remain connected with him or her, some others will leave, and some new network members will be added. Second, even when peer groups remain stable, there can be change in the organizing feature of the group. For example, initially, there may have been a shared interest in basketball, which changed to a common interest in hanging out at public places. Third, individual peer group members will show developmental changes themselves. Fourth, the quality of children's relationships with others, or their relation to the entire group may change, and a specific child may become more of a "core" or more of a "fringe" member (cf. Gest et al., 1991).

In addition, any of these changes may interact with the other kinds of changes. For example, when some members of a child's network change in a way that makes them incompatible with the group's organizing feature (e.g., interest in the other gender), this may affect the target child, some members of his or her group, or the entire network, and lead to eliminating these children or to adding new children who fit to the new organizing feature of the group.

Mechanisms That Produce Peer Group and Individual Change Across Time

For the current discussion, three mechanisms are of particular interest that are commonly regarded as most influential in producing peer group and individual change across time (cf. Cairns et al., 1989; Cohen, 1977; Kandel, 1978a), namely, peer selection, elimination, and socialization processes.

Selection and elimination processes address issues of peer group membership. These processes also highlight one form of influence that children can have on their peer contexts that goes far beyond traditional approaches to studying within-context development: With regard to almost all other important contexts, such as parents, siblings, or teachers, children can exert almost no selection or elimination influences themselves.

Selection refers to the extent to which individual children exhibit associative preferences for specific others or groups, the extent to which groups have preferences for specific individuals, and the extent to which, once children belong to a group, its members strive to maintain group consistency by inclusion of new members. Conversely, processes of *elimination* are those in which new candidates or existing members are excluded or in which an individual child leaves the peer group.

When we have identified the individuals who make up a child's network at several points in time, we also know the specific peers who left the group, who moved in, or who remained constant group members. By combining this information with the groups' psychological profiles across time, we can examine the nature of selection and elimination processes, their consequences for group profiles, and whether specific features around which groups are organized at one point in time become stronger or weaker criteria for selection and elimination across time.

The third mechanism of interest here is that of *socialization* influences within peer groups. Selection and elimination processes determine who becomes a member of a group (and who does not), socialization processes influence what individuals and groups actually do to and with each other (e.g., in terms of activities and in terms of establishing or maintaining group norms).

Often socialization processes are expected to be directed toward group homogeneity, similarly to selection and elimination processes. However, socialization may also influence children towards taking on specific functions or roles within their peer groups (Cairns et al., 1989; Youniss, 1986). The nature, strength, and direction of socialization influences will depend on factors within the individual, such as a child's age, gender, self-confidence, autonomy, independence, as well as on factors that originate from his or her group, such as the length of time a child has been with a specific group, the stability of other members, or affective qualities among group members. Although it is beyond the scope of this chapter, it should be noted that influencing factors may also originate from outside agents, such as parents or teachers.

Again, by combining information about those others who are important socializing contexts with their psychological profiles, we are able to examine whether interindividual differences in children's contexts at one point in time are related to changes in their own characteristics across time. This represents the classical pathway of socialization studies.

Examining Mutual Processes of Influence Across Time

In the example study, children's self-reports on engagement were again obtained in all four classrooms within the last weeks of the school year. In one fourth-grade classroom ($n = 28$), peer group network information was also collected at this time, which was used to form composite maps of social networks at the end of the year.

Across time, mechanisms of *selection and elimination* were expected to lead to specific patterns of group stability and change, both in terms of group memberships and in the groups' organization with regard to psychological variables. Turnover of peer group members was used as an indicator of the amount of selection and elimination processes at work. Member turnover was relatively high; at the end of the year, on the average, about 50% of a child's peer network members had remained stable members, whereas about 30% of his or her initial group members were lost.

Selection Effects. The effects of group member turnover on the group profiles were examined using *teacher reports* on children's engagement in the one fourth-grade classroom, for which longitudinal group information was available. To hold constant children's intraindividual changes and to focus only on changes that were due to selection processes, reports from the beginning of the year were used for computing children's peer group profile scores for both Fall and Spring.

The specific expectation was that new members would be added and old members eliminated in ways that preserved the groups' initial homogeneity. Thus, high stability in peer group scores was expected over time, despite changes in actual group memberships. This expectation was supported. The results showed that group scores for Fall and Spring were highly correlated ($r = .80$, $p < .001$; $n = 25$); analyses of variance showed no mean level changes in children's group profiles. Hence, it was concluded that although turnover had led to marked changes in the specific individuals that made up children's peer groups, it had produced little effect on the psychological profiles of their groups.

However, even if group homogeneity was preserved, this does not mean that change in group profiles was entirely absent. It was assumed that nevertheless, the "rich" would become "richer" over time, whereas the "poor" would become "poorer." Hence, it was expected that changes in children's group profiles across the year were related to how these children had been motivated themselves at the beginning of the year. Students who were initially highly motivated were expected to be associated with peer groups that, due to membership changes, became more motivated across the year, and vice versa. Multiple regressions were used to examine whether group profiles in the Spring could be predicted from individuals' motivation in the Fall, over and above the contribution of the groups' initial profiles. However, in this general form, this assumption was not supported.

Selection and elimination effects can be affected by the stability within peer groups; they should be most salient for children whose peer groups had shown a high amount of membership turnover. Hence, selection effects were further examined by weighting individual children's scores with the number of classmates that were added to their network across time, and elimination effects by weighting their scores with the number of group members lost. Using weights for the proportion of new peer group members gained, changes in children's motivational group profiles across the year were significantly predicted by their own initial motivation at the beginning ($\beta = .37$, $t = 2.42$, $p < .05$, $n = 25$). However, this was not the case when the number of group members lost was used as a weight.

This indicates that diverging developmental trends existed for children who differed in the amount of new group members they were able to attract. The higher a child's initial motivation, and the higher the number of new group members this child was able to include in his or her network across time, the more likely was his or her network to change in a positive direction.

Socialization Effects. Hypotheses about socialization processes were examined along a complementary route. The question was whether a child's own development was influenced by the characteristics of his or her peer group members, or, more specifically, whether children's motivational gains or losses across time were related to their initial peer group profile. Children's self-reported engagement in school was used as the outcome variable. A multiple regression analysis showed that children's own motivation at the end of the school year could be predicted by the composition of their peer groups from the Fall before, over and above their own motivation at the beginning of the year (β = .15, t = 2.06, $p < .05$, n = 96). Children who had initially been with peer groups that were highly motivated changed in a positive direction, and vice versa.

Differential analyses can again help examine those group characteristics that could make specific groups particularly powerful socializing agents, or characteristics of individuals that could make them more susceptible to influences from their peers. For example, socialization effects may often not be expected to be of equal strength for all groups or individuals, and stronger effects can be expected for groups of children who stay together for a longer period of time. However, in the smaller subsample of children whose groups were followed up longitudinally, this hypothesis was not supported. Children's initial group scores, weighted with the amount of stability within their groups across time, did not predict changes in their own school motivation across the year.

CHILDREN'S PEER RELATIONSHIPS AS A SAMPLE CASE
FOR THE STUDY OF PERSON-CONTEXT RELATIONS

Although in theory, peer contexts have often been accorded a major role for children's development (cf. Piaget, 1959; Vygotsky, 1962), methodological problems have largely prohibited the study of their influences. Parents and teachers generally believe that those others with whom children choose to affiliate are of major developmental importance, but empirical analyses have usually been restricted to examining influences of children's close friends, children's sociometric status in the classroom, or to the study of what children think about their peers. In comparison with the extensive research traditions on adults' socialization influences on children, relatively little is known about the influences of children's self-selected peer contexts.

Two major obstacles to our attempts to include natural peer contexts in our picture of childhood socialization processes are consequences of children's own involvement in the development of these contexts. The first difficulty lies in the question of how to determine which children, among a group of peer candidates, can be considered to be important for a given child, and which not. The second difficulty lies in the question of how indices for the psychological characteristics of those important others can be formed.

This chapter presented avenues to overcome these obstacles. A method was presented that allows us to differentiate "buddies" from "bystanders" in natural settings, and thus to distinguish more important socialization agents in children's lives from their less important counterparts. It was also suggested to use composite peer group profiles as a means of representation of the psychological characteristics of peer contexts. In their combination, both methods allow us to study processes of children's development within natural peer groups across time. Models were suggested for examining the impact of peer group characteristics on individuals, as well as the influences of individuals on their groups, although both individuals and their networks change across time.

On a larger scale, efforts to include the study of peer contexts in investigations of childhood socialization processes are consistent with current trends that direct our attention towards the study of development of ecological systems (Bronfenbrenner, 1989), of social relationships (Hinde, 1992; Kindermann & Skinner, 1992; Maccoby, 1992), or of processes of social construction (or coconstruction) of developmental pathways by joint efforts of individuals and their contexts (Valsiner, 1987; Wozniak & Fischer, 1993). Peer contexts, much more than contexts that are biologically or culturally assigned, are contexts that are defined by the very people in whom we want to study their influences, are contexts that change with the same pace as our target individuals under study, and are contexts whose patterns of change, both in terms of the identities of contextual agents, as well as of change within these agents, are results of reciprocal influences among active individuals and their social partners. These features make the study of children's self-selected peer contexts a major challenge. However, attention to these features may also be helpful in our efforts to better understand the implications that contextual changes may have for developing individuals.

ACKNOWLEDGMENTS

I want to thank Robert B. Cairns from the University of North Carolina at Chapel Hill, who developed the network assessment method described in this chapter, Jaan Valsiner for sharing his conceptual and methodological insights for context-inclusive analyses, and Jean-Louis Gariepy for his valuable discussions of network quantification methods. Special thanks go to Ellen A. Skinner from Portland State University for her suggestions for models of analysis. Thanks for help with data formatting and analyses go to Caroline Bettridge, Shelly Jackson, Tanya McCollam, and Julie Reynolds from Portland State University, and to Beate Metzler, who was an exchange student from the University of Frankfurt, Germany; Roland Kwee deserves many thanks for his help in writing the NETWORKS analysis program. The work on this chapter was supported by a Faculty Development Grant and a Research and Publications Grant from Portland State University.

REFERENCES

Adams, R. G. (1989). Conceptual and methodological issues in studying friendships of older adults. In R. G. Adams & R. Blieszner (Eds.), *Older adult friendship: Structure and process* (pp. 17–41). Newbury Park, CA: Sage.

Asher, S. R., & Coie, J. D. (Eds.). (1990). *Peer rejection in childhood.* New York: Cambridge University Press.

Asher, S. R., Hymel, S., & Renshaw, P. D. (1984). Loneliness in children. *Child Development, 55,* 1457–1464.

Berndt, T. J. (1989). Friendships in childhood and adolescence. In W. Damon (Ed.), *Child development today and tomorrow* (pp. 332–348). San Francisco: Jossey-Bass.

Berndt, T. J., Laychak, A. E., & Park, K. (1990). Friends' influence on adolescents' academic achievement motivation: An experimental study. *Journal of Educational Psychology, 82,* 664–670.

Bierman, K. L., Smoot, D. L., & Aumiller, K. (1993). Characteristics of aggressive-rejected, aggressive (nonrejected), and rejected (nonaggressive) boys. *Child Development, 64,* 139–151.

Bronfenbrenner, U. (1989). Ecological systems theory. In R. Vasta (Ed.), *Annals of child development* (pp. 187–249). Greenwich, CT: JAI Press.

Bryant, B. K. (1985). The neighborhood walk: Sources of support in middle childhood. *Monographs of the Society for Research in Child Development, 50* (Serial No. 210).

Bukowski, W. M., & Hoza, B. (1989). Popularity and friendship: Issues in theory, measurement, and outcome. In T. J. Berndt & G. W. Ladd (Eds.), *Peer relationships and child development* (pp. 15–45). New York: Wiley.

Cairns, R. B. (1983). Sociometry, psychometry, and social structure: A commentary on six recent studies of popular, rejected, and neglected children. *Merrill-Palmer Quarterly, 29,* 429–438.

Cairns, R. B., Cairns, B. D., Neckerman, H. J., Gest, S. D., & Gariepy, J.-L. (1988). Social networks and aggressive behavior: Peer support or peer rejection? *Developmental Psychology, 24,* 815–823.

Cairns, R. B., Gariepy, J.-L., & Kindermann, T. A. (1990). *Identifying social clusters in natural setting.* Unpublished manuscript; University of North Carolina at Chapel Hill, Social Development Laboratory.

Cairns, R. B., Neckerman, H. J., & Cairns, B. D. (1989). Social networks and shadows of synchrony. In G. R. Adams, R. Montemayor, & T. P. Gullota (Eds.), *Biology of adolescent behavior and development* (pp. 275–305). Newbury Park, CA: Sage.

Cairns, R. B., Perrin, J. E., & Cairns, B. D. (1985). Social structure and social cognition in early adolescence: Affiliative patterns. *Journal of Early Adolescence, 5,* 339–355.

Cillessen, A. H. (1991). *The self-perpetuating nature of children's peer relations.* Kampen, The Netherlands: Mondiss.

Cillessen, A. H., van Ijzendoorn, H. W., van Lieshout, C. F., & Hartup, W. W. (1992). Heterogeneity among peer rejected boys: Subtypes and stabilities. *Child Development, 63,* 893–905.

Cohen, A. K. (1977). Sources of peer group homogeneity. *Sociology of Education, 50,* 227–241.

Cohen, Y. A. (1961). *Social structure and personality.* New York: Holt, Rinehart & Winston.

Coie, J. D., Dodge, K. A., & Coppotelli, H. (1982). Dimensions and types of social status. *Child Development, 59,* 815–829.

Dodge, K. A. (1983). Behavioral antecedents of peer social status. *Child Development, 54,* 1386–1399.

French, D. C. (1988). Heterogeneity of peer-rejected boys: Aggressive and non-aggressive subtypes. *Child Development, 59,* 976–985.

Furman, W. (1989). The development of children's social networks. In D. Belle (Ed.), *Children's social networks and social support* (pp. 151–172). New York: Wiley.

Gariepy, J.-L., & Kindermann, T. A. (1989, April). *Quantitative techniques for the identification of social subgroups in natural settings.* Paper at the 1989 Meetings of the Society for Research in Child Development, Kansas City.

Gest, S., Graham-Bermann, S. A., & Hartup, W. (1991, July). *Social network affiliations and social reputations of 2nd and 3rd grade children.* Poster at the 11th Biennial Meetings of the International Society for the Study of Behavioral Development, Minneapolis.

Hallinan, M. T., & Williams, R. A. (1990). Students' characteristics and the peer-influence process. *Sociology of Education, 63,* 122–132.

Hammer, M. (1980a). Predictability of social connections over time. *Social Networks, 2,* 165–180.

Hammer, M. (1980b). Social access and clustering of personal connections. *Social Networks, 24,* 305–325.

Hartup, W. W. (1978). Children and their friends. In H. McGurk (Ed.), *Childhood social development* (pp. 181–271). London: Methuen.

Hartup, W. W. (1983). Peer relations. In P. H. Mussen (Gen. Ed.), *Handbook of child psychology* (Vol. 4), E. M. Hetherington (Ed.), *Socialization, personality, and social development* (pp. 103–196). New York: Wiley.

Heller, K., & Swindle, R. W. (1983). Social networks, perceived social support, and coping with stress. In R. D. Felner, L. A. Jason, J. N. Moritsugu, & S. S. Faber (Eds.), *Preventive psychology: Theory, research, and practice* (pp. 87–103). Elmsford, NY: Pergamon.

Hinde, R. A. (1992). Developmental psychology in the context of other behavioral sciences. *Developmental Psychology, 28,* 1018–1029.

Kahn, R. L., & Antonucci, T. C. (1980). Convoys over the life course: Attachment, roles, and social support. In P. B. Baltes & O. G. Brim (Eds.), *Life-span development and behavior* (Vol. 3, pp. 253–286). New York: Academic Press.

Kandel, D. B. (1978a). Homophily, selection, and socialization in adolescent friendships. *American Journal of Sociology, 84,* 427–436.

Kandel, D. B. (1978b). Similarity in real-life adolescent friendship pairs. *Journal of Personality and Social Psychology, 36,* 306–312.

Kindermann, T. A. (1993). Natural peer groups as contexts for individual development: The case of children's motivation in school. *Developmental Psychology, 29,* 970–977.

Kindermann, T. A., & Skinner, E. A. (1992). Modeling environmental development: Individual and contextual trajectories. In J. B. Asendorpf & J. Valsiner (Eds.), *Stability and change in development: A study of methodological reasoning* (pp. 155–190). Newbury Park, CA: Sage.

Kindermann, T. A., McCollam, T. L., & Gibson, E. (in press). Peer networks and students' classroom engagement during childhood and adolescence. In K. Wentzel & J. Juvonen (Eds.), *Social motivation: Understanding children's school adjustment.* New York: Cambridge University Press.

Kupersmidt, J. B., Coie, J. D., & Dodge, K. A. (1990). The role of poor peer relationships in the development of disorder. In S. R. Asher & J. D. Coie (Eds.), *Peer rejection in childhood* (pp. 274–305). New York: Cambridge University Press.

Ladd, G. W., & Asher, S. R. (1985). Social skill training and children's peer relations. In L. L'Abate & M. A. Milan (Eds.), *Handbook of social skills training* (pp. 219–244). New York: Wiley.

Ladd, G. W., Price, J. M., & Hart, C. H. (1990). Preschoolers' peer networks and behavioral orientations: Relationship to social and school adjustment. In S. R. Asher & J. D. Coie (Eds.), *Peer rejection in childhood* (pp. 90–115). New York: Cambridge University Press.

Le Bon, G. (1896). *The crowd.* London: Fisher Unwin.

Maccoby, E. E. (1992). The role of parents in the socialization of children: A historical overview. *Developmental Psychology, 28,* 1006–1017.

Matthews, S. H. (1986). *Friendships through the life-course.* Newbury Park, CA: Sage.

McGrath, J. E. (1984). *Groups: Interaction and performance.* Englewood Cliffs, NJ: Prentice-Hall.

Moreno, J. L. (1934). *Who shall survive? A new approach to the problem of human interrelations*. Washington, DC: Nervous and Mental Diseases Publishing.

Moreno, J. L., & Jennings, H. H. (1945). Sociometric measurement of social configurations: Based on deviations from chance. *Sociometry Monographs, 3*. New York: Beacon House.

Morrison, P., & Masten, A. S. (1991). Peer reputation in middle childhood as a predictor of adaptation in adolescence: A seven year follow-up. *Child Development, 62*, 991–1007.

Newcomb, A. F., & Bukowski, W. M. (1984). A longitudinal study of the utility of of social preference and social impact sociometric classification schemes. *Child Development, 55*, 1434–1447.

Newcomb, A. F., Bukowski, W. M., & Pattee, L. (1993). Children's peer relations: A meta-analytic review of popular, rejected, neglected, controversial, and average sociometric status. *Psychological Bulletin, 113*, 99–128.

Parker, J. G., & Asher, S. R. (1987). Peer relations and later personal adjustment: Are low-accepted children at risk? *Psychological Bulletin, 86*, 357–389.

Piaget, J. P. (1959). *The language and thought of the child*. London: Routledge & Kegan.

Pope, A., Bierman, K. L., & Mumma, G. H. (1991). Aggression, hyperactivity, and inattention-immaturity: Behavior dimensions associated with peer rejection in elementary school boys. *Developmental Psychology, 27*, 663–671.

Putallaz, M., & Wasserman, A. (1990). Children's entry behavior. In S. R. Asher & J. D. Coie (Eds.), *Peer rejection in childhood* (pp. 60–89). New York: Cambridge University Press.

Rubin, K. H., LeMare, L. J., & Lollis, S. (1990). Social withdrawal in childhood: Developmental pathways to peer rejection. In S. R. Asher & J. D. Coie (Eds.), *Peer rejection in childhood* (pp. 217–249). New York: Cambridge University Press.

Sherif, M., Harvey, O. J., White, B. J., Hood, W. R., & Sherif, C. W. (1961). *Intergroup conflict and cooperation: The robbers cave experiment*. Norman, OK: Institute of Group Relations.

Skinner, E. A., & Belmont, M. J. (1993). Motivation in the classroom: Reciprocal effects of teacher behavior and student engagement across the school year. *Journal of Educational Psychology, 85*, 571–581.

Skinner, E. A., Wellborn, J. G., & Connell, J. P. (1990). What it takes to do well in school and whether I've got it: The role of percieved control in children's engagement and school achievement. *Journal of Educational Psychology, 82*, 22–32.

Tarde, G. (1903). *The laws of imitation*. New York: Holt.

Tesser, A., Campbell, J., & Smith, M. (1984). Friendship choice and performance: Self-esteem maintenance in children. *Journal of Personality and Social Psychology, 46*, 561–574.

Valsiner, J. (1987). *Culture and the development of children's action*. Chichester: Wiley.

Von Eye, A. (1990). *Introduction to configural frequency analysis: The search for types and antitypes in cross-classifications*. New York: Cambridge University Press.

Vygotsky, L. S. (1962). *Thought and language*. Chicago: MIT Press.

Wasserman, S., & Galaskiewicz, J. (Eds.). (1994). *Advances in social network analysis*. Thousand Oaks, CA: Sage.

Wellborn, J. G. (1991). *Engaged vs. disaffected action: Conceptualization and measurement of motivation in the academic domain*. Unpublished dissertation, Graduate School of Human Development and Education, University of Rochester, Rochester, NY.

Wellman, B., & Berkowitz, S. D. (1988). *Social structures: A network approach*. New York: Cambridge University Press.

Wozniak, R. H., & Fischer, K. W. (Eds.). (1993). *Development in context: Acting and thinking in specific environments*. Hillsdale, NJ: Lawrence Erlbaum Associates.

Youniss, J. (1986). Development in reciprocity through friendship. In C. Zahn-Waxler, E. M. Cummings, & R. Iannotti (Eds.), *Altruism and aggression: Biological and social origins* (pp. 88–106). Cambridge, England: Cambridge University Press.

Directions for the Study of Developing Person–Context Relations

Thomas A. Kindermann
Portland State University

Jaan Valsiner
University of North Carolina at Chapel Hill

Our goal with this volume was to outline conceptual and methodological suggestions for an approach to the study of human development that is based on notions of developing person-context relations. This framework, in our view, can complement current trends toward systemic orientations in the study of human development. As all the authors of this volume acknowledge, systemic frameworks are a step in the right direction: Developmentalists will increasingly need to consider people and their environments as interconnected systems. What the current view adds, however, is an emphasis on the study of context development itself. Two assumptions were basic to the frame of this volume: First, there is the assumption that both individuals and their contexts are integral parts of processes of human development, and second, it is assumed that to describe and explain developmental processes we would need to focus as much on people's contexts as we traditionally have on individuals.

Systems frameworks have led to three major conceptual refinements in developmental psychology: There is widely held agreement that individuals' development occurs within many different ecological systems that often overlap among each other, that different kinds of systems differ with regard to their complexity, and that these systems have self-organizing potential of their own. What the current volume intended to add is a perspective on change and development of those systems. In Bronfenbrenner's (1989) terms, this means to regard all ecological systems as *chronosystems*, that is, as systems that are characterized by change and development in individuals and their contexts at the same time.

THE CLASSICAL VIEWPOINT: CONTEXT ENVELOPES AND LAUNCH PROCESSES

From the traditional viewpoint on a contextual understanding of human development, contexts are assumed to be given, and often, to exist independently of individuals. Typically, variations in contextual antecedents are assumed to be responsible for variations in individuals' patterns of change. This assumption is usually presented as if it constitutes an analogy to classical experimental epistemology: Pre-existing context variation is used in quasi-experimental designs (as if it were an independent variable) to reveal co-variations with differences between individuals.

However, within this framework, context variation has the status of an index variable at best. A prototypical case is the so-called *social address* model (Bronfenbrenner & Crouter, 1983): "One looks only at the *social address*—that is, the environmental label—with no attention to what the environment is like, what people are living there, what they are doing, or how the activities taking place could affect the child" (pp. 382–383). In general, a person's social address is a poor candidate for developmental descriptions and explanations (similar arguments have been made with regard to age, another index variable of vast interest to developmentalists; see Baltes, Reese, & Nesselroade, 1982; Wohlwill, 1973). The task for developmentalists is then to examine the psychologically relevant process variables that are responsible for context-correlated change across time. These process variables would need to be identified to allow meaningful interpretations and explanations of any developmental change.

In addition, context envelopes that surround the person are traditionally treated as more or less stable. Typically, context change across time is considered either irrelevant or is explicitly controlled; the focus is on interindividual differences that are examined as consequences of differences in earlier (or simultaneous) context conditions. This has been called the *launch model* approach to examining contextual influences (e.g., Connell & Skinner, 1990; Kindermann & Skinner, 1992; see Fig. E.1). In the following, we use this metaphor for discussing the implications of including processes of context change in the study of human development.

It may not be an overstatement to depict the launch model as the most popular model guiding developmental investigations. Prominent examples for its application are studies of the effects of early traumatization, of developmental outcomes of early childrearing styles, or of the consequences of early childhood attachment. To take an example from research on parental

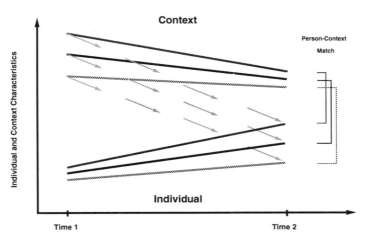

FIG. E.1. The launch model of studying context influences on human development: Context variations as predictors of interindividual differences and intraindividual change (adapted from Kindermann & Skinner, 1992; copyright Sage Publishers; adapted by permission).

childrearing styles, we may assume the context variable to be mothers' amount of help and support for their children and the individual variable to be the children's independence. Data would likely show that maternal support is positively related to childhood independence: Highly supportive mothers would have highly independent children, and vice versa (see Fig. E.1). Two features of this model are most central for our current discussion: Variation across contexts is taken as indicative of differences between individuals, and after the "launch" process is initiated, individuals' further development is assumed to proceed independently of further context influences.

Launch models do not necessarily confine us to studying just interindividual differences. Developmentalists are increasingly intererested in *intraindividual change*—in addition to differences among individuals—and there is a growing literature on the use of growth curves as indices of change for individuals across time (Asendorpf, 1993; Bryk & Raudenbush, 1992; McArdle & Epstein, 1987; Rogosa & Willett, 1985; Willett, 1994, in press). Research designs that target intraindividual change in launch processes combine longitudinal information on individuals' development with information on initial contexts. In terms of the previous example, we may find (as indicated in Fig. E.1) that initial differences between contexts are also positively related to how individuals change: Mothers who are highly supportive have children who turn out to be most independent and who gain the most in independence (note that for a growth curve approach, more than two points of individual measurement would be needed). Although in the example scenario both kinds of results lead to a similar conclusion, namely that support is positively related to growing independence, the relations between context variations and interindividual differences versus intraindividual change may differ depending on the target phenomenon under study. Conceptually, patterns of intraindividual change need to be understood as independent from differences between individuals (e.g., Schmitz & Skinner, 1993).

BEYOND THE LAUNCH MODEL: TOWARD THE STUDY OF DEVELOPING PERSON-CONTEXT RELATIONS

There is a strong argument for continuing to use launch models and for continuing to regard contexts as stable entities that do not change across individual development: The theoretical basis and the methodological strategies needed for empirical studies are much more simple. As Thorngate (chap. 4) has pointed out, the complications of a person-context relational approach are enormous. We may decide to continue to avoid these issues and leave the problems associated with context change for historians and sociologists.

However, the simplicity argument is problematic; as developmentalists, we may be quite concerned with the possibility that some of our views may be inaccurate, even if they are simple. Along these lines, Lerner (chap. 1) has argued strongly for the case that change in person-context relations needs to be regarded as the *basic process* of development; Valsiner and Herbst (chaps. 3 and 4) have addressed the logical and historical basis for regarding person-context relations as units of analysis. Following these lines of thought, launch models would likely be inaccurate in many instances. Most important, the kinds of explanations that can be based on launch designs are usually linear and direct, rather than systemic and catalyzed (cf. Sameroff, 1983; Valsiner, 1987, 1989; Winegar & Valsiner, 1992), although it is these latter kinds of causality that are able to take into account mutual interdependencies of persons and their contexts along the path of development.

What we would gain from a person-context relational model would primarily be a perspective on the *interconnectedness* and *temporal coordination* of developmental processes in individuals and in their environments (Bergson, 1911; Valsiner, 1993). Long-standing theoretical claims that the most powerful contexts in individuals' development are social and consist of other people would become central to our research endeavors (e.g., Baldwin, 1897/1902; Piaget, 1923/1959; Vygotski, 1934/1978). Our focus would be on processes of individuals' adaptation to changing contexts, as well as on processes of context adaptation to changing individuals, and on individuals' potential to instigate and shape the development of their contexts, as well as on contexts' potential to instigate and shape the developmental pathways of individuals (Kindermann & Skinner, 1992).

As many of the contributors to this volume have pointed out, a systemic interpretation of individuals' development within contexts is central to a framework of development in person-context relations. What the current volume tries to add to existing systemic frameworks is a focus on environments, including considerations for refining our conceptualizations of what environments are (and what they do), and for refining our methodological strategies for their study accordingly. Individuals and contexts are viewed as parts of dynamic systems, which reciprocally influence each other.

Three recommendations for further directions in the study of person-context relations can be delineated from the contributions to the current volume: The need to include context change across time in the designs of developmental studies, the need for specification of context characteristics and processes of influence, and the need for studying the organization of person-context relations and their change across time.

Examining Context Change and Development. As most of our readers will agree, contexts are rarely static envelopes. A decision to include contextual change in developmental descriptions and explanations involves foremost a change in study designs: Both individuals and contexts would need to be assessed at several points of measurement.

This is more than a cosmetic refinement. Assuming that contexts can change and incorporating respective extensions in our designs may lead to findings that can be at odds with findings of launch designs. It is possible that results would lead us to an entirely different interpretation of the developmental changes observed. In the scenario of Fig. E.1, two features should be highlighted: First, within individuals and their contexts, maternal support is negatively related to children's growth in independence; support decreases whereas independence increases across time. Second, the amount of change in mothers is also negatively related to the amount of change seen in children; highest decreases in mothers occur together with highest increases in children. Nevertheless (as discussed earlier), highly supportive mothers tend to have highly independent children, and highly supportive mothers tend to have children that grow most in independence. It should be noted that this must not necessarily be the case; questions about the relations between intracontext change and intraindividual change, and about the relations between those and intercontext or interindividual differences are empirical in nature; all four characteristics can be independent of one another.

Although Fig. E.1 should be taken as a metaphor only, as such, it may nevertheless be instructive for discussing the implications of the contributions this volume. Context change may occur in several ways; the psychological characteristics of contexts may change, as well as the specific agents, settings, or life circumstances that comprise a person's context at a point in time. As soon as we include context change as an additional parameter in developmental studies, we will have to broaden our understanding of the role of contexts beyond that of a launch mechanism.

Examining Contexts' Psychological Characteristics. As many authors of this volume have pointed out, context should rarely be treated as an index variable. Reducing context to an index variable is a mental construction that serves the purpose of examining between-context differences. Usually, this does not help much beyond this one purpose; we may assume that people's surroundings serve as fuel or raw material for their development, or that different categories that we use to characterize these surroundings are an aggregate index of many kinds of detailed differences that are causing differences among individuals. In short, index variables do not tell us much about these surroundings themselves, and what their "active" ingredients are.

Overall, developmental researchers have become increasingly dissatisfied with "passive exposure" concepts of environments (Wohlwill, 1983), or the social address model (Bronfenbrenner, 1989), which simply reference locations or the presence or absence of specific features, objects, or philosophies. These views of environments are appropriately criticized as notions of a "stimulus soup" that is full of potential "causes of behavior" (chap. 2, this volume), or as an "amorphous and haphazard collection of forces" (Dannefer 1992, p. 90).

Developmentalists have increased their efforts to overcome these problems. Recent trends in how contexts are conceptualized show a progression from the use of descriptive markers toward the inclusion of explanatory hypotheses; classifications of contexts in the form of "unitary" and "monolithic entities" (Wohlwill, 1983) have given way to increasingly more theory-based and multifaceted conceptualizations. This pertains to all levels of complexity of contexts. Most prominently, efforts to accord individuals the role of active agents who participate in their own development are applied to contexts as well. This goes together with widespread agreement that the influences that environments exert on individuals usually feed back into the environment and serve to influence further environmental change; similarly, influences that individuals exert on their contexts also feed back into the pathway of individual development (Lerner, 1991; Lerner & Busch-Rossnagel, 1981; Wohlwill, 1983). New questions focus on the characteristics of contexts that are relevant for individual development at different points in time, and the processes that might be involved in context-individual and individual-context transmissions. Along these lines, a social constructivist perspective has emerged in which development is characterized by individuals' active efforts to make use of their contexts by way of constructing and reconstructing meaning, and taking actively part in their own devlopmental change (cf. Valsiner, 1993; Yarrow, Rubenstein, & Pedersen, 1975).

Overall, increasing attention is being paid to examine the "nature of nurture" (Wachs, 1992), the cultural organization of environments (Valsiner, 1987, 1989), and the psychologically relevant characteristics and functions that contexts possess in contributing to individuals' development. This includes efforts to recognize the "psychological structure" of environments (cf. Sameroff, 1983), the "affordances" that environments provide for individuals' actions (Gibson, 1982), the agenda that contexts may hold for individuals (Goodnow, 1984; Kindermann & Skinner, 1988, 1992; Sigel, 1985, 1990), and the mechanisms by which environments influence psychological development (cf. Wohlwill, 1983).

Several authors in this volume have underscored the importance of the psychological characteristics and functions that contexts possess for individuals. Three avenues for further study should be mentioned. As the contributions by Claar (chap. 5) and Trommsdorff (chap. 6) show, one avenue is the the study of *contextual frames* themselves and of the cultural guidance systems that contexts provide for individuals' development. Focal areas may be the study of the environmental conditions for children's emotional, cognitive, and behavioral development, but also investigations of what children learn in a given culture or across cultural transitions, and of how children try to make sense of cultural frames.

This may include the study of historical change that occurs in macrocontext frames (chap. 5), but also change in person-context relations when the context itself remains comparably stable. Co-constructive theorizing would lead one to expect that even in cases in which there is no change in context agents or macrocontext conditions themselves, change in individuals would nevertheless constitute a change in the relationship between individuals and their contexts (e.g., Rogoff, 1993; Valsiner, 1993).

A second avenue for studying the psychological characteristics of environments can be seen in the contributions by Batchelder (chap. 8) and Kindermann (chap. 9). Both chapters focus on the psychological characteristics of specific context *agents.* Within such a framework, the focus is on the psychologically relevant characteristics of people's close affiliates and on the functions that social partners may have for developing individuals. Attention to context change would entail the study of the belief systems or agenda that context agents may hold for individuals, but also the study of what the detailed messages are that developing individuals receive from contexts in guiding their development at different points in development (cf. Goodnow, 1984; Sigel, 1985, 1990), and what individuals and contexts "do" for and with each other (cf. Heckhausen, 1987; Kindermann, 1993; Kindermann & Skinner, 1988). For example, strategies established in social interaction research (e.g., Bakeman & Gottman, 1986; Bornstein & Bruner, 1989) can be used to study change in socializing interactions between children and their social partners. It seems likely to expect that these lines of research will highlight processes of mutual coadaptation and reciprocal attunement between individuals and their contexts (e.g., Field, 1992; Kindermann & Skinner, 1992).

A third area of investigating changing person-context relations is in the field of critical life events (chap. 7). Life event researchers (cf. Brim & Ryff,

1980; Filipp, 1982; Hultsch & Plemons, 1979) have argued that some events that people encounter along the path of their development exert drastic influences on their further development. Von Eye and colleagues provide a perspective on how the organization of these context changes can be examined, with specific attention to the sequential organization and temporal spacing of these events as contexts for individuals' development.

Examining the Organization of Person-Context Relations. Conceptually, to assume that contexts change with changes that occur in developing individuals is a comparably easy refinement, as long as the contextual agents involved stay the same across time. Thus, it is of no suprise that the contexts studied traditionally have been mostly families and schools. Family contexts have "generated their own" individual, and usually the system remains stable in terms of its members for a larger time span; school contexts have their individuals assigned by culture, typically also for predictable time frames.

Psychologists have not always regarded parent-child relations as the prototypical case for studying human development; Wundt, for example, had reservations whether child psychology would be the ultimate means for resolving developmental questions (1912; see Reinert, 1976). Nevertheless, developmental psychology has been dominated by the study of childrearing processes and the study of institutionalized education since the early years of this century. Consequently, the study of how individuals and contexts become connected to one another, beyond instances of normative biological or cultural assignments, has been accorded minor importance.

Thorngate's example of the developmental pathway of a swimmer (chap. 2) provides an intriguing case for the role of changes in the matching of people and contexts across time. The example is about a girl who has high abilities in swimming and participates in competitions. Across time and with increasing context support (i.e., from parents and trainers), she is able to participate and succeed in competitions at increasingly higher levels, but with increasingly narrower margins between her and her competitors. Finally, she ends up in a stage where neither differences in abilities nor differences in context support are responsible for whether she will win or not, but sheer luck (the reader may envision this as a variant of Fig. E.1, in which both individual and context trajectories have positive slopes and would converge across time).

Of critical importance here is the fact that only some contexts are assigned to individuals in a normative fashion through biology or culture (cf. Baltes, 1989). Nevertheless, there may be systematic change in the sequential patterning of how individuals become exposed to these non-normative contexts. In Thorngate's example, the most important characteristics of context change are self-selected by the developing individual herself; in the field of life-event research (e.g., see chap. 9) the temporal sequence, patterning, and duration of life events that happen to individuals is of interest. Within launch models, typically no attention is paid to how a connection comes about between an individual and his or her context. However, in many cases, the nature and organization of pathways of person-context relations may be a key process that needs to be studied.

In the area of life-span developmental psychology and gerontology, the concept of *selective optimization with compensation* has gained much attention (cf. Baltes & Baltes, 1990); the concept appears to be closely related to Thorngate's principle of cross-context proliferation. Usually, selective optimization is discussed in terms of individuals' efforts to maximize most valued competencies at the expense of less valued ones, and especially with regard to individuals' success in managing their life in the face of functional decline in old age (Heckhausen & Schulz, 1993). However, the concept may also provide a viable perspective on the development of person-context relations. Lawton's (1987) view that people engage in processes of *proactive construction* of their social world across age, or Carstensen's (1992) formulation of a *socioemotional selectivity theory* that postulates that people optimize their social relationships according to age-related changes in their own needs, are very consistent with the views expressed in this volume.

With regard to childhood, peer group and friendship researchers have a similar interest in processes of how individuals select contexts for their own development (e.g., Berndt, 1989; Cairns, Neckerman, & Cairns, 1989; Dunphy, 1963; see also Kindermann, chap. 9). Typically, children are found to hold associative preferences for specific other children with whom peer affiliations are sought. Those others are recognized as social context agents who have personality characteristics, belief systems, and behavior tendencies of their own, and peer selection processes are portrayed as proceeding according to criteria of similarity in these characteristics between target individuals and context candidates.

In general, questions of the nature of the connection between individuals and their contexts may be considered to be of minor importance as long as we stay within the classical fields of developmental studies, namely, parental socialization and education. However, the point may be more general. For example, behavior-genetic researchers (e.g., Plomin, DeFries, & Loehlin, 1977; Scarr & McCartney, 1983) argue along similar lines that individuals actively seek out environments that support their own genetic proclivities. These active selection processes would deserve our attention in addition to "passive" and "reactive" genotype-environment covariations, which have been in the focus of classical socialization studies.

Likewise, age-graded changes even in biologically or institutionally assigned contexts may allow children increased freedom in selecting or attending to specific contexts above others. An example may be taken from the field of education; when children shift from elementary to middle or junior high school, they typically change from having one primary teacher to having multiple teachers, sometimes as many as six or seven. This shift is not only likely to dilute the influence of any one teacher but also allows children to concentrate attention and engagement selectively, depending on their own developing preferences (Altman, 1993). Similarly, Batchelder's study (chap. 8, this volume) can be taken as an example for such selection processes during families' development.

A Word of Encouragement

We began this volume by pointing out a line of thought that has been there all along in developmental psychology but never has acquired more than the status of a general critique of developmental research practice, namely, the strong inclination of developmentalists to separate individuals from their contexts and to regard both as separate entities. Despite a rich tradition of theories on the sociogenic nature of development (e.g., Baldwin, Lewin), developmental psychology has remained predominantly the study of isolated individuals that change within context envelopes that are assumed to stay static across time (cf. Asendorpf & Valsiner, 1992; Hetherington & Baltes, 1988; Valsiner, 1993). Things must not necessarily stay that way. There is a new resurgence of systemic frameworks for the study of human development (e.g., Bronfenbrenner, 1989; Ford & Lerner, 1992; Lerner, 1991), and there are indications that developmentalists are trying to take seriously their belief that "individuals develop within changing contexts."

It is obviously quite a troublesome problem that contextual change likely involves several kinds of change at the same time. We must assume that development within individuals is likely to potentiate changes in the psychological characteristics of their environment and, hence, changes in person-context relations, even if context agents and individuals' life circumstances stay entirely constant. We also need to consider that context agents may change themselves, simultaneously with target individuals under study, and that different context agents become involved when transitions occur across developmental settings. Finally, individuals change also in the extent to which they are able themselves to determine which kinds of transitions to undertake, which contexts to join, and which context agents to choose for interpersonal relationships. As soon as we acknowledge that contexts may change, we will have to deal with the combination of these changes. Developmental questions, then, will need to focus less on change within individuals, and more on the interrelations between change within people and change within their contexts. Based on the contributions to this volume, key questions will likely be concerned with how people and contexts become related to one another, how they seek out each other (or miss or avoid each other), how they acquire and perform specific functions for one another, and how people and contexts adapt to each others' changing characteristics across time.

What we attempted with this volume was to try to shed light on the promises that a person-context relational approach may hold for developmentalists. We hoped to be able to identify some of its conceptual and methodological consequences, and to outline strategies for its empirical investigation. As indicated by many of the contributions to this volume, this is not a goal that is easy to reach. However, we all expect that it is a goal that is promising enough to exert the effort needed for its pursuit. If any of our readers would concur, the purpose of this book will be achieved.

REFERENCES

Altman, J. H. (1993). *How do proximal and distal school contexts influence teacher motivation? A study on the effects of student engagement and school climate on elementary and middle school teachers' motivation in the classroom.* Unpublished dissertation, Graduate School of Education and Human Development, University of Rochester, Rochester, NY.

Asendorpf, J. B. (1992). Beyond stability: Predicting interindividual differences in intra-individual change. *European Journal of Personality, 6,* 103–117.

Asendorpf, J. B., & Valsiner, J. (Eds.). (1992). *Stability and change in development: A study of methodological reasoning.* Newbury Park, CA: Sage.

Bakeman, R., & Gottman, J. M. (1986). *Observing interaction: An introduction to sequential analysis.* Cambridge, England: Cambridge University Press.

Baldwin, J. M. (1902). *Social and ethical interpretations in mental development: A study in social psychology* (3rd ed.). New York: Macmillan. (Original work published 1897)

Baltes, P. B. (1989). Theoretical propositions of life-span developmental psychology: On the dynamics between growth and decline. *Developmental Psychology, 23,* 611–626.

Baltes, P. B., & Baltes, M. M. (1990). Psychological perspectives on successful aging: The model of selective optimization with compensation. In P. B. Baltes & M. M. Baltes (Eds.), *Successful aging: Perspectives from the behavioral sciences.* Cambridge, England: Cambridge University Press.

Baltes, P. B., Reese, H. W., & Nesselroade, J. R. (1982). *Life-span developmental psychology: Introduction to research methods.* Hillsdale, NJ: Lawrence Erlbaum Associates.

Bergson, H. (1911). *Creative evolution.* New York: Holt. (Original work published 1907)

Berndt, T. J. (1989). Friendships in childhood and adolescence. In W. Damon (Ed.), *Child development today and tomorrow* (pp. 332–348). San Francisco: Jossey-Bass.

Bornstein, M. H., & Bruner, J. S. (1989). *Interaction in human development.* Hillsdale, NJ: Lawrence Erlbaum Associates.

Brim, O. G., & Ryff, C. D. (1980). On the properties of life-events. In P. B. Baltes & O. G. Brim (Eds.), *Life-span development and behavior* (Vol. 3, pp. 368–388). New York: Academic Press.

Bronfenbrenner, U. (1989). Ecological systems theory. In R. Vasta (Ed.), *Annals of child development* (pp. 187–249). Greenwich, CT: JAI Press.

Bronfenbrenner, U., & Crouter, A. C. (1983). The evolution of environmental models in developmental research. In P. H. Mussen (Ed.), *Handbook of child psychology* (Vol. 1); W. Kessen (Ed.), *History, theory, and methods* (pp. 357–414). New York: Wiley.

Bryk, A. S., & Raudenbush, S. W. (1992). *Hierarchical linear models: Applications and data analysis models.* Newbury Park, CA: Sage.

Cairns, R. B., Neckerman, H. J., & Cairns, B. D. (1989). Social networks and shadows of synchrony. In G. R. Adams, R. Montemayor, & T. P. Gullota (Eds.), *Biology of adolescent behavior and development* (pp. 275–305). Newbury Park, CA: Sage.

Carstensen, L. L. (1992). Social and emotional patterns in adulthood: Support for socioemotional selectivity theory. *Psychology and Aging, 7,* 331–338.

Connell, J. P., & Skinner, E. A. (1990, April). *Predicting trajectories of academic engagement: A growth curve analysis of children's motivation in school.* Paper presented at the annual meeting of the American Educational Research Association, Boston.

Dannefer, D. (1992). On the conceptualization of context in developmental discourse: Four meanings of context and their implications. In D. L. Featherman, R. M. Lerner, & M. Perlmutter (Eds.), *Life-span development and behavior* (Vol. 10, pp. 83–110). New York: Academic Press.

Dunphy, D. C. (1963). The social structure of urban adolescent peer groups. *Sociometry, 26,* 230–246.

Field, T. M. (1992). Psychobiological attunement in close relationships. In D. L. Featherman, R. M. Lerner, & M. Perlmutter (Eds.), *Life-span development and behavior* (Vol. 11, pp. 1–25). Hillsdale, NJ: Lawrence Erlbaum Associates.

Filipp, S.-H. (1982). Kritische Lebensereignisse als Brennpunkte einer angewandten Entwicklungspsychologie des mittleren und höheren Erwachsenenalters [Critical life events as focal points of an applied developmental psychology of middle and late adulthood]. In R. Oerter & L. Montada (Eds.), *Entwicklungspsychologie* [Developmental psychology] (pp. 769–788). München: Urban & Schwarzenberg.

Ford, D. H., & Lerner, R. M. (1992). *Developmental systems theory: An integrative approach.* Newbury Park, CA: Sage.

Gibson, E. (1982). The concept of affordances in development: The renascence of functionalism. In W. A. Collins (Ed.), *The concept of development* (pp. 55–81). Hillsdale, NJ: Lawrence Erlbaum Associates.

Goodnow, J. J. (1984). Parents' ideas about parenting and development. In M. E. Lamb, A. E. Brown, & B. Rogoff (Eds.), *Advances in developmental psychology* (pp. 193–242). Hillsdale, NJ: Lawrence Erlbaum Associates.

Heckhausen, J. (1987) Balancing for weaknesses and challenging developmental potential: A longitudinal study of mother-infant dyads in apprenticeship interactions. *Developmental Psychology, 23,* 762–770.

Heckhausen, J., & Schulz, R. (1993). Optimisation by selection and compensation: Balancing primary and secondary control in life span development. *International Journal of Behavioral Development, 16,* 287–303.

Hetherington, E. M., & Baltes, P. B. (1988). Child psychology and life-span development. In E. M. Hetherington, R. M. Lerner, & M. Perlmutter (Eds.), *Child development in life-span perspective* (pp. 1–19). Hillsdale, NJ: Lawrence Erlbaum Associates.

Hultsch, D. F., & Plemons, J. K. (1979). Life-events and life-span development. In P. B. Baltes & O. G. Brim (Eds.), *Life-span development and behavior* (Vol. 2, pp. 1–37). New York: Academic Press.

Kindermann, T. A. (1993). Fostering independence in everyday mother-child interactions: Changes in contingencies as children grow competent in developmental tasks. *International Journal of Behavioral Development, 16,* 513–535.

Kindermann, T. A., & Skinner, E. A. (1988). Developmental tasks as organizers of children's ecologies: Mothers' contingencies as children learn to walk, eat, and dress. In J. Valsiner (Ed.), *Child development within culturally structured environments* (Vol. 2, pp. 66–105). Norwood, NJ: Ablex.

Kindermann, T. A., & Skinner, E. A. (1992). Modeling environmental development: Individual and contextual trajectories. In J. B. Asendorpf & J. Valsiner (Eds.), *Stability and change in development: A study of methodological reasoning* (pp. 155–190). Newbury Park, CA: Sage.

Lawton, M. P. (1987). Environment and the need satisfaction of the aging. In L. L. Carstensen & B. A. Edelstein (Eds.), *Handbook of clinical gerontology* (pp. 33–40). Elmsford, NY: Pergamon.

Lerner, R. M. (1991). Changing organism-context relations as the basic process of development. *Developmental Psychology, 27,* 27–32.

Lerner, R. M., & Busch-Rossnagel, N. A. (Eds.). (1981). *Individuals as producers of their development: A life-span perspective.* New York: Academic Press.

McArdle, J. J., & Epstein, D. (1987). Latent growth curves within developmental structural equation models. *Child Development, 58,* 110–133.

Piaget, J. (1959). *The language and thought of the child.* London: Routledge & Kegan. (Original work published 1923)

Plomin, R., DeFries, J. C., & Loehlin, C. (1977). Genotype-environment interaction and correlation in the analysis of human behavior. *Psychological Bulletin, 84,* 309–332.

Reinert, G. (1976). Grundzüge einer Geschichte der Human-Entwicklungspsychologie [Prolegomena to a history of developmental psychology]. In H. Balmer (Ed.), *Die Psychologie des 20. Jahrhunderts, Vol. 1, Die europäische Tradition. Tendenzen, Schulen, Entwicklungslinien* [The psychology of the 20th Century: Tendencies, schools, developmental trends] (pp. 862–896). Zürich: Kindler.

Rogoff, B. (1993). Children's guided participation and participatory action appropriation in sociocultural activity. In R. H. Wozniak & K. W. Fischer (Eds.), *Development in context: Acting and thinking in specific environments* (pp. 121–153). Hillsdale, NJ: Lawrence Erlbaum Associates.

Rogosa, D. R., & Willett, J. B. (1985). Understanding correlates of change by modeling individual differences in growth. *Psychometrika, 50,* 203–228.

Sameroff, A. J. (1983). Developmental systems: Contexts and evolution. In P. H. Mussen (Ed.), *Handbook of child psychology* (Vol. 1); W. Kessen (Ed.), *History, theory, and methods* (pp. 237–294). New York: Wiley.

Scarr, S., & McCartney, K. (1983). How people make their own environments: A theory of genotype-environment effects. *Child Development, 54,* 426–435.

Schmitz, B., & Skinner, E. A. (1993). Perceived control, effort, and academic performance: Interindividual, intraindividual, and multivariate time series analyses. *Journal of Personality and Social Psychology, 64,* 1010–1028.

Sigel, I. E. (1985). *Parental belief systems: The psychological consequences for children.* Hillsdale, NJ: Lawrence Erlbaum Associates.

Sigel, I. E. (1990). *Parental belief systems: Consequences for children's development.* Hillsdale, NJ: Lawrence Erlbaum Associates.

Valsiner, J. (1987). *Culture and the development of children's action.* Chichester: Wiley.

Valsiner, J. (1989). *Human development and culture.* Lexington, MA: Heath.

Valsiner, J. (1993). Culture and human development: A co-constructive perspective. In P. van Geert & L. Mos (Eds.), *Annals of theoretical psychology* (Vol. 10). New York: Plenum.

Valsiner, J. (1993, July). *Irreversibility of time and the construction of historical developmental psychology.* Paper presented at the XII Biennnial Meetings of the International Society for the Study of Behavioural Development, Recife, Brazil.

Vygotsky, L. S. (1978). *Mind in society.* Cambridge, MA: Harvard University Press. (Original work published 1934)

Wachs, T. D. (1992). *The nature of nurture.* Newbury Park, CA: Sage.

Winegar, L. T., & Valsiner, J. (Eds.). (1992). *Children's development within social context. Vol. 2. Research and methodology.* Hillsdale, NJ: Lawrence Erlbaum Associates.

Willett, J. B. (1994). Measuring change more effectively by modeling individual growth over time. In T. Husen & T. N. Postlethwaite (Eds.), *The international encyclopedia of education* (2nd ed.). Elmsford, NY: Pergamon.

Wohlwill, J. F. (1973). *The study of behavioral development.* New York: Academic Press.

Wohlwill, J. F. (1983). Physical and social environment as factors in development. In D. Magnusson & V. L. Allen (Eds.), *Human development: An interactional perspective* (pp. 111–129). New York: Academic Press.

Wundt, W. (1912). *Elemente der Völkerpsychologie: Grundlinien einer psychologischen Entwicklungsgeschichte der Menschheit* [Elements of Cultural-Psychology: Toward a psychological history of the development of mankind]. Leipzig: Kröner.

Yarrow, L. J., Rubenstein, J. L., & Pedersen, F. A. (1975). *Infant and environment: Early cognitive and motivational development.* New York: Wiley.

Author Index

Subject Index